50 Fast Final Cut Pro® 3 Techniques

TIM MEEHAN

50 FAST FINAL CUT PRO® 3 TECHNIQUES

WILEY

Wiley Publishing, Inc.

50 Fast Final Cut Pro® 3 Techniques

Published by
Wiley Publishing, Inc.
909 Third Avenue
New York, NY 10022

www.wiley.com

Library of Congress Control Number: 2002110274

ISBN: 0-7645-2446-1

Manufactured in the United States of America

10 9 8 7 6 5 4 3 2 1

1V/RV/QR/QT/IN

Published by Wiley Publishing, Inc., Indianapolis, Indiana
Published simultaneously in Canada

For Ray, the spotted wonder-pup.

For my niece, who appears in this book with the gracious permission of her parents.

For my assistants and support staff who worked so hard to help me get this project off the ground and flying smoothly.

For my parents and my extended family, who encourage and support me.

For the pilots and friends who fly with me. Your spirit keeps my spirit in motion.

For you. For me. For everyone who has been creatively inspired by the new capabilities this technology brings to us.

PREFACE

As the title of this book implies, there are 50 fast digital video techniques to explore in the pages of this volume. While it would have been an easy task to fill the pages with 50 relatively simple, useful digital video and editing techniques, this effort presents 50 fast, easy and FUN techniques for digital video. All are easily accomplished by using any camcorder or video recording device, from home-use consumer models to high-end production cameras and Apple's Final Cut Pro 3 video editing software.

This book is for anyone who has a camcorder, a Macintosh, and Final Cut Pro and wants to shoot extraordinary footage and special effects without the unreasonable investment of a full-on Hollywood studio back-lot and editing suite. This book is for everyone who has grown up with the American movie experience and thought to themselves, "Why aren't there any 50-foot-tall house pets in MY neighborhood?" This book, in short, is for anyone who wants to produce great video, great effects, and great fun with their Macintosh, their camcorder, and Final Cut Pro.

If you're new to the world of digital video, you'll love this book for its simplicity and approachability. If you're an experienced video-editing professional, you'll love this book for its clarity and straightforward explanation of effects and techniques that you've always done the hard way with other systems.

Every effect and technique shown in this book has a place in the digital video realm, whether for commercial broadcast, home video, or distribution on the World Wide Web. Final Cut Pro, your Macintosh, your imagination, and this recipe book for special effects and techniques are all you need to create compelling and entertaining video content.

WHY THIS BOOK WAS WRITTEN

Since the beginning of the personal computer revolution, digital technology has brought to the masses new expressions of media and distribution of knowledge and creativity. In the early '80s, we saw the birth of the desktop publishing, graphics, and print media revolution with the Apple Macintosh computer, laser printers, and software, such as the Aldus PageMaker. The world has never been the same since.

The '90s saw the maturation of print and publishing with computer-based tools from Apple and Adobe. Fine arts, graphic, and print production all saw major leaps forward in productivity and creativity thanks to the benefits of powerful solutions made possible by Apple. As these technologies matured, new media distribution methods were born as graphic media content crossed over from traditional conventional print media to electronic digital graphics distribution on the World Wide Web.

Today we're enjoying new media and creative expression with the birth of Web publishing and the mutation of print distribution into the electronic and interactive world of the Web, which has become a large and inextricable part of our everyday lives. Again, with Apple Macintosh computers, software tools from Adobe and Macromedia, and the adoption of the creative and publishing communities, uses are at the forefront of another revolution in the way we create, publish, and consume media and knowledge.

Now we are witness to another new media expression and distribution medium in desktop digital video, again made possible through superior tools such as Final Cut Pro and powerful Macintosh computers from Apple. Final Cut Pro enables us to create compelling and inspiring creative content in the world of full-motion, broadcast-quality video — as well as bandwidth-efficient, Web-distributable video media. Here is your tool for making it your own.

WHY ME?

As witness to the revolution since 1984, I've enjoyed and taken advantage of the benefits of the technologies presented to us, and ultimately made a rewarding living out of finding ways to bring the inspiration and fun that these new technologies and capabilities represent to the world through books, presentations, workshops, and classes.

As an early adopter with a solid background in graphics, I saw the potential that this combination of tools and media had for transforming the lives and careers of design professionals everywhere. My first books were among the first to bring the world of desktop computer graphics production to the creative and consumer markets.

Today, the field of desktop digital video is exploding as new media and distribution models are changing the way we create, distribute, and receive information. Products such as the Apple Macintosh, Final Cut Pro, and DVD Studio Pro are bringing new capabilities and methods of creative expression to everyone from the novice home user to the most advanced editing professionals. And again, I am seeing the potential these new tools have for impacting the lives of computer users and video producers everywhere.

THIS BOOK IS NOT LIKE ANY OTHER FINAL CUT PRO BOOK ON THE SHELVES TODAY

Your local bookstore is filling shelves with a growing number of "how-to" titles about new computer-based video-editing tools such as Final Cut Pro. Look at each of them. Take this one home with you.

This book is filled with simply presented, step-by-step recipes for creating compelling video techniques and effects. You will appreciate the straightforward presentation and the clear-cut, brief descriptions as you learn how easy it is to create stunning video with your home camcorder and personal computer running Final Cut Pro.

Each of the techniques presented is easily scalable, allowing you to build your own effects and styles to suit your needs and tastes. You can layer effects on one another, making them as simple (or complex) as you like. You can even save the effects and techniques in the native Final Cut Pro format for use on other future video projects as your skills and capabilities develop.

This book is the perfect video cookbook for you.

WHY USE FINAL CUT PRO?

Apple's Final Cut Pro video software is a powerful near-line editing, composition, and production product. Comparable to a fully equipped video-editing studio suite, yet costing a fraction of the price of the tools found in the conventional video-editing world, Final Cut Pro offers the professional as well as the amateur a complete editing and production solution. A professional-level tool, with an industrial-strength feature set, Final Cut Pro is also surprisingly approachable and comfortable to work with, making it the perfect solution for anyone from full-time professional editors and producers to home and consumer users. Final Cut Pro is the perfect companion for anyone with a camcorder.

No matter which current model Macintosh you own, from a consumer-level iMac to the portable iBook and PowerBook to state-of-the-art desktop workstations, you have some form of video-editing tool on your computer right out of the box. The Apple iMovie software is preinstalled with every system.

While powerful in its own right, iMovie is a great introduction to digital video editing. Final Cut Pro brings full-power professional-level tools to you to help you take your next step, taking your video creations to the next level. In this book, you find techniques to help you perform basic enhancements and correction as well as full-on movie-studio digital special effects.

WHAT COMPUTER HARDWARE AND SOFTWARE DO YOU NEED?

Final Cut Pro: Fortunately for you, Final Cut Pro runs on almost any current Macintosh model in production today. Apple recommends a PowerPC Macintosh with at least 256MB of RAM and a large enough hard drive to accommodate the installation of the software and a reasonable amount of captured video media.

Macintosh: Apple lists the requirement for Final Cut Pro as a Macintosh computer with a 300 MHz or faster PowerPC G3 or G4 processor and built-in FireWire connectivity.

To take advantage of real-time effects, you need:

- 500 MHz or faster single or 450 MHz dual processor Power Mac G4 or PowerBook G4. To take advantage of "real-time" effects in DV format:
    - 667 MHz PowerBook G4
    - Mac OS 9.2.2 or Mac OS X v10.1.1
    - QuickTime (included) with every system
    - 256MB of RAM, 384MB recommended for G4 real-time effects (512MB in the real world. Too much is never enough.)
- 40MB of available disk space required for installation.

A note about hard disk requirements: Hard disk drives come in all sizes and flavors. The conventional wisdom for hard disk storage is you can never have enough hard disk space. Consider that at video resolutions, each minute of captured video will consume over 200MB of hard disk space.

Capture vs. storage: With such voluminous storage requirements for video, it makes sense to have a large, fast hard drive as your capture drive. However, storing your projects and source footage has never been more efficient with all the inexpensive external drives available in this market.

Windows users: Tough luck. No Windows-compatible versions of Final Cut Pro are available anywhere. Conventional wisdom would suggest that given the cost of purchasing a new Macintosh with Final Cut Pro compared to the cost of purchasing, maintaining, and running a comparably configured Windows-based PC, the choice is simple and compelling. Get to your nearest Apple authorized reseller and buy a new Mac. You'll be glad you did, and you'll never look back.

CONVENTIONS USED IN THIS BOOK

The best way to present 50 fast (and fun) digital video techniques is in a simple, straightforward, easy-to-follow, step-by-step, recipe-book format. You'll find that each of the techniques shown in this book is brief, concise, and specific in the presentation.

The first page of each technique shows a before and after peek at the effect presented. Or, at least as much as is possible in the static print format of a book. As the world of video is a world of motion and the presentation of this world is being given in a static print medium, to help compensate for this shortcoming for each technique you'll find that a small QuickTime clip of the results of each technique accompanies the lesson material.

The project demonstration media is supplied to you in QuickTime digital video format, in a relatively small frame, slow frame rate, and highly compressed in order to fit as much as possible on the CD that ships with the book. All are of an appropriate format for import and inclusion in all the technique demonstrations.

Each step of each technique is illustrated with a screen-capture snapshot of the sample project as it progresses so that you can compare your results on-screen with those generated in creating the material. You may find that there are occasionally subtle (and often not-so-subtle) differences between what you see on your computer screen and what is shown in the book. There are certain inescapable differences in how pixels are recorded and how video is captured and shown on-screen. Keep your thoughts focused on the concepts being presented and allow for those differences.

Wherever an image is referenced as a figure, and when the image is also shown in the color insert section, a color-plate number is shown in parentheses following the image reference. For example, an illustration showing Figure 12 in Chapter 7, listed as 7.12, in black and white in the text has the figure number with the initials CP in parentheses following it, as 7.12 (CP 7.12), alerting you to its presence in the color-plate section of the book.

Many of the steps shown in the process of performing these techniques involve selecting menu commands, which have layers of pop-up or submenu commands associated with them. This process is shown with the suggestion to choose as:

menu command ➢ submenu command ➢ pop-up submenu command.

For example:

choose Modify ➢ Composite Mode ➢ Screen.

Where appropriate, a keyboard shortcut is often listed or recommended as well.

ACKNOWLEDGMENTS

Creating any published work, getting it produced, published, marketed, distributed, and ultimately into the hands of the public who will make the best use of it is invariably a huge undertaking. "Time-consuming" and "arduous" are the two terms I would use to most accurately describe the process.

In the case of every title that's had my name on the cover, the indispensable involvement and contributions of a team of competent professionals has always been the key to any success I have enjoyed. Any great endeavor is often the result of dedicated and supportive teamwork. In this case, my ideas were supported, endorsed, and championed by some incredibly talented and committed professionals.

It is with great thanks and appreciation that I acknowledge the assistance and support of all who were involved in this project with me. Without you, it could not have come into being.

The dedicated professionals at Waterside Productions; my agent, advocate, and representative, Danelle Jatlow, who acted as buffer, translator, negotiator, and interpreter for me in this challenging world of book publishing.

Mike Roney, acquisitions editor for Wiley, a true professional in this often competitive and challenging field. Amanda Munz Peterson, the project editor who kept me coherent and on schedule throughout the process. The technical, media, CD-ROM, and production editors, John Matson, and Jerelind Charles, and all who labored in the engine rooms, figuratively shoveling the tons of coal necessary to drive the engines of production.

Thanks also to my staff of good friends and associates: Jon Kantor, who helped turn my excited ramblings about the magic of Final Cut Pro into a cohesive and understandable flow of information; Dan Haskin, who labored through the tedium of play-testing and screen capturing each of the effects and techniques.

I can't forget friends, family, models, and patrons who supported, encouraged, contributed, and understood all my distractions in getting this project into the world. And for all who very graciously afforded their likenesses in modeling for the video demonstrations on the CD: my baby niece Payton Meehan (arguably the cutest baby on the planet), Ray the spotted wonder-pup, the various and assorted fearless pilots and renegade flying monkeys in the skies above Aspen and Golden, Colorado, the ducks in my backyard, my little wind-up toy robot, and the 20th Anniversary Macintosh.

And of course the magicians at Apple who made all of this possible. Where would any of us be today without the Macintosh?

CONTENTS AT A GLANCE

CONTENTS

Final Cut Pro File Edit View Mark Modify Sequence Effects Tools Window Help
F2
I
O
J
K
L

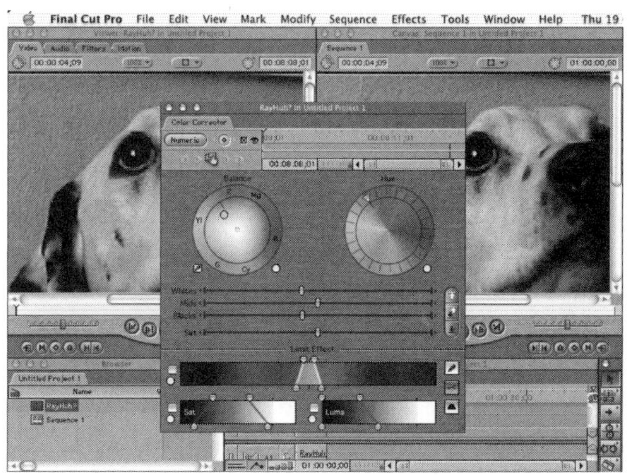

Final Cut Pro File Edit View Mark Modify Sequence Effects Tools Window Help Thu 19

Speed
Speed: 200 percent
Duration: 00:00:36,23
Reverse
Frame Blending
Cancel
OK

Cartoon Balloons.mov
Chocolate?
GRACO
00:00:00

Canvas: Planets&Moons in Chapter5Projects
Planets&Moons
00:00:05;28
100%
01:00:00;00

Viewer: Slug
Video
Audio
Filters
Motion
00:02:00:00
100%
00:00:00:00

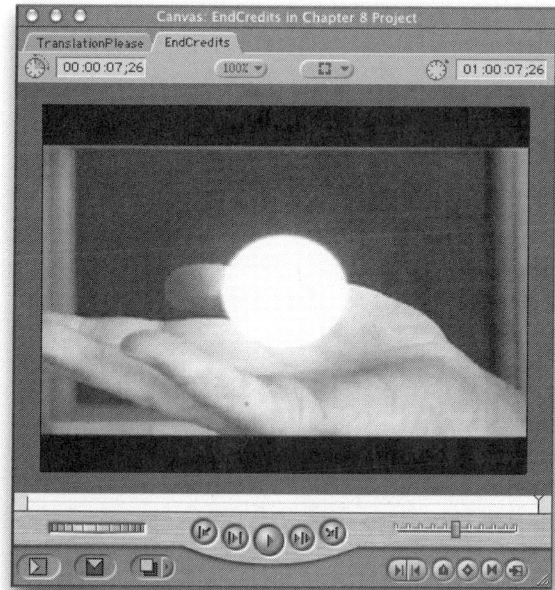
Canvas: EndCredits in Chapter 8 Project
TranslationPlease
EndCredits
00:00:07;26
100%
01:00:07;26

CHAPTER 8: ADVANCED TEXT AND TILTING TECHNIQUES 211

INTRODUCTION

Welcome to the exciting world of digital video editing with Final Cut Pro 3 and your Macintosh. This book brings you 50 fast and fun techniques to help improve your video project and to add some fun effects and techniques to the video projects you shoot.

All you need is a suitable Macintosh computer, the Apple Final Cut Pro 3 software, and a camcorder to get started. If your camcorder has FireWire (IEEE1394) connectability, the the process is even easier still. FireWire allows for a two-way communication between your computer and your camcorder.

Of course illustrating motion in still imagery is difficult, so this book includes a CD-ROM full of demonstration and sample material to help you along in your learning process. You'll find the examples easy to follow and the sample materials a valuable addition to your desktop digital video-editing toolbox.

WHAT IS DIGITAL VIDEO?

No matter how your video image has been captured, with a little effort and the right cables you can easily capture (or transfer) your video to your computer's hard disk for processing with Final Cut Pro and ultimately export to a variety of different media types from regular analog video (VHS), digital video (DV), or QuickTime media for the Web.

After your video is captured, it exists in a digital format on your hard drive, making it easy for a powerful solution such as the Macintosh and Final Cut Pro to manipulate, enhance, improve, and export the data. Modern digital video cameras have the capability to capture digital video, still video images, and still digital images (there's a difference) in a variety of formats and resolutions.

Consult your camera's owner's manual for connectivity and compatibility with Final Cut Pro on the Macintosh. Most cameras sold in the United States today include FireWire connectivity, though it may be referred to by different trade names, such as IEEE1394 or iLink, allowing the camera to connect and transfer data between it and your computer easily and reliably.

The real beauty in FireWire, however, is in its ability for two-way communication between the camera and the computer. Not only can the video data be captured in the computer, but also the computer can send signals, data, and commands back to the camera, making Final Cut Pro especially useful in capturing and producing video in discontinuous batches to and from tape.

TECHNIQUES OVERVIEW

These 50 fast and fun digital video techniques are presented in eight chapters. Feel free to browse and wander through the book for techniques that interest you. You don't necessarily have to follow any order or sequence in your explorations; however, the techniques progress through the chapters in gradually increasing levels of complexity. The examples in each chapter are grouped by concept and progress, technique by technique, building on each concept.

Chapter 1: Practical workflow techniques. How to gather, capture, assemble, and store clips for easy retrieval and construction.

Chapter 2: Basic enhancement and improvement techniques. Not at all unlike the kinds of enhancements and improvements you might apply to a still image in your standard image-editing software such as Photoshop. In fact, the menu commands and the concepts behind them are remarkably similar in most respects.

Chapter 3: Time and speed effects. How to create the illusion of altered time passage. Fast motion, slow motion, stop motion, and so forth.

Chapter 4: Superimposition techniques. How to work with layers in Final Cut Pro. Again, not at all unlike layers in Adobe Photoshop. If you've ever used Photoshop, you'll be comfortable with the concepts presented here.

Chapter 5: Superimposing visual effects. Building on the layering concept, you learn how to integrate filter effects with layers to achieve some interesting illusions.

Chapter 6: Advanced special effects. Using matte windows to enhance and improve your already-interesting layering techniques.

Chapter 7: More advanced special effects. Even more fun with mattes and windows. You simulate simple size deceptions and matte window effects.

Chapter 8: Advanced text and titling effects. You learn how to add professional text and titling effects by using tools entirely within Final Cut Pro 3.

THINGS YOU SHOULD KNOW BEFORE STARTING THE PROJECTS

You should be comfortable with the basic operation of your computer. You should be familiar with using your favorite input device, whether that's a mouse, a pen tablet, a trackpad, or a trackball. You should know how to navigate the file system and be able to save and retrieve files and know where to look for and find them after you save them. You should be comfortable navigating within the application. Take the Final Cut Pro tour, and do the Final Cut Pro tutorial projects so that you're comfortable with the interface elements, such as pull-down menus and floating palette windows.

You should be familiar with your digital camcorder, knowing how to turn it on and off, switch between capture and playback mode. You should also be familiar with the FireWire cable connection between the camcorder and your computer.

Be sure to consult your owner's manual and reference guides for all of your computer, software, and camera devices for any information you're not immediately familiar or comfortable with.

Wherever possible, when a menu command has a keyboard shortcut associated with it, a description is included with the text as a Note or Tip.

BE AWARE OF SOME CAVEATS

There are certain fundamental differences between the graphics world and the digital video world. In fact, there are bound to be differences between versions of software, operating systems, and even brands of cameras when it comes to connectivity and operability.

Be aware that the color space and even pixel density between the graphics world and the video world have some basic differences and can produce some unexpected results. This is especially visible when viewing your video media on a computer screen and on a regular NTSC color TV monitor. Consult your reference materials for specifics on how to compensate for these differences.

If you've been using a Macintosh for any length of time, you'll notice that the basic interface for Final Cut Pro is substantially different from what you're used to seeing on a Macintosh. Getting used to it is easy, but the differences may initially be challenging for you.

Keyboard shortcuts are not always the conventional command key + types of shortcuts you're accustomed to. Many rely on nonstandard combinations of shift, option, control, and command (and if you're using a PowerBook, the function) keys. In fact, many keyboard shortcuts do not require a command or modifying key at all.

You may want to consider printing the Final Cut Pro keyboard shortcut guide as a handy assistant. You'll find it in the PDF documentation that ships with the product.

It may take some time, but you will likely become quickly familiar and comfortable with the new media and functionality that Final Cut Pro has to offer. My recommendation is always to learn your favorite techniques well and compile a personal "bag of tricks" that you can draw from as needed. As is most often the case, the techniques you know best can help you learn new techniques when challenged. In short, what you know is the best foundation for what you want to learn.

And finally, if you become confused, run out of ideas, or can't find the answers in the help files, plenty of resources are readily available and easily accessible for learning more about Apple, the Macintosh, and Final Cut Pro on the Internet.

CHAPTER 1

GETTING READY: PREPARING YOUR VIDEO CLIPS

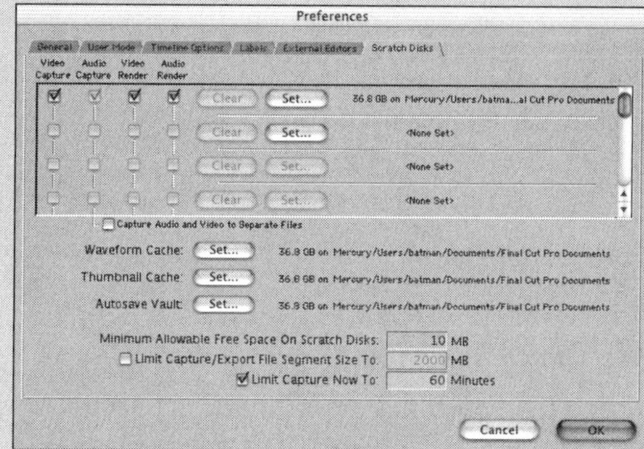

This chapter leads you through the basics of preparing your video clips for editing in Final Cut Pro. From techniques as easily quantifiable as establishing "Handle" length value and determining where to store your clips while you compose your video to more subjective topics such as "How to plan your shots for special effects," this chapter helps you make better decisions earlier in the production process.

The decisions you make about settings, which you establish at the beginning of your video project, are the foundation on which you build your production and special effects. Good decisions now help to smooth out your production process and make editing your Final Cut Pro projects easier as you assemble your final projects.

Establishing your initial presets and project settings should be performed as you initially install and set up Final Cut Pro on your computer. Also, the setting you choose for device control is entirely specific to the type and brand of camera or digital video devices you're using. Consult the Final Cut Pro documentation and your camera's owner's manual for this initial installation and setup information.

This chapter starts with a simple explanation and demonstration of how to capture all of the clips on a tape, then how to specify and set "handles" for your clips, and finally how and where to store all the clips you captured.

Onward!

import media
batch capture
set handle length
store clips
F2
I O
J K L

TECHNIQUE 1

"BATCH" CAPTURE YOUR VIDEO CLIPS

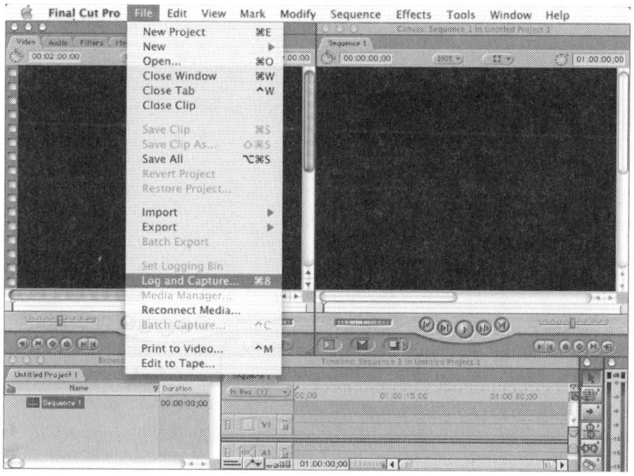

1.1

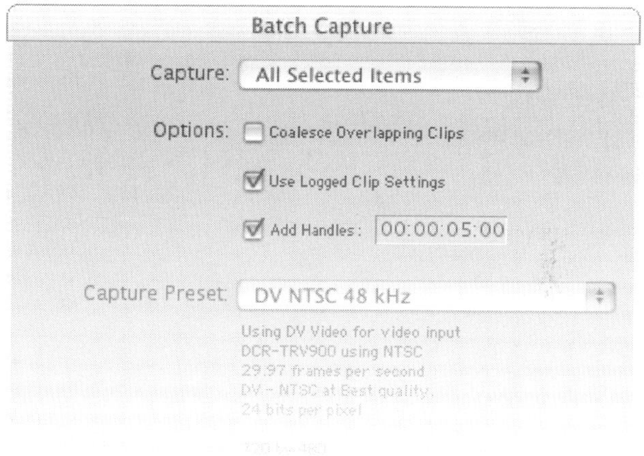

1.2

Your first step in creating a compelling video project is to capture all your video data from your camcorder or video source to your computer's hard drive. This prospect can be tedious if you're playing through your tapes, making edit decisions, rewinding, capturing, naming, and annotating your files. The process is time-consuming and known to cause madness in even the most experienced professionals.

Final Cut Pro allows you to play through your tape, marking your preferred edit points as you go, and then command the program to do all the tedious capturing work for you while you attend to more interesting tasks (such as answering your e-mail, doing your laundry, returning your agent's phone calls, and so forth).

The steps are simple and easy to learn.

ENCODING A TAPE

First things first. Before you begin to record on any tape, it should be "encoded" so that it will have a complete timecode sequence from start to finish. The timecode is what tells Final Cut Pro and your camcorder where every clip is on the tape. Without a continuous timecode throughout the tape, you are likely to encounter problems in capturing your video media to the computer. Final Cut Pro is designed to alert you whenever it encounters a break in the timecode on the tape.

To encode a tape, simply place the tape in the camcorder. Make sure the lens cap is on tightly, covering the lens and preventing any video capture. Start recording. Let the camera record the inside of the lens cap for its entire length. Doing this places a timecode signal throughout the entire length of the tape.

After the encoding is done, simply rewind and mark the tape as encoded. Now you're ready to record video onto it.

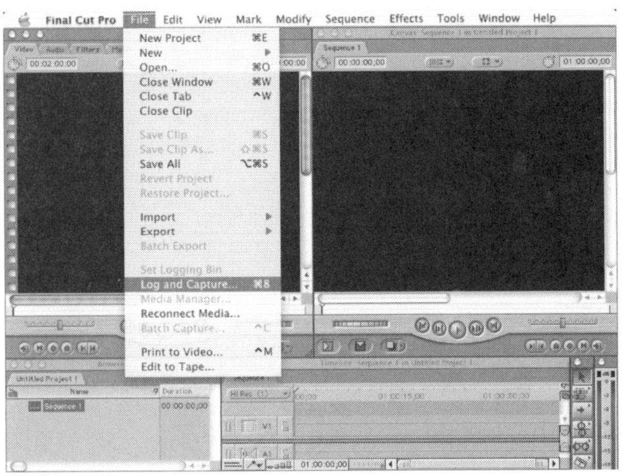

1.3

STEP 1: MARK YOUR CLIPS

Before you begin, set your camera to VTR mode, make sure your FireWire cable is connected properly to your Macintosh and launch Final Cut Pro.

- Choose **File ➢ Log & Capture** (Command+8) as shown in **Figure 1.3**.

STEP 2: SET YOUR REEL AND SCENE INFORMATION

TIP

If you label your tapes as you record them, naming the clips, reel, and bin collections with the same title as the one you wrote on the tape label makes good sense. Imagine having to look through your vast collection of tapes for that one clip on a tape that is labeled differently from the bin in your Final Cut Pro project!

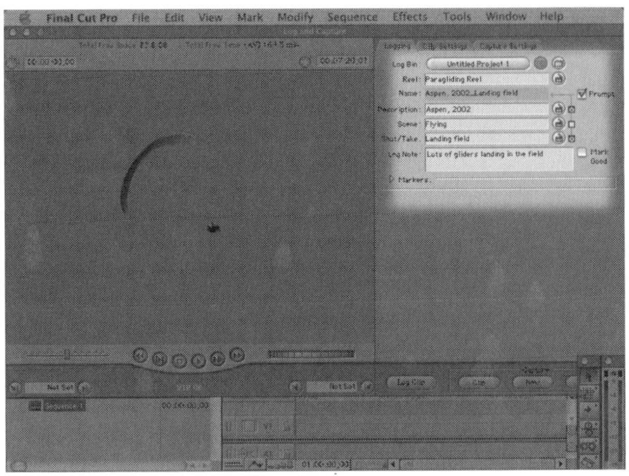

1.4

STEP 3: LOG YOUR CLIPS AND THEN MARK YOUR IN AND OUT POINTS

If you storyboard your production, you can use your hand-drawn sketches in front of you as a guide for how and where to set your in and out points for each scene or clip you're capturing.

As you're viewing your raw media on tape, begin setting the in and out points for each clip that you want to capture as shown in **Figure 1.4**.

In and *Out points* shown in **Figure 1.5** are markers that Final Cut Pro uses to know where to begin and end capturing clips of video media from your tape. Final Cut Pro allows you more than one way to mark your clips. You can use the handy intuitive on-screen buttons in the viewer window, or you can use the handy intuitive keyboard commands.

At this moment, all you're doing is telling Final Cut Pro where on the tape to start and stop capturing video data after you give it the batch capture command. You can easily shuttle-jog your tape back and forth, playing and marking your clips by using the following keyboard shortcuts:

L: Play the tape from the current location.
K: Stops the tape playing.
J: Rolls tape in reverse.
I: Marks an in point.
O: Marks an out point.
F2: Logs the clip and displays a dialog box allowing you to name the clip.

Note that the JKL key positions in **Figure 1.6** allow for easy one-handed control of the reverse, stop, and play commands.

Each time you press the F2 key to mark your clip, you see a dialog box asking you to name the clip and add a notation if you want.

You also see a clip icon appear in the browser window in **Figure 1.7**.

TIP

Device control must be enabled in the Audio/Video settings for you to be able to control your camcorder by using the keyboard shortcuts. You can open the Audio Video settings by hitting Option+Command+Q.

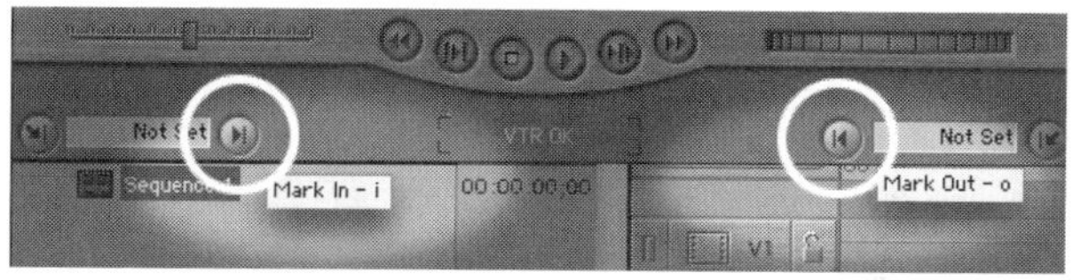

1.5

1.6

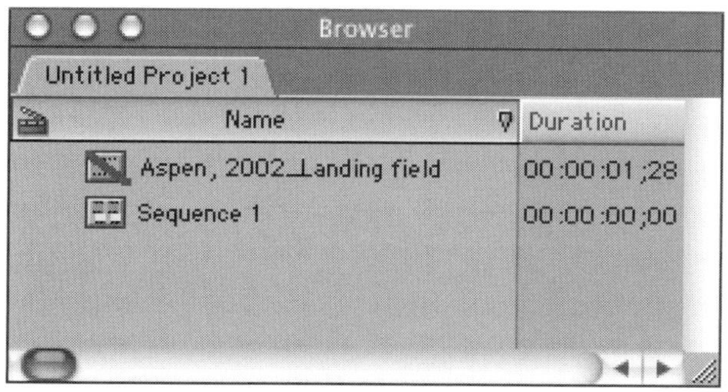

1.7

Note that all of your captured clip icons have red lines running diagonally across them, indicating that they have been marked, but not yet captured.

STEP 4: CLOSE THE LOG AND CAPTURE WINDOW

- Click the Close button on the log and capture window or just choose **File ➢ Close Window**.

STEP 5: SELECT THE CLIPS YOU WANT TO CAPTURE

Figure 1.8 shows your Browser bin. This shows you icons with a diagonal red line through them for each of the logged but uncaptured clips you marked on this tape, indicating that they are logged, but not yet actually captured from the tape to your hard drive.

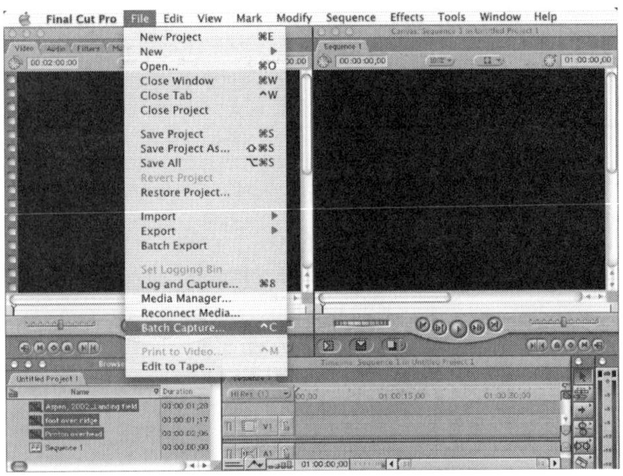

1.8

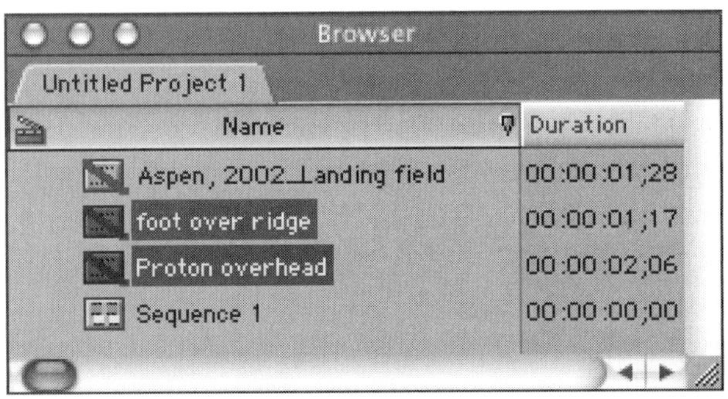

1.9

- You can select all or only some of the clips to capture by choosing each sequentially while holding down the Control key or by drawing a selection rectangle around a group selection as shown in **Figure 1.9**.

STEP 6: BATCH CAPTURE

- Click to select the browser window, then choose **File ➢ Batch Capture...** (Control+C) as shown in **Figure 1.10**.

STEP 7: GET A CUP OF COFFEE

- After the capture process has completed, you see your captured clips in the browser window without the red line through the icons in **Figure 1.11**.

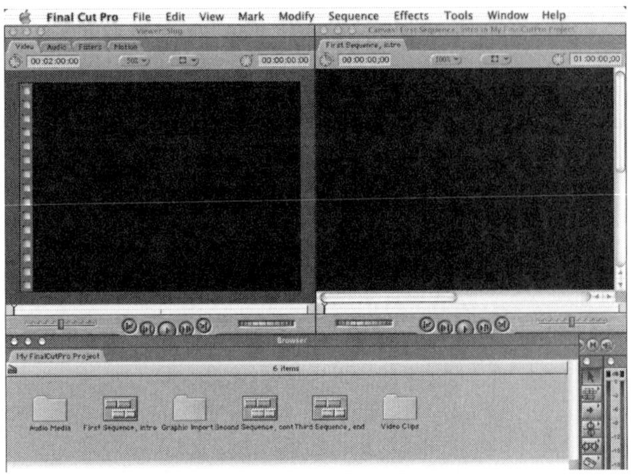

1.10

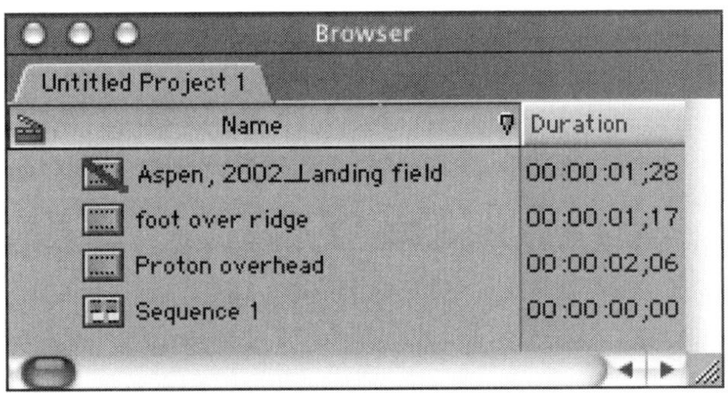

1.11

TECHNIQUE **2**

SETTING "HANDLE" LENGTH

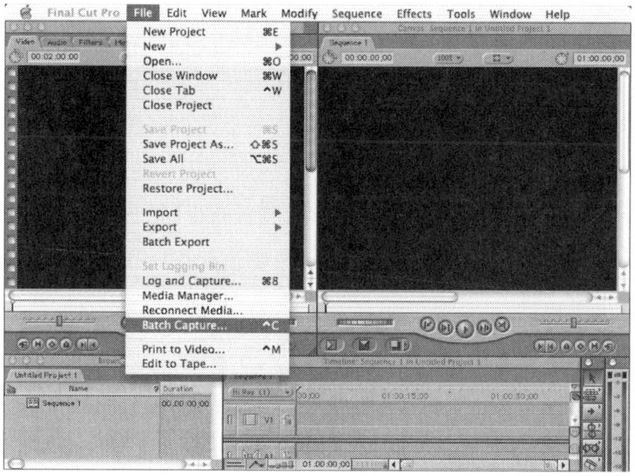

2.1

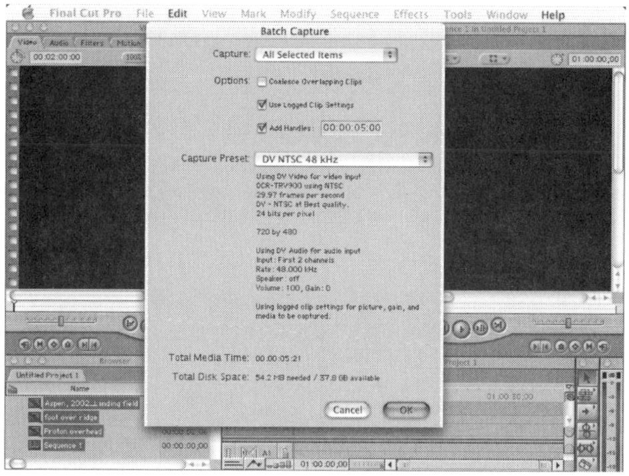

2.2

Handles are extra frames of media saved at the beginning and the end of a captured clip. The handle allows you to, in effect, "color outside the lines," giving you a few extra seconds or a defined number of additional frames of captured video data with which to transition between scenes, clips, or effects.

Final Cut Pro enables you to establish a value for these handles, measured in frames – or in seconds of video data when you begin the actual capture from tape process. Final Cut Pro enables you to specify the handle length when you choose the Batch Capture command.

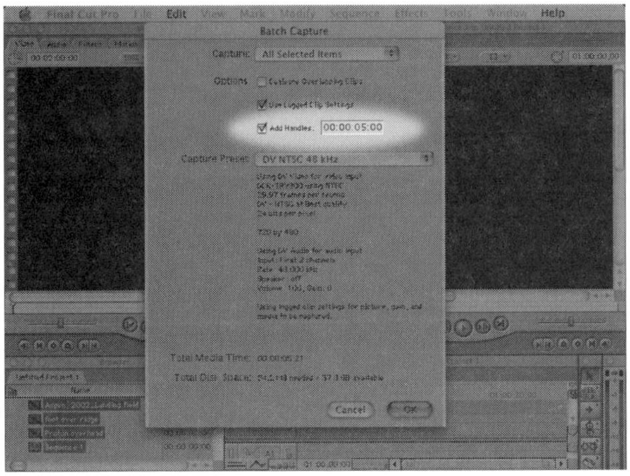

2.3

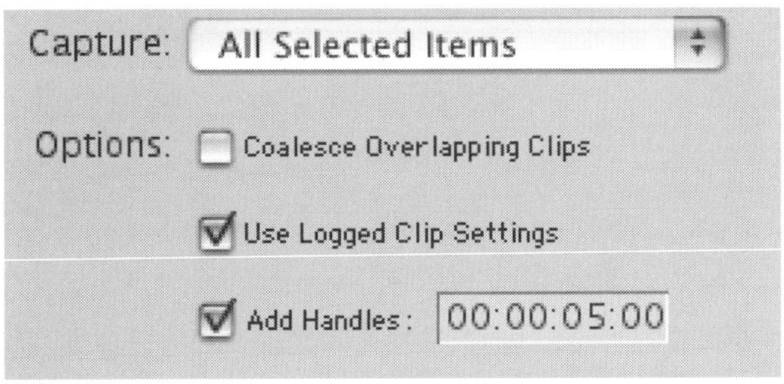

2.4

STEP 1: SET HANDLE LENGTH

After choosing File ➢ Batch Capture. . ., Final Cut Pro presents you with a series of batch capture preferences. One of the most important is the Handle Length setting.

Handle length defines the amount of time or frames of video data that precedes and follows the marked in or out point of your capture.

- Click the Add Handles button shown in **Figure 2.3**.

STEP 2: SPECIFY YOUR HANDLE LENGTH

Just as in the graphics world, where a little margin space around the outside of an image allows you room to adjust the cropped area of the image, in the video world, handles give you a little extra space at either end of your clip with which to adjust the in and out (or start and end) points of your video clip.

- In the handle length field, type in **00:05:00** seconds (shown in **Figure 2.4**) of handle length for the clips you are capturing.

STEP 3: FINISH THE STEP

Click the OK button. Now you have established a handle length for this sequence of captured clips.

TECHNIQUE 3

STORING YOUR CLIPS ON YOUR HARD DRIVE

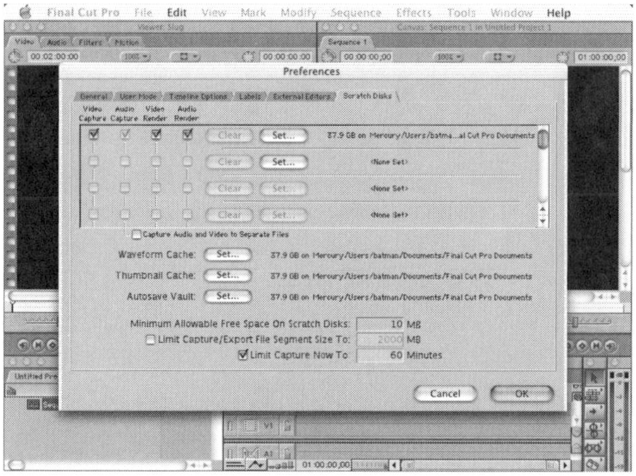

3.1

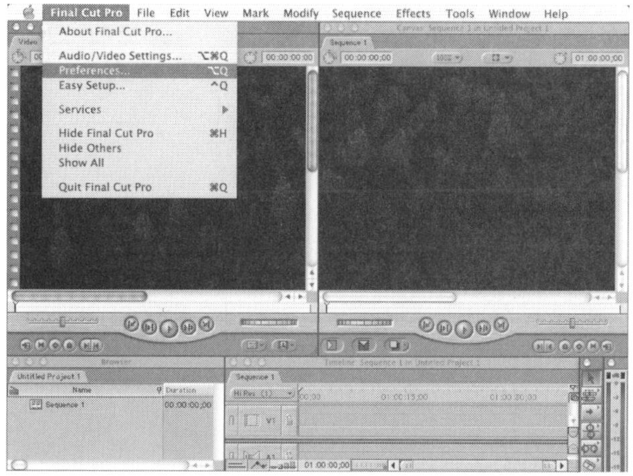

3.2

Final Cut Pro presents just the right mix of freedom and structure in allowing you to determine where and how you store your captured clips.

By default, Final Cut Pro stores your captured video clips in the Final Cut Pro Documents folder found in your `users/documents/Final Cut Pro Documents` directory of your main hard drive. However, you are not limited to this location.

You can tell Final Cut Pro to store your project and rendering files anywhere that is convenient or practical for you. At any time in the production of your project you can choose a new location for the storage of captured clips. This storage is called your *scratch disk*.

Storing your captured media in the device with the largest contiguous free space available generally makes sense, as does storing all the relevant and related clips together in the same directory.

- Choose **Final Cut Pro ➢ Preferences...** (Option+Q).

The dialog box has six tabs controlling different aspects of Final Cut Pro's general preferences.

- Choose the **Scratch Disks** tab.

CONTIGUOUS FREE SPACE

When information is recorded onto your hard drive, the fastest, most efficient way for the information to be stored and retrieved is if all the tiny little data packets are right next to each other. Although modern computers are very good at keeping track of where all the data is on your hard drive, even if it ends up in unconnected segments on opposite ends of the hard drive map, for high-bandwidth applications like video editing large segments of contiguous (geographically adjacent) drive space can offer a faster data flow and fewer dropped frames when recording.

To find out how much contiguous free space is available on your hard drive, you'll need to use a commercial drive maintenance software utility like those from Norton, FWB, or Micromat. They will investigate your drive map and allow you to optimize the placement of the data.

Alternatively, if you are recording or storing your video media to a separate internal or external hard drive, you can take the step that many professionals do when starting or finishing a project. Completely re-format your primary storage drive prior to beginning the capture process!

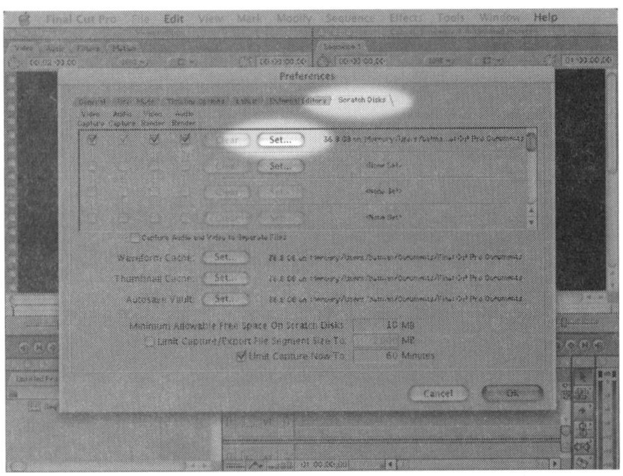

3.3

This tab lets you specify where you want to store your captured clips for later processing.

- Choose the Set button (shown in **Figure 3.3**) next to the first scratch disk setting and navigate to the folder where you want your media stored during capture.

Final Cut Pro enables you to define up to five different connected media storage devices. As each one in the series fills up, Final Cut Pro automatically begins storing new data on the next available specified drive.

A good strategy is to collect and keep your video clips for each project together on some high-density fast external devices while you're working on your project. This method allows you to move and process data back and forth across your system as efficiently as possible. After the project is complete, you can archive your media on a reliable, permanent removable media, such as DVD-RAM or Tape Backup.

STORAGE DEVICES

Your choices for types of storage devices is rather limited. They fall into three easy-to-remember families of devices: USB, FireWire, and SCSI. USB (universal serial-bus) has the slowest transfer speeds and given the volume of data to store, is the least practical of the three.

FireWire is a generic trade name used to describe the IEEE-1394 serial data transfer scheme. Hard drives with Firewire bus connectivity offer convenience of hot-swappability and easy plug-and-play connections, as well as reasonable transfer speeds. While FireWire-enabled hard drives make for a great storage medium, an external FireWire drive is generally not the best choice for media capture. The nature of its serial communications as the data passes through the computer's on-board bus to the external drive, makes it prone to dropped frames while capturing. The current generally accepted wisdom is that a fast SCSI capture device offers the best reliability for capturing high-density, high-speed data, such as video.

TECHNIQUE 4

ORGANIZING YOUR CLIPS

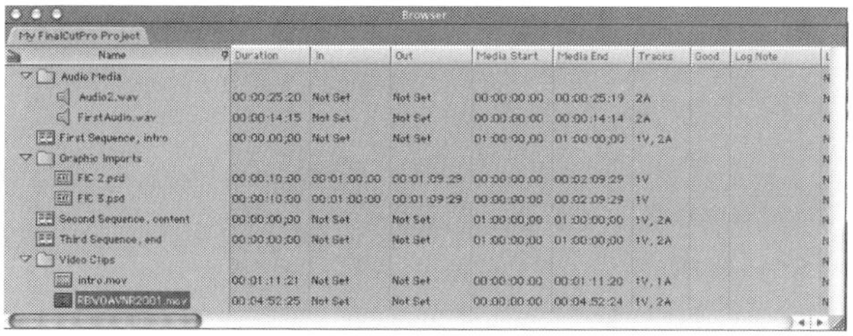

4.1

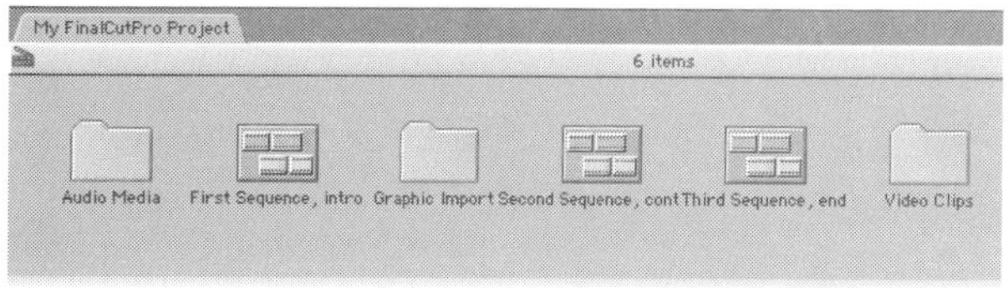

4.2

Because Final Cut Pro offers great flexibility in organizing your data, it's easy for you to create your own storage scheme for keeping track of which clips and which media types belong to which sequence of video you're editing.

You can think of your storage scheme the same way that you think of the filing system of any computer system (which in turn is analogous to real world filing cabinets): folders within folders within folders.

Your Project exists as a tab in the browser window. You can create folders within that browser window, called Bins, to store and organize your different media types and clips.

You might categorize your clips by media type, storing all your audio clips in a bin labeled "Audio," your video clips in a bin labeled "Video," and so on, with bins for effects, still frames, artwork, mattes, and so on.

You might also store your individual scenes as a bin, containing sub-bins for the media that exists in each scene. For example, "Opening Scene" would then contain bins for audio and video media that are part of that scene.

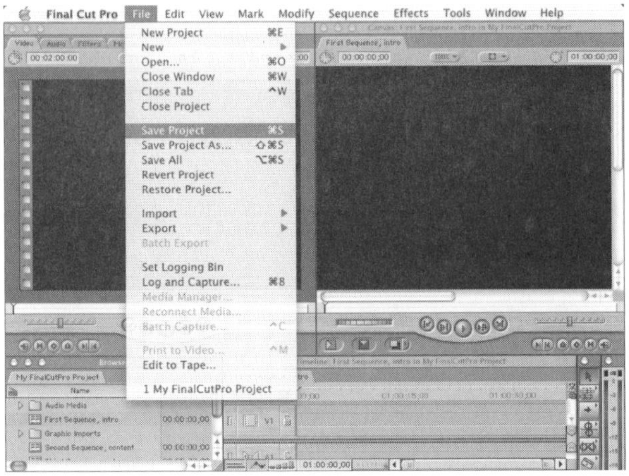

4.3

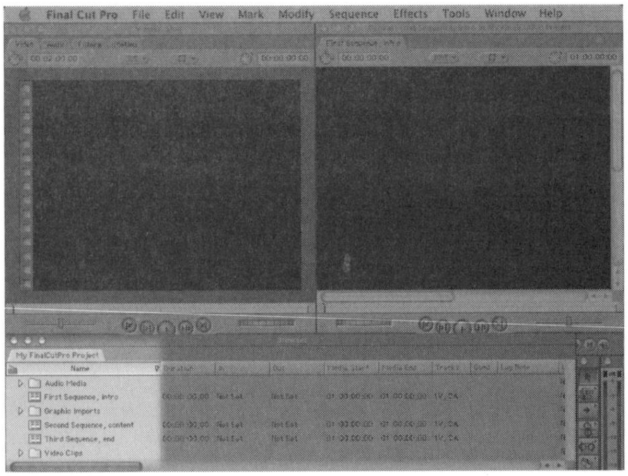

4.4

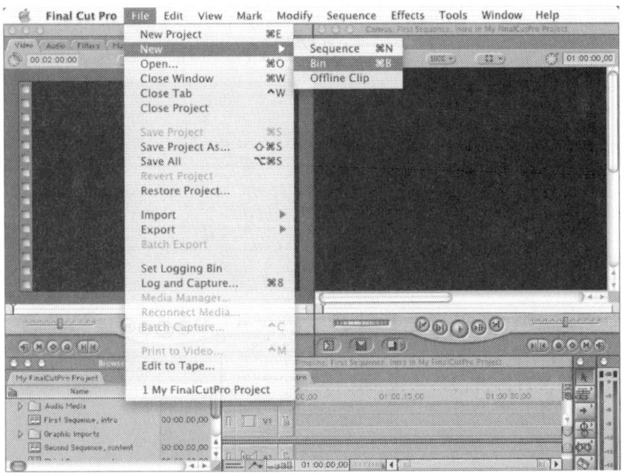

4.5

STEP 1: SAVE AND NAME YOUR PROJECT

You must save your project in order to name the Project tab.

- As shown in **Figure 4.3**, choose **File ➢ Save Project . . . .**

You see that the name of your project now appears as the name of the tab in your browser window.

STEP 2: CREATE A NEW BIN

- Choose **File ➢ New ➢ Bin** (Command+B). As shown in **Figure 4.4**, a new bin with a folder icon appears in the browser window.

STEP 3: NAME YOUR NEW BIN

As the new bin appears in the browser window in **Figure 4.5**, the default name assigned to it highlights and is ready for you to type in a new name as you see in **Figure 4.6**. Easy!

- Press return to confirm the new name.

You can as easily rename a bin in your browser window by double-clicking on the bin name and typing in a new name for it. Press Enter or Return to finalize the step.

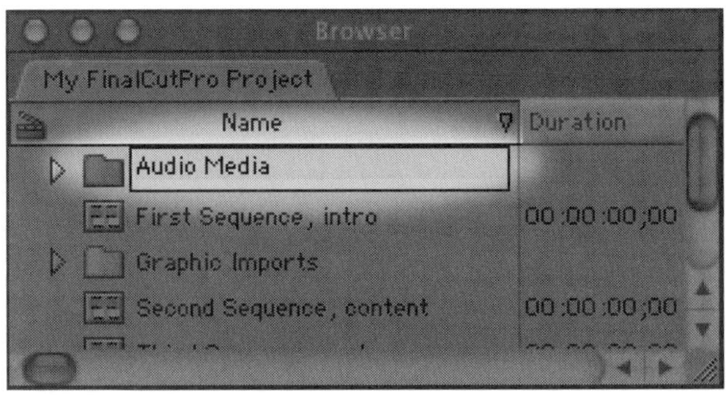

4.6

STEP 4: CREATE MORE NEW BINS

- Repeat the previous steps to create two more new bins. Name one "Video" and the other one "Audio."

This step creates a few more bins, intuitively named, to store your audio and video media for your project.

STEP 5: IMPORT YOUR MEDIA

Importing media to Final Cut Pro is as easy as any drag-and-drop operation on the Macintosh.

- From a finder window, simply click to select the files you want to add to your project and drag them into the appropriate bin in your Browser.

You can also import media to your browser window by using a menu command or keyboard shortcut. Do this by choosing File ➢ Import ➢ Files (Command+I) (shown in **Figure 4.7**).

Items imported and stored in Final Cut Pro Project are not necessarily embedded into the project. Instead, they are marked and tagged with an invisible link to the location of the actual media as shown in **Figure 4.8**. You might think of the icons shown in the browser window as an alias, or a pointer to the original file, as you would in the Mac's Finder.

WARNING

Once the media has been imported, if it is moved from its original location, Final Cut Pro will prompt you to locate and re-link the media to your project.

TIP

Final Cut Pro gives each media type a unique icon that is easily recognizable for efficient media management and storage. Audio media has a unique audio icon, as does video media.

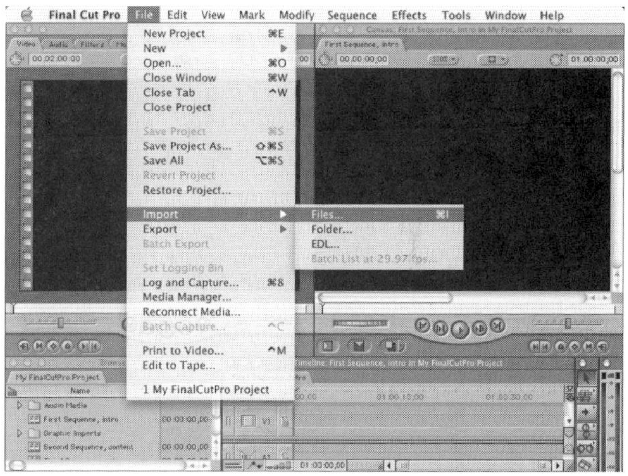

4.7

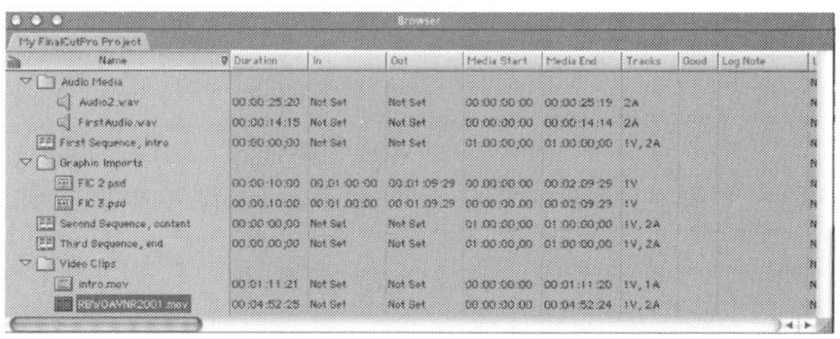

4.8

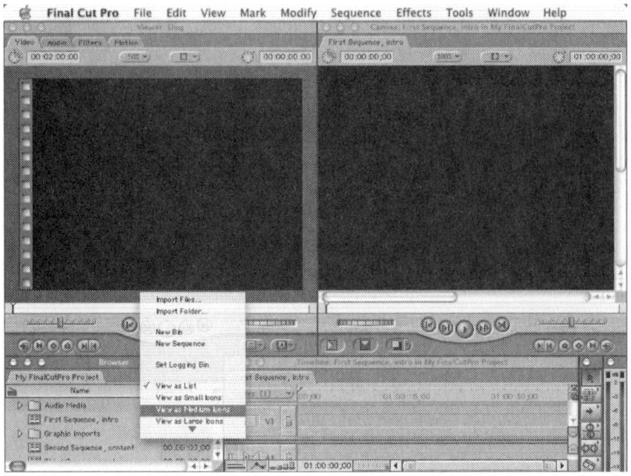

4.9

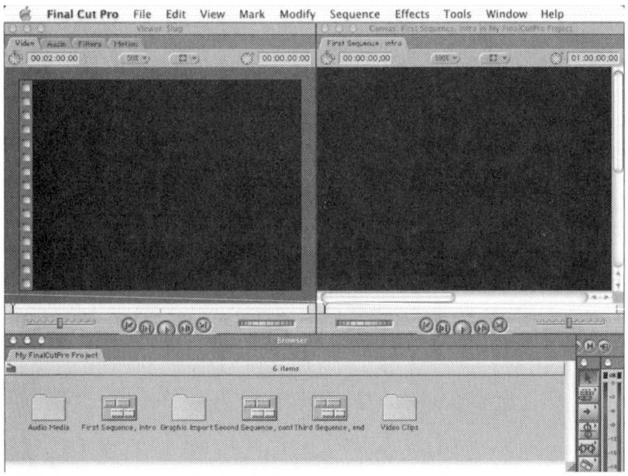

4.10

STEP 6: LOGICALLY ORGANIZE YOUR MEDIA

No matter how you imported your media items, or where they are currently stored, you can rearrange and reorganize the media clips in the Project tab.

- Click to select your media clips in the browser window. Then drag and drop them into the bin icons where they make the most sense.

That's not all!

Final Cut Pro also lets you change the appearance of the icons in your browser window to make it even easier for you to organize all your media clips. Simply hold down the Control key while clicking the browser window to reveal the contextual pop-up menu as you see in **Figure 4.9**. From this menu you can choose from several different view options, as well as choose other commands relevant to the Browser as shown in **Figure 4.10**.

CHAPTER 2

TECHNIQUES FOR IMPROVING YOUR VIDEO PICTURE

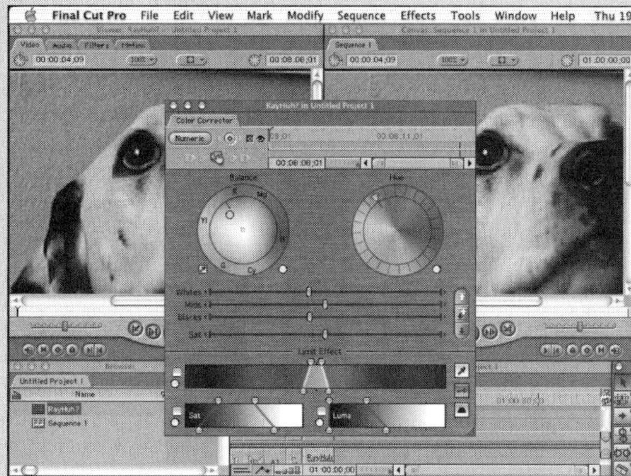

Final Cut Pro lets you enhance the look of any video image through the application of filters in much the same way that you're used to applying filters to images in Adobe Photoshop. The difference in Final Cut Pro is that the filter effects are time-based, meaning that you can apply and adjust the filter's effects over the course of time.

If you're familiar with Adobe Photoshop, then you already know how powerful the concept of corrective filter commands can be for image enhancement and adjustment. Final Cut Pro offers a suite of powerful filter enhancements that enable you to adjust your video images in much the same way as the filter effects of Photoshop enhance still images and graphics.

Many times a simple one-step filter effect or basic image control is all that is needed to improve the basic visual quality of your video image in Final Cut Pro. For example, image corrections such as color balance, saturation, and contrast are often only a simple menu command away.

You can get as sophisticated and complex as you want with these techniques and build layers on top of layers of corrective filter effects onto your clips. However, the demonstrations that follow are good starting points to help show you the simple techniques available to you through the video filter effects menus.

You might be amazed at the breadth and diversity of the effects you can create with these simple video variations.

Color Corrector
Filters
Video Filters
Sharpen
Amount
Sequence
Effects
Tools
Window
Help
Video Transitions
Favorites
Default - Cross Dissolve
Set Default
Clear Default
Video Filters
Favorites
Audio Transitions
Favorites
Default - Cross Fade (+3dB)
Set Default
Clear Default
Audio Filters
Favorites
Motion Favorites
Blur
Border
Channel
Color Correction
Distort
FXScript DVE's
FXScript Layered DVE's
Image Control
Key
Matte
Perspective
QuickTime
Sharpen
Stylize
Video
Brightness and Contrast (Bezier)
Color Balance
Desaturate
Gamma Correction
Levels
Proc Amp
Sepia
Tint
colorcorrection
00:00:02;05
100%

A SIMPLE SHARPEN FILTER

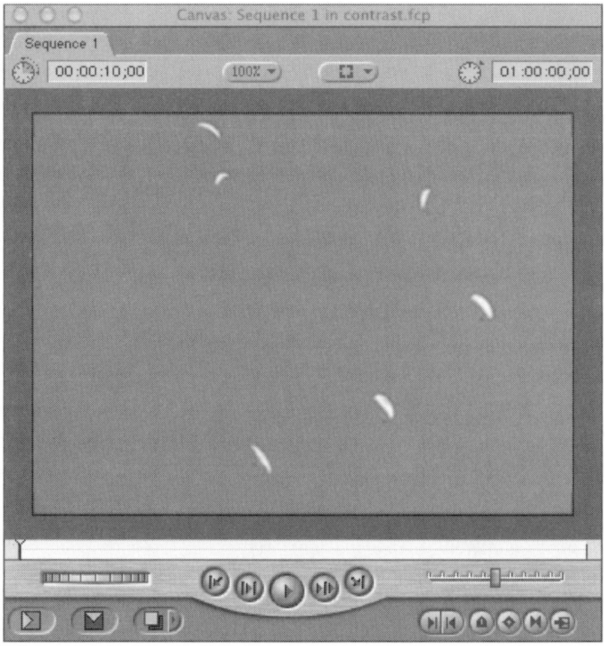

5.1

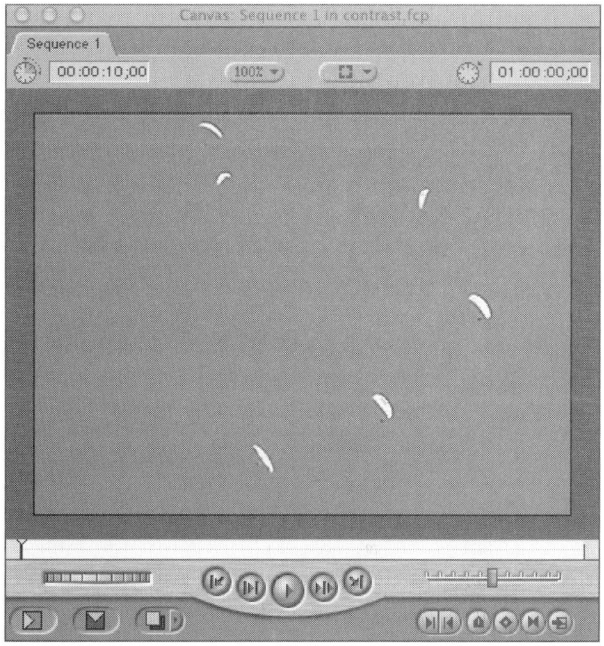

5.2

To play along with these demonstrations, you need to open some of the files included on the CD-ROM that ships with this book. The sample files accentuate some common failings of current video camera technology and the techniques here lead you through the simple steps required to correct them.

A simple sharpening of an image can be useful when you want to accentuate some of the contrast detail in a video image.

■ Open the file in the Chapter 2 Project folder named **sharpenme.fcp**.

■ Choose **File ➢ Open** as shown in **Figure 5.3** and choose the file from the navigation window that appears (shown in **Figure 5.4**). Alternatively, you can also simply drag the file from the finder into the browser window for your project.

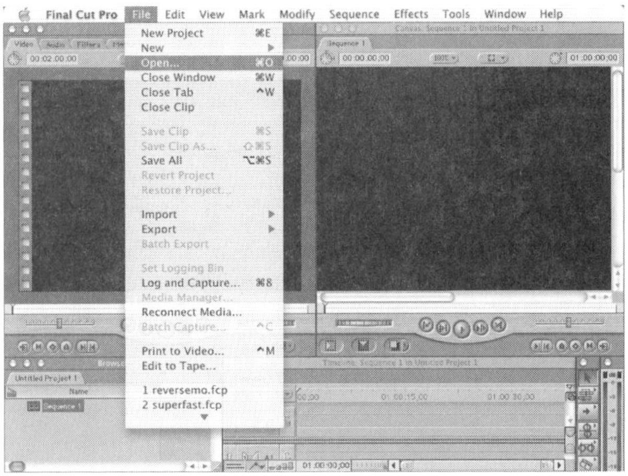

5.3

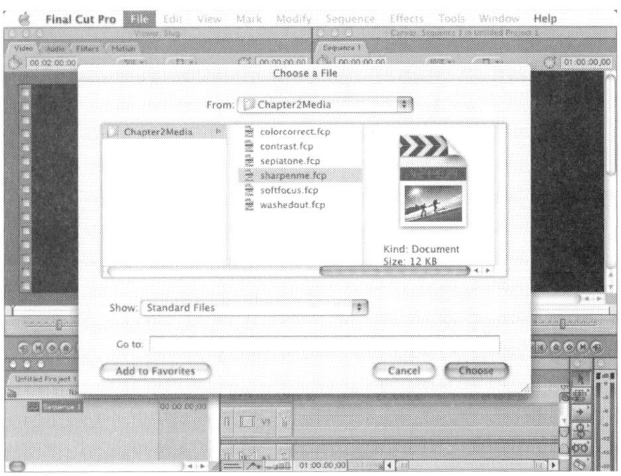

5.4

As you scrub back and forth with the play head through this short clip, you can see how the video image in this clip could use a little improvement.

■ Double-click the imported clip in the bin to see it in the viewer window.

■ Choose **Effects ➢ Video Filters ➢ Sharpen ➢ Sharpen**, as shown in **Figure 5.5**.

You immediately see the effect of the sharpen filter applied to the video clip. Yikes! It looks terrible! Of course, you want to mitigate the super-heavy-handed application of this video filter by controlling it in the video tab of the viewer window.

■ Click the **Filters** tab of the viewer window in **Figure 5.6** to show all the currently applied video filters. This filter is the only one.

■ Expose the controls for this video filter by clicking the **delta** next to the check box that appears to the left of the filter name.

■ Here's where you can adjust the level of filter application to the selected clip. Click and drag the **slider** to the left in **Figure 5.7** to reduce the effect of the sharpen filter application on the sample video clip.

5.5

In order for you to see the effects of the filter application immediately as you apply or change it, you can separate the tabs in the viewer window and view them both side by side.

Remember to apply your filters judiciously. A few light applications of a filter almost always yields better results than a heavy-handed application.

> **NOTE**
>
> **"Scrubbing" or "to scrub" is a simple term used to describe the manual movement of the play head through the timeline. When you manually drag the play head through the timeline using the mouse or keyboard shortcuts to place the play head at a desired location in the timeline, you are scrubbing.**

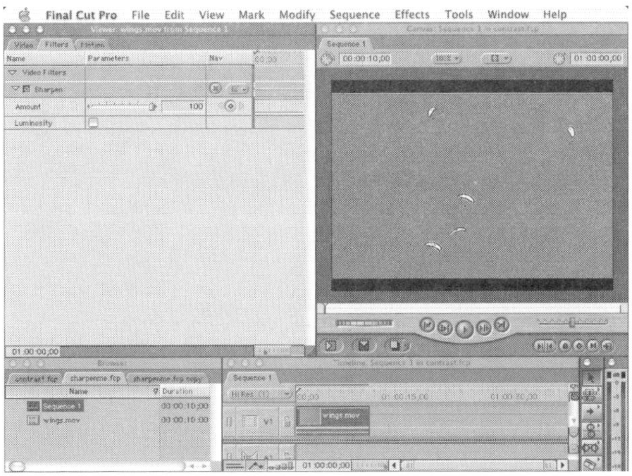

5.6

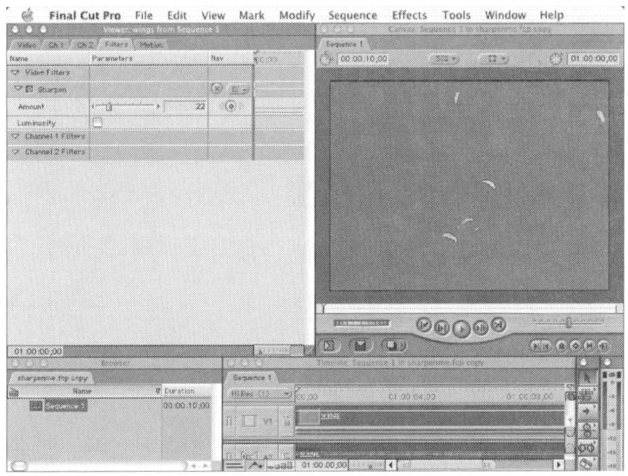

5.7

TECHNIQUE 6

SIMPLE CONTRAST CORRECTION

6.1 (CP1)

6.2 (CP2)

For this demonstration, you make another simple image correction by using a single application of a video filter. Enhancing contrast can add a hint of sharpness and boost the color energy in a video image. In doing so, it might also add a feeling of drama and surrealism that you might not see anywhere else.

■ Open the file in the Chapter 2 folder named **contrast.mov**, as shown in **Figure 6.3**. Choose **File ➢ Open.**

This video image looks a little flat and lifeless.

■ Double-click the **imported** clip in the bin to see it in the **viewer** window.

■ From the Effects menu, choose **Effects ➢ Video Filters ➢ Image Control ➢ Brightness and Contrast** as you see in **Figure 6.4**.

■ Again, make sure that your video image is visible in the viewer window while your controls for this filter are visible in the filter window.

■ You can control the level of filter application by moving the slider back and forth manually. For this demonstration, set the brightness amount to **11** and the contrast setting to **22**. Remember, a little goes a long way with video filters.

Figure 6.5 has too much brightness and contrast. However, **Figure 6.6** is just right.

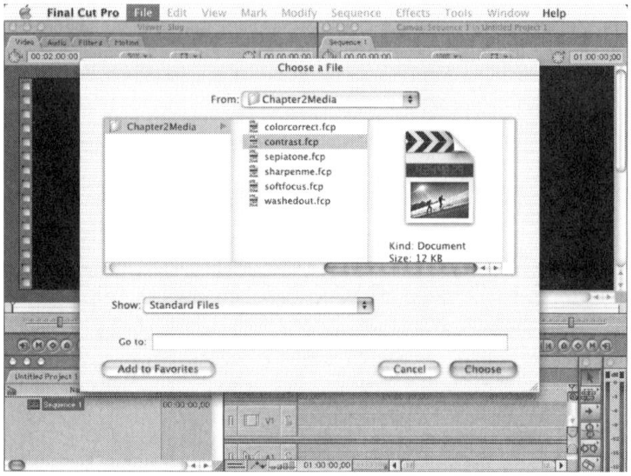

6.3

6.4

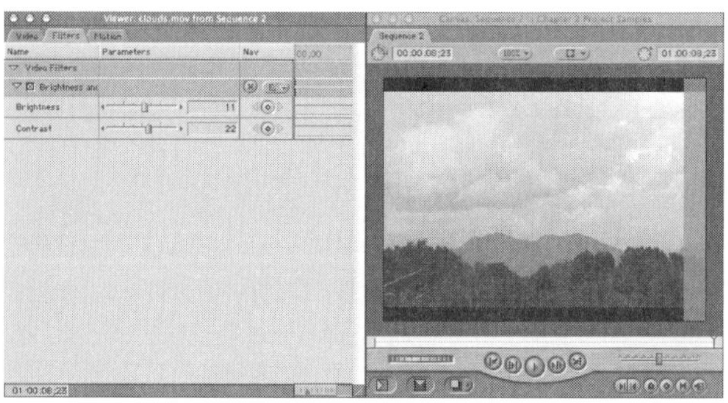

6.5

6.6

TECHNIQUE 7

ADDING A SOFT FOCUS EFFECT TO YOUR VIDEO

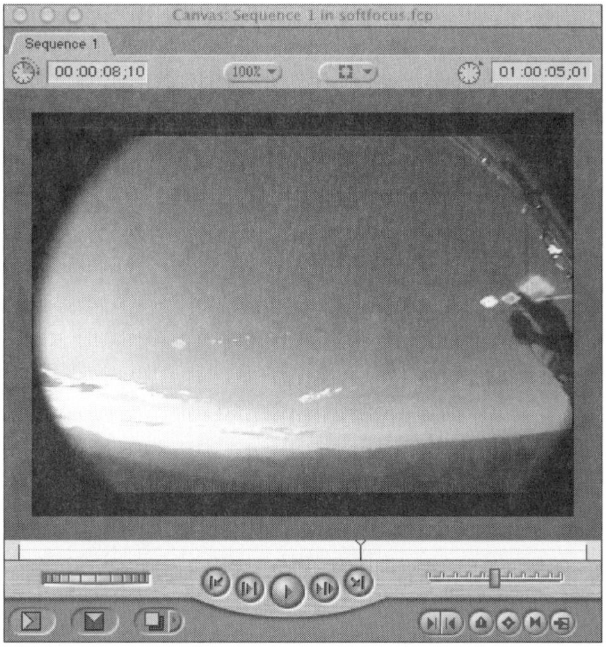

7.1

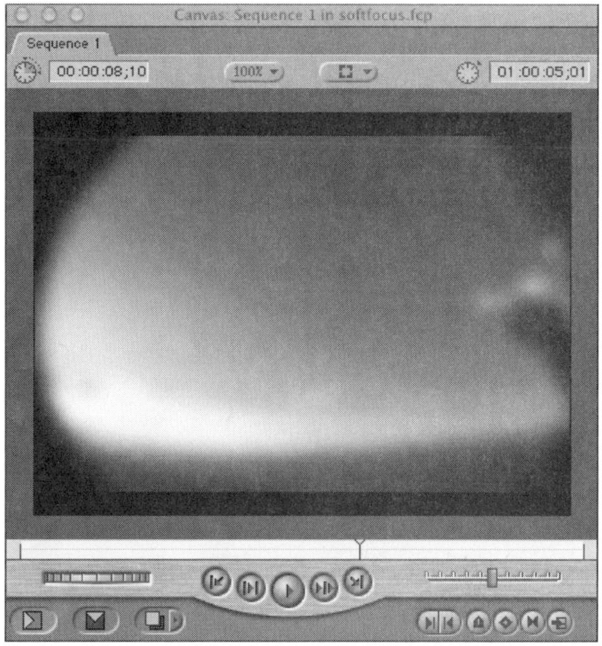

7.2

This technique shows you how to use a simple, one-step video filter to add a stylish mystical or ethereal mood to any video clip. A blurry, softly-focused image may convey the feeling of a memory flashback or romanticized view of an event.

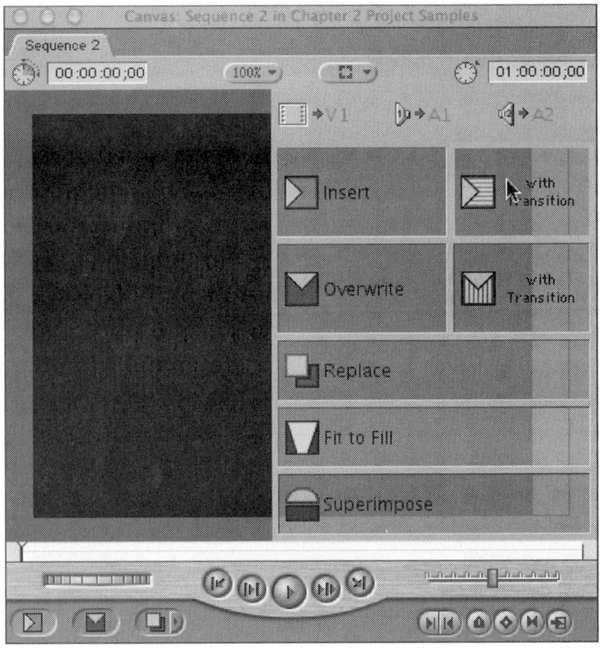

7.3

STEP 1: OPEN THE CLIP

- Open the file named **softfocus.fcp** in the Chapter 2 Project folder.
- Add the clip to the timeline by dragging its icon onto the canvas window and choosing the **with transition** overlay as you see in **Figure 7.3**.

STEP 2: APPLY THE FILTER

- Select the clip and choose Effects ➢ Video Filters ➢ Blur ➢ Gaussian Blur as shown in **Figure 7.4**.

7.4

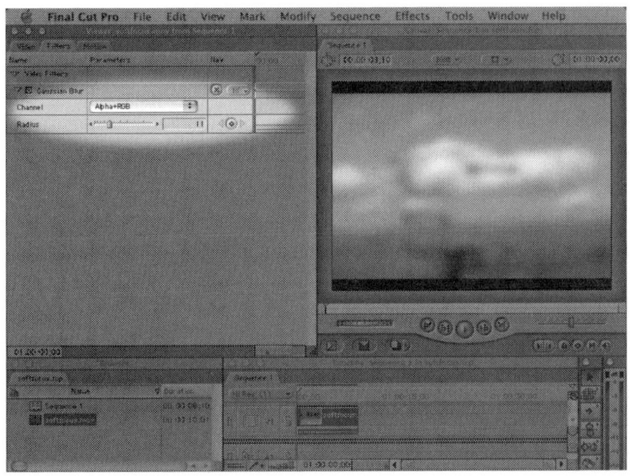

7.5

STEP 3: SET THE SETTINGS

Set the amount of blur to a degree of softness that you like.

- Double-click the clip in the timeline and choose the **Filters** tab in the viewer window.

Here you can change the degree of softness of the blur by sliding the slider or by choosing a value in the value field in **Figure 7.5**.

Figure 7.6 shows a Gaussian blur value of 22. Elements of the image are indistinct.

Figure 7.7 shows a Gaussian blur value of 44.

Even more Gaussian blur is applied to the video image in **Figure 7.8**. This radius value has been set to 66.

STEP 4: RENDER THE CLIP

See how your clip has transformed.

In order for you to preview the work you've done so far, you'll need to render the work. Final Cut Pro renders the media, allowing you to play it back in real-time.

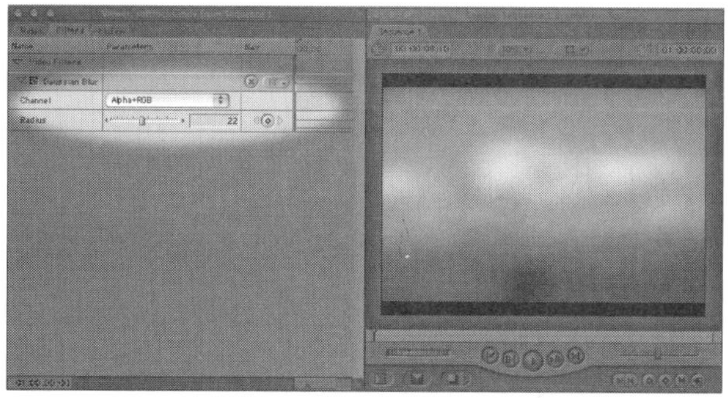

7.6

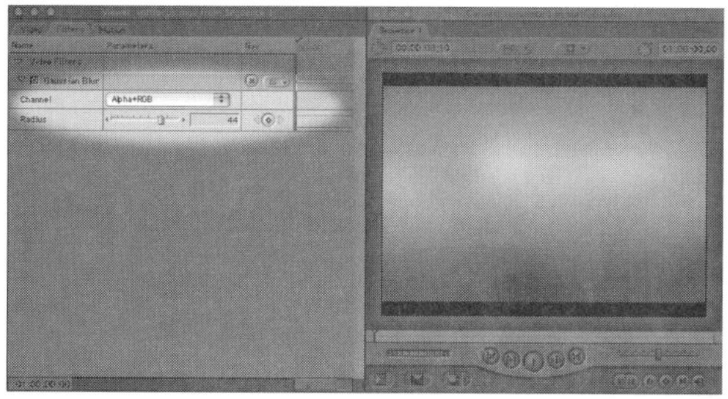

7.7

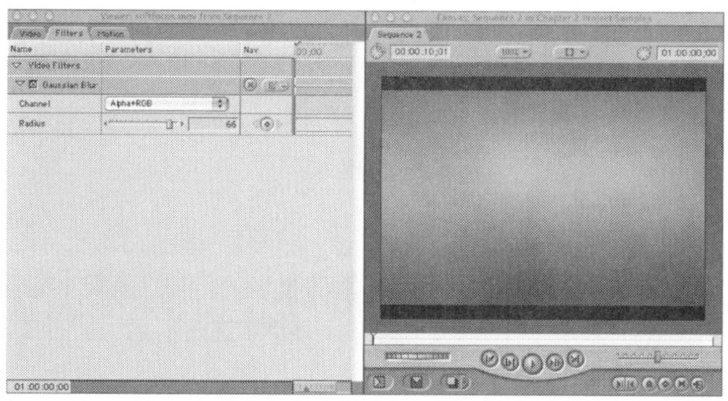

7.8

TECHNIQUE

8

CREATING A WASHED OUT VIDEO BACKDROP

8.1

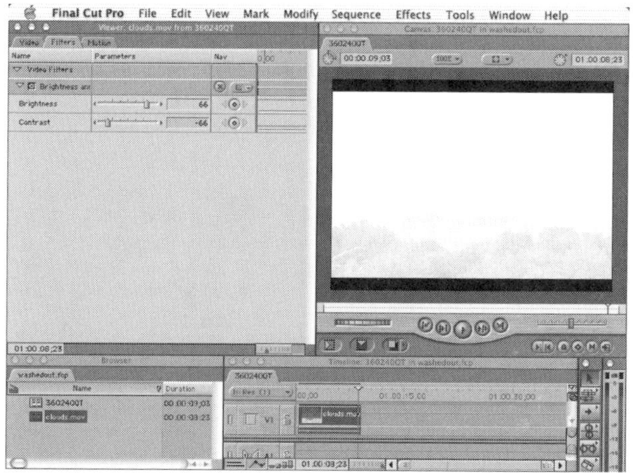

8.2

Here's another simple, yet powerful filtering technique that you can use to add visual texture to your video images. In this technique, you use the contrast controls filter to create a washed out, ethereal background effect.

The effect requires only a single menu command that is precisely controllable and the results can add pure magic to your video.

STEP 1: OPEN THE FILE

- You find a Final Cut Pro file named **washedout.fcp** shown in **Figure 8.3** in the Chapter 2 Project folder.
- Double-click on the clip in the timeline and choose the **Filters** tab in the viewer window.

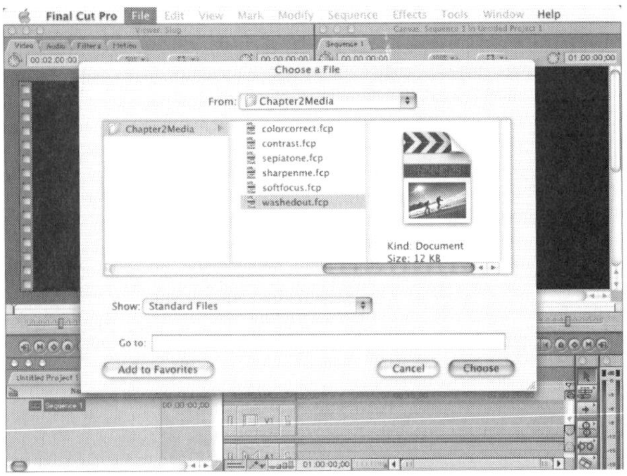

8.3

STEP 2: APPLY THE EFFECT

- Choose **Effects ➢ Video Filters ➢ Image Control ➢ Brightness & Contrast**, as shown in **Figure 8.4**.
- In the **Filters** tab in the viewer window, you see the sliders that control the amount of filter effect that you apply to your clip. Drag the Brightness slider up to **77** as you see in **Figure 8.5**.

Of course, you can also always tab through the value fields to apply your filter amounts as well.

STEP 3: RENDER THE FILE

- Choose **Sequence ➢ Render All** (Option+R).

NOTE

This techniques works equally well in the opposite direction. You can as easily create a darker, more ominous background by dialing down the brightness and contrast controls.

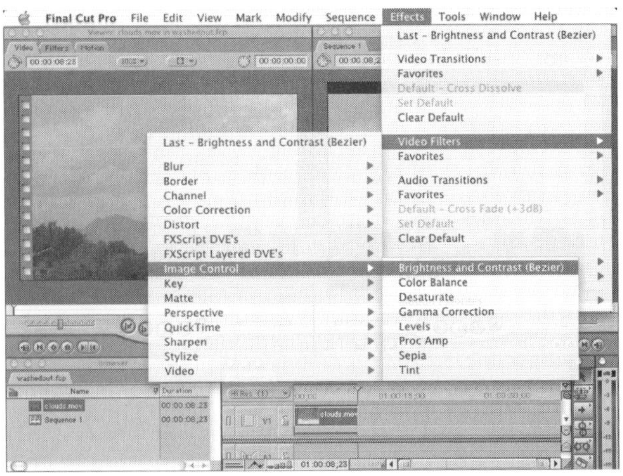

8.4

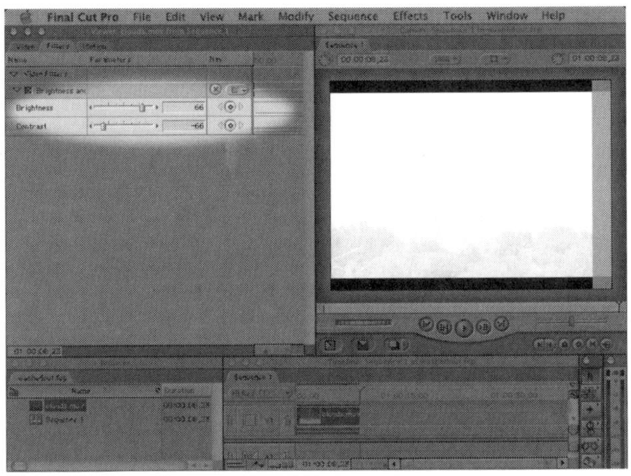

8.5

COLOR CORRECTION WITH FINAL CUT PRO

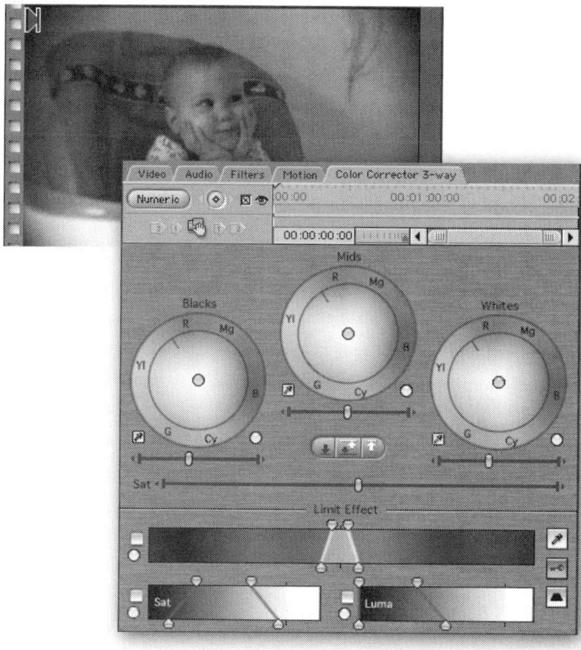

9.1

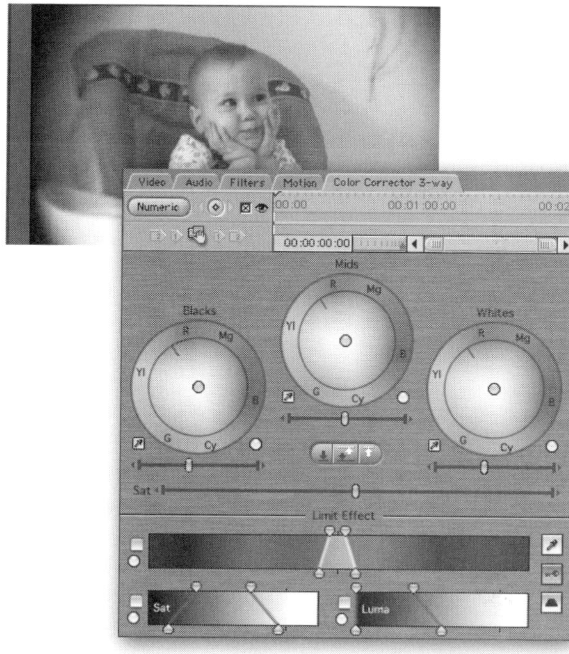

9.2

New color correction capabilities are among the most powerful new features that Final Cut Pro has to offer. With a few simple clicks in a new menu interface, you can compensate for differences in individual clips between varied lighting and camera conditions. You can balance colors, correct for color shifts due to environmental conditions, and even correct for the subtle color shifts that occur under different types of electric lights.

The differences between lighting conditions can sometimes be painfully apparent between clips. You may not immediately notice how green the

9.3

light from fluorescent lighting is until you see your clip played adjacent to a clip shot under the strong yellow of incandescent lights. And similarly, the character of light shot at different times of day can easily affect the mood of a shot.

Final Cut Pro offers you tools to make your representation of color more consistent throughout your video project.

In this technique, you see how easy and precise the color correction controls in Final Cut Pro are to use.

STEP 1: LOAD THE SAMPLE CLIP IN THE VIEWER

- Choose **File ➢ Open** to get the file named **colorcorrect.fcp** in the Chapter 2 Project folder.
- Double-click the clip in the timeline to load it into the viewer window as shown in **Figure 9.3**.

9.4

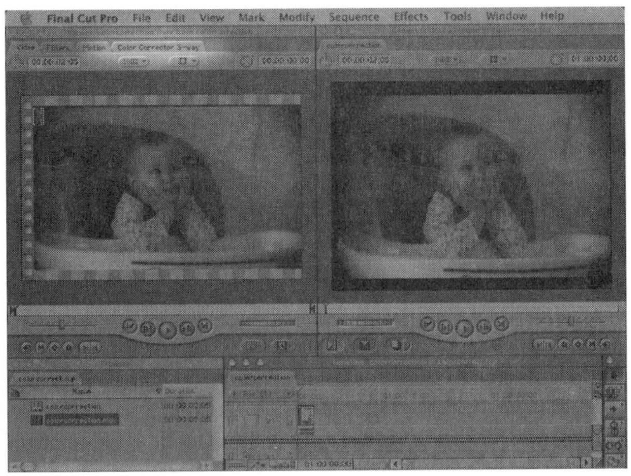

9.5

STEP 2: OPEN THE COLOR CORRECTOR FILTER

- Choose **Effects menu ➢ Video Filters ➢ Color Correction ➢ Color Corrector 3-way**, as shown in **Figure 9.4**.
- The color corrector filter appears as an additional tab in the viewer window. Click the **tab** to bring it forward.

Bringing the Color Correcting 3-Way tab forward hides the video in the viewer window, but the color changes you will be making will be reflected in the canvas window.

The Color Corrector filter in **Figure 9.5** enables you to make subtle (or even profound) changes to the overall look of your video clip.

You can change the color balance by choosing a new reference white point, black point, and mid-point of the colors present in this clip by using the tools that the color corrector brings to Final Cut Pro.

Click the white point eyedropper and then click (as shown in **Figure 9.6**) here to see an overall change in the color balance of your video image.

STEP 3: SIMPLE CLICKS

To balance the colors in your video image, all you need to do is click the eyedropper button for each tonal group, as **Figure 9.7** shows.

- Click the **white point eyedropper** icon and then click the **brightest point** you can see in your video frame. Watch for a change in the overall color cast of your video image.
- Click the **black point eyedropper** icon near the left color wheel and click the **darkest point** you can see in your video frame.
- Click the **midpoint eyedropper** icon in the center color wheel and choose a representative **midtone color** in your video image.

Watch for subtle changes in the location of the center target indicators in the color wheels.

You can also make your color correction changes in the color correction filter window by using numerical values.

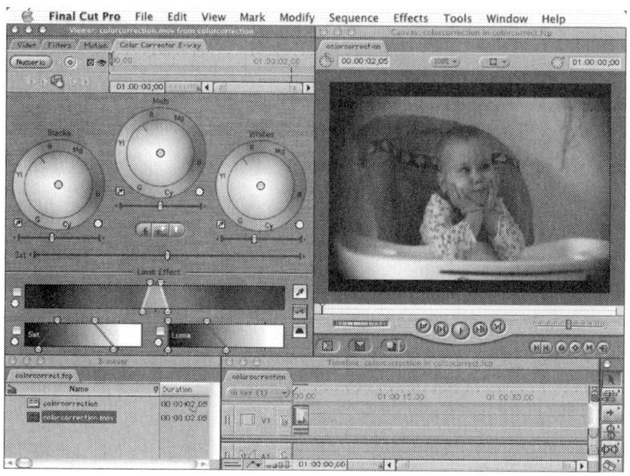

9.6

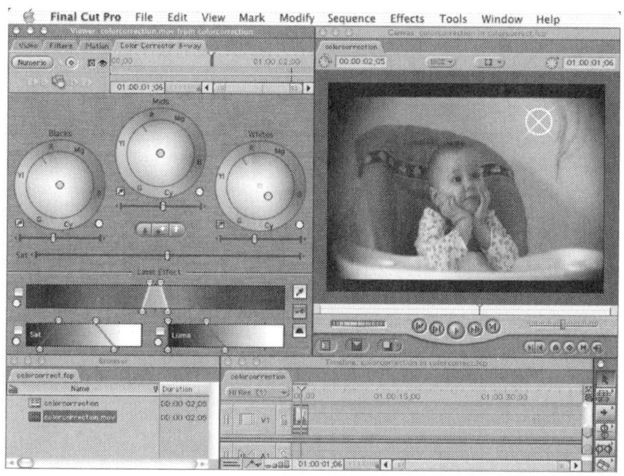

9.7

TECHNIQUE **10**

SEPIA TONE AND AGED FILM

10.1 (CP3)

10.2 (CP4)

Here's a chance to take your first steps to use the techniques shown in this chapter. In this technique, you shift the colors and saturation in your video image by using a series of a few simple filter effects to simulate the look of an old-time, aged film look, or a very artistic sepia-toned moving photograph.

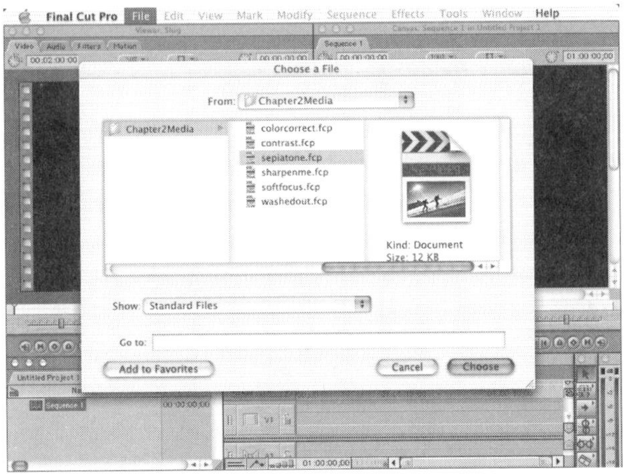

10.3

STEP 1: OPEN THE PROJECT FILE

- Choose **File ➢ Open** and look for the file named **sepiatone.fcp** in the Chapter 2 Project folder as **Figure 10.3** shows.

STEP 2: ADJUST THE COLOR USING A VIDEO EFFECT FILTER

- Select the video clip in the timeline by double-clicking on it, which displays the video image in the viewer window.
- Choose **Effects ➢ Video Filters ➢ Image Control ➢ Sepia** as shown in **Figure 10.4**.
- Click the **Filters** tab in the viewer window (shown in **Figure 10.5**).

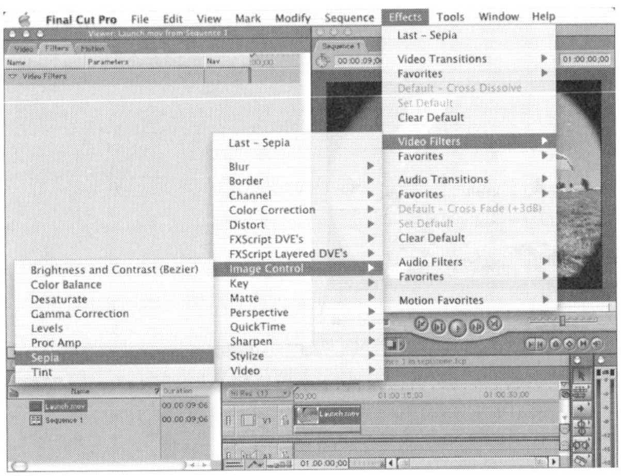

10.4

10.5

STEP 3: CUSTOMIZE THE VIDEO FILTER EFFECT

- Drag the settings sliders in the **Filter** tab to adjust the look of your sepia effect to something a little more muted. Or, just type in new values to adjust the image as shown in **Figure 10.6** and **Figure 10.7**.

10.6

STEP 4: RENDER THE CLIP

- Choose **Sequence ➢ Render All** to render the clip.
- Click the **Play** button to see the results of your work.

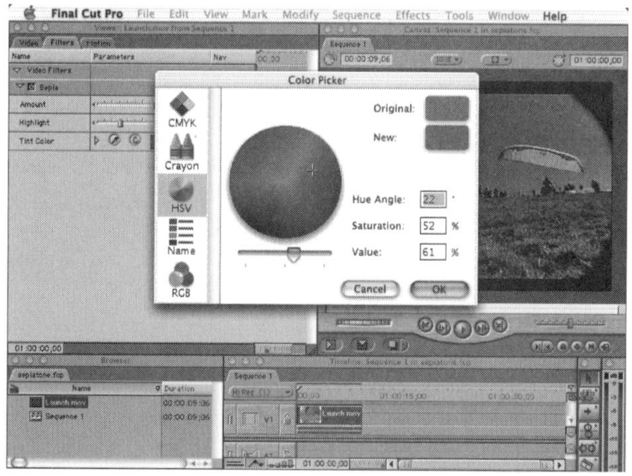

10.7

STEP 5: AN ADDED ENHANCEMENT

For this technique, you add a supplemental effect that isn't technically a part of Final Cut Pro, but rather a feature enhancement to the Apple QuickTime media format. QuickTime offers a rich, diverse, and versatile feature set of enhancements that are included with its "Pro" installation with Final Cut Pro.

- After rendering your project, choose **File ➢ Export ➢ QuickTime**, as shown in **Figure 10.8**.
- With the export window open, choose the **Options** button.

10.8

> **WARNING**
>
> **The size option does not constrain the aspect ratio of your video export proportionally. If you change the frame size disproportionately to the original size, you'll stretch your video image.**

The Options dialog box in **Figure 10.9** allows you to define a number of export options for the QuickTime media format. If you're exporting your video for use in multimedia applications or for the World Wide Web, then becoming familiar with the various options present in this dialog box is absolutely crucial.

- Click the **Settings** button to adjust the options for image compression and frame rate.
- Click the **Size** button to adjust the output frame size.
- Click the **Filters** button to apply a broad variety of filter effects to the QuickTime export.
- Choose the **Film Noise** option and choose your settings to make the film as old, grainy, and damaged as you can tolerate.
- Click the **OK** button.

> **NOTE**
>
> **A good rule of thumb to follow when applying filter effects to your video images is to think of the degree of filter applied as corresponding to your intention for the filter. Lightly applied, a filter is corrective and improves the image. Heavily applied, the filter creates an "effect," changing entirely the look and feel of the image. Keep this in mind as you plan your production and create impressive video projects.**

STEP 6: RENDER THE FILE

- Choose **Sequence ➢ Render All** (Option+R), as shown in **Figure 10.10**.

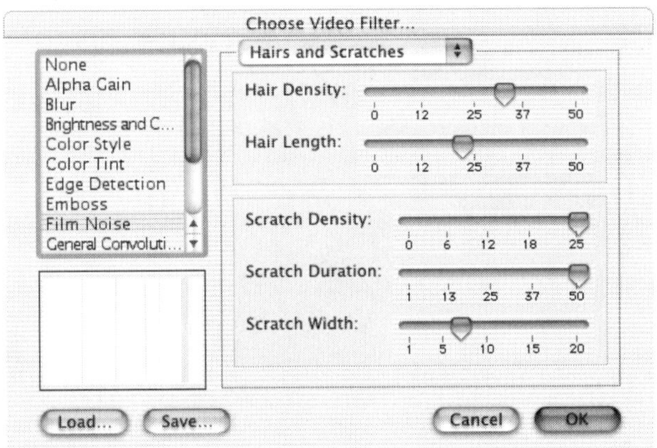

10.9

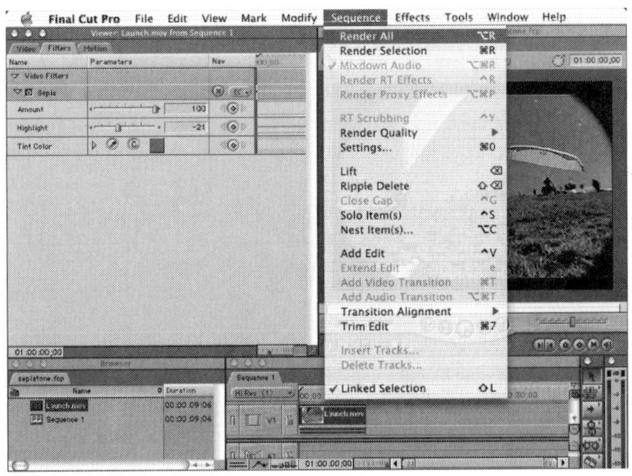

10.10

CHAPTER 3

TIME AND SPEED EFFECTS

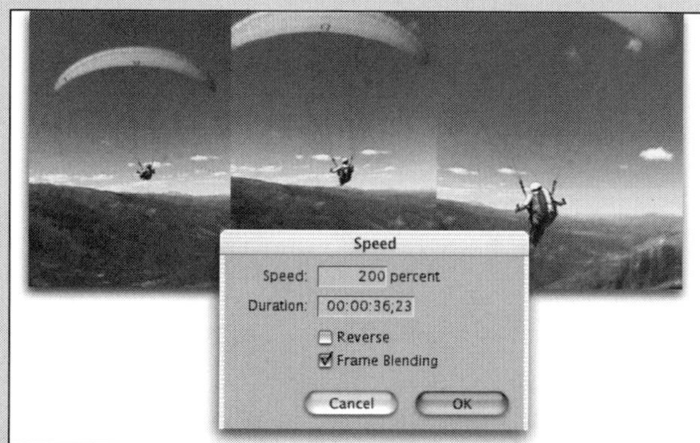

Final Cut Pro gives you precise control over the speed that your video clips are played. Speeding up or slowing down video clips can profoundly affect the mood that your piece conveys. Add a sense of drama to a scene with an extended slow-motion sequence, or conversely liven up a scene by speeding up the action, adding a little comic brevity.

More than just varying the speed that frames are played (known as frame rate), Final Cut Pro actually calculates the digital transitions between frames, blending pixels together seamlessly so that the ultimate final rendering of the video plays pack smoothly and naturally.

The techniques shown in this chapter show you the mechanics of adjusting the playback speed of your video clip. It's remarkably easy.

slow motion effects

fast-motion effects

reverse motion

TECHNIQUE **11**

SLOW MOTION EFFECTS

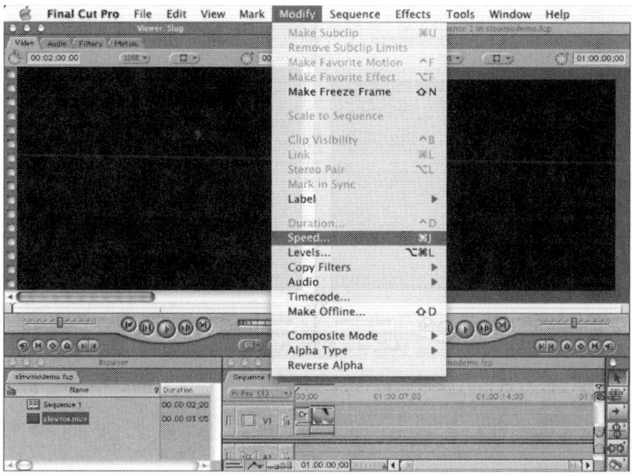

11.1

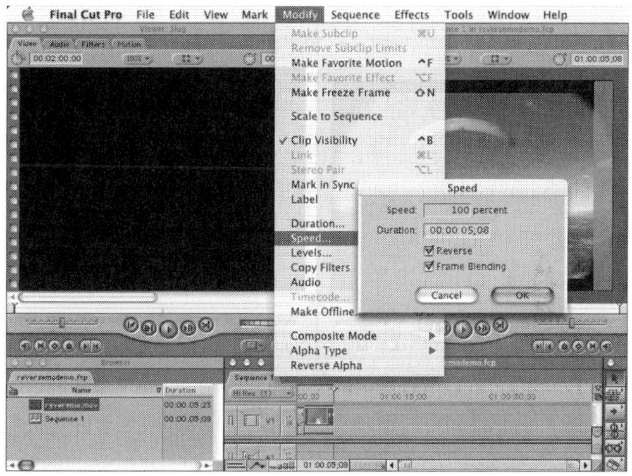

11.2

Add a sense of drama and poetry to a scene by slowing down the action and allowing the images to linger in your viewer's imagination. Final Cut Pro makes it easy with a simple command under the Modify menu.

For this demonstration, use the sample clips on your CD-ROM in the Chapter 3 Projects folder. Start by copying this folder to your hard drive first.

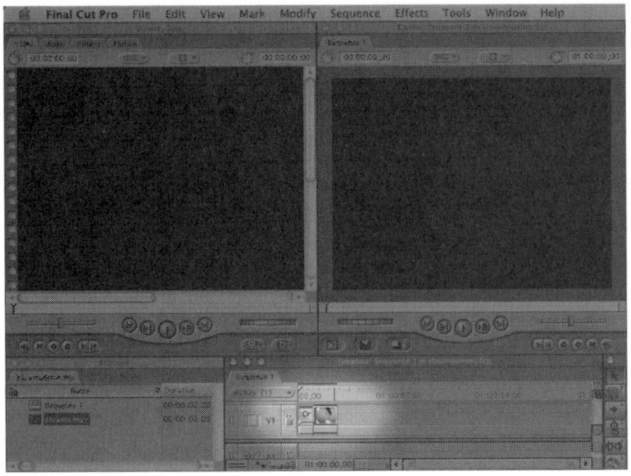

11.3

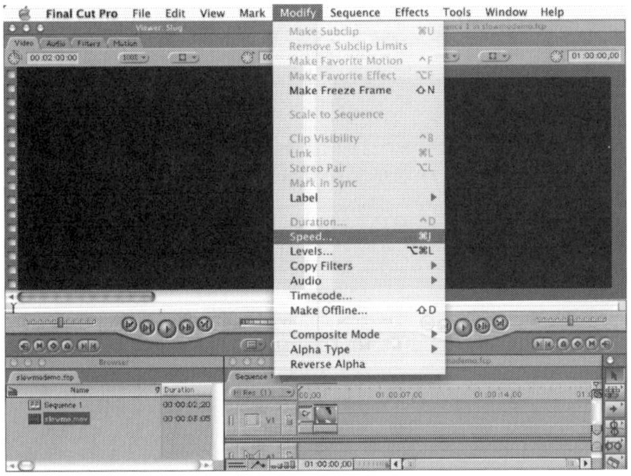

11.4

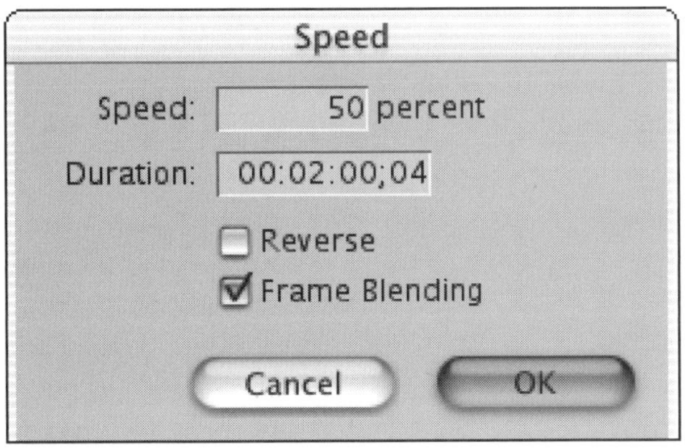

11.5

STEP 1: OPEN THE SEQUENCE

■ Open the Final Cut Pro file named **slowmodemo.fcp** in the Chapter 3 Projects folder on your CD-ROM.

STEP 2: SELECT THE CLIP IN THE TIMELINE

■ Click once on the clip to select it in the timeline, as shown in **Figure 11.3**.

If the clip appears short, too short to manipulate easily with your mouse, then you can use the keyboard shortcut Command + to enlarge your view of the media in the window. This shortcut works with any open window in Final Cut Pro. In the canvas and viewer windows, your view of the video image enlarges. In the timeline window, your view of the clips enlarges.

STEP 3: SLOW IT DOWN

■ Choose **Modify ➢ Speed** (shown in **Figure 11.4**) and set the speed of the clip to **50** in **Figure 11.5**. The value you choose is the percentage of the original clip speed. Setting the speed to 50 tells Final Cut Pro to slow the speed down to 50% of the original playback speed.

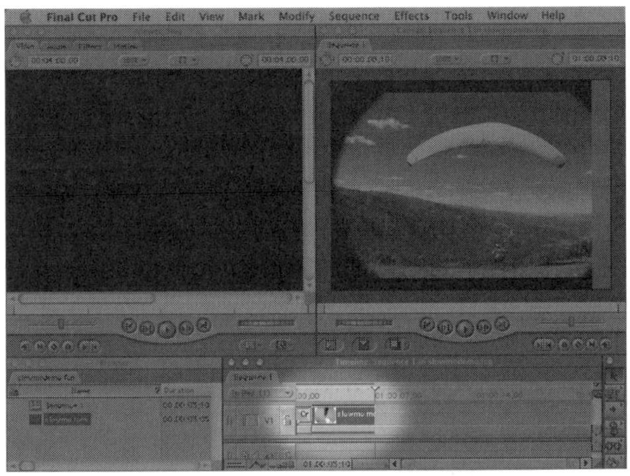

11.6

Setting the speed to 50 tells Final Cut Pro to slow the playback speed down so that the clip takes twice as long to play.

The length of the clip has stretched out in the timeline (shown in **Figure 11.6**), which is a visual indicator that the clip will play back slower.

STEP 4: RENDER THE CLIP

Even though the sample clips provided on the CD are relatively low resolution, not all computers may be able to play the clip back without dropping frames or skipping. You may want to render the clip in order to see the results of this operation as **Figure 11.7** shows.

11.7

TIP

When working on higher-resolution projects or longer clips, you can also choose Tools ➢ QuickView. QuickView forces a low-resolution preview of the clip in its own window.

TECHNIQUE **12**

FAST MOTION EFFECTS

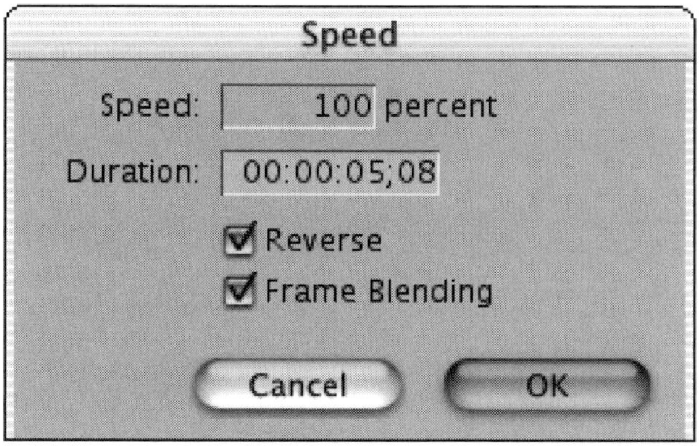

12.1

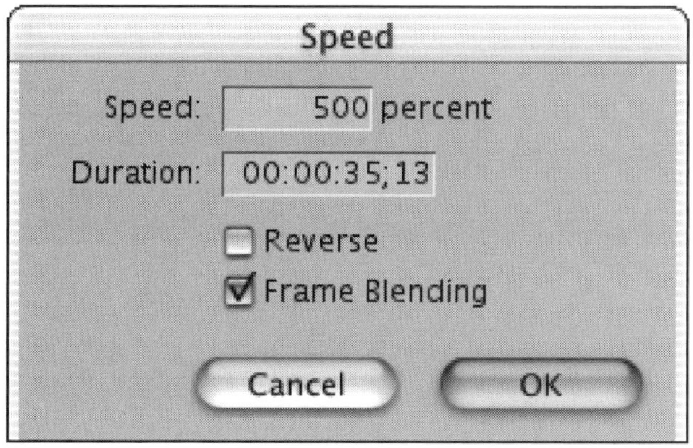

12.2

Marginally increasing the playback speed of a clip can add a comic influence to the mood of the scene with people scurrying about. However, adjusting the speed in increasing amounts, can also add some artistic urgency and excitement to a clip.

Adding super-speed to a long clip, such as in time-lapse clips can add a feeling of surreal time passage. Seeing the sun set in five seconds, highway traffic moving at unreal speeds, or clouds moving overhead are all creative uses of Final Cut Pro-enhanced time compression.

In this demonstration, you experiment with two different applications of the speed setting to achieve two very different feelings in the sample clips.

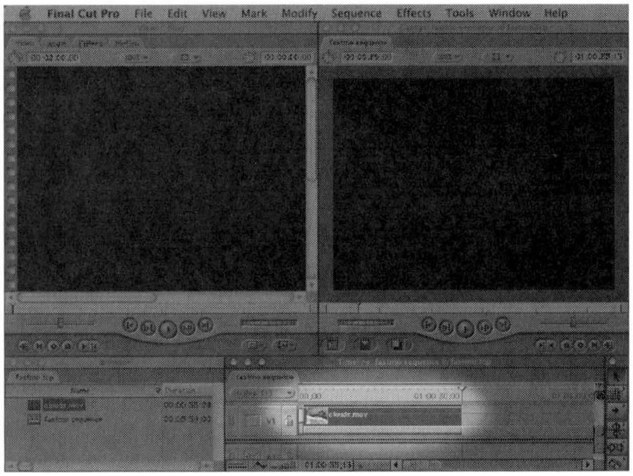

12.3

STEP 1: SELECT THE CLIP TO THE TIMELINE

- Open the sample file in the Chapter 3 Projects folder called **fastmodemo.fcp**, as shown in **Figure 12.3**.
- Click once on the clip to select it.

STEP 2: SET THE SPEED

- From the **Modify** menu, choose **Speed**, as shown in **Figure 12.4**.
- Set the speed value to **500** (or 500% of the original playback speed), as shown **Figure 12.5**.

The speed value of 500 tells Final Cut Pro to play this clip back at 500%, or five times its original speed.

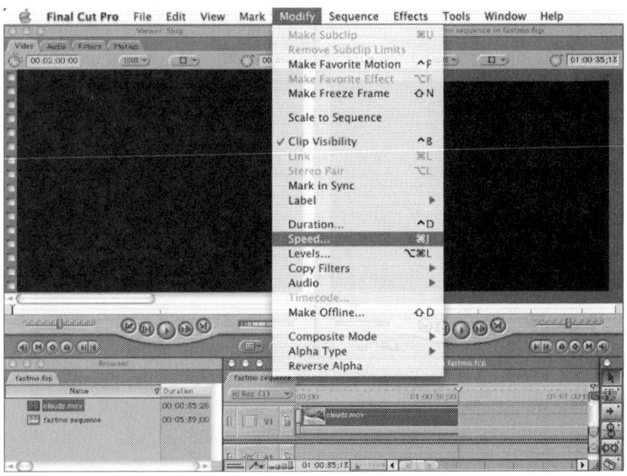

12.4

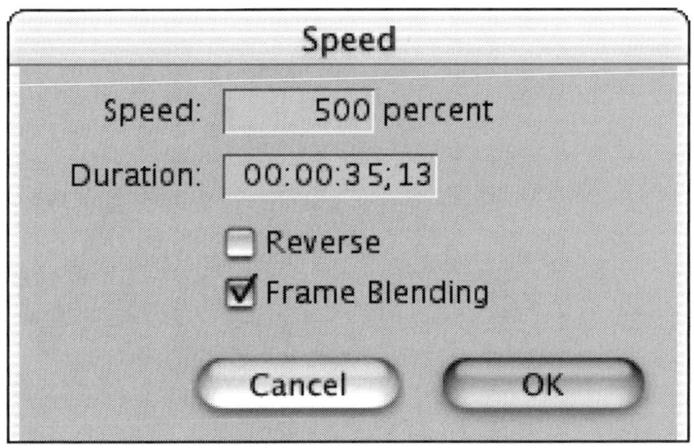

12.5

STEP 3: RENDER THE CLIP

- From the **Sequence** menu, choose **Render All** (shown in **Figure 12.6**) to see results of your playback speed adjustment.

Because clouds move so slowly, played back at five times its original speed, the action on the clip is still recognizable and gives a more dramatic feeling of time passage to the subject matter.

> **TIP**
>
> **Rendering the clip to see the results is more practical, in this case, than option-scrubbing the play head because of the heavy computational load required to show the increased speed of the clip.**

12.6

TECHNIQUE 13

SUPER FAST MOTION EFFECTS FOR EXCITEMENT

13.1

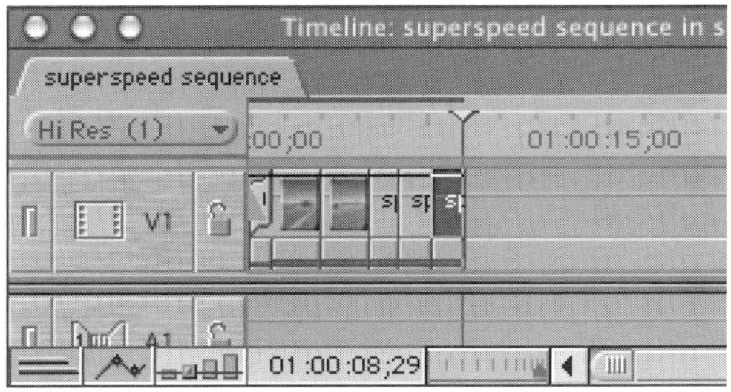

13.2

By increasing the playback speed in incremental stages, you can add a level of excitement to a video clip. Creating the illusion of time-space acceleration.

This technique is a little more involved than the previous demonstration and involves judicious use of the Blade tool. Follow along with each of the steps, using the sample clips provided in the file named **superfastmodemo.fcp**.

13.3

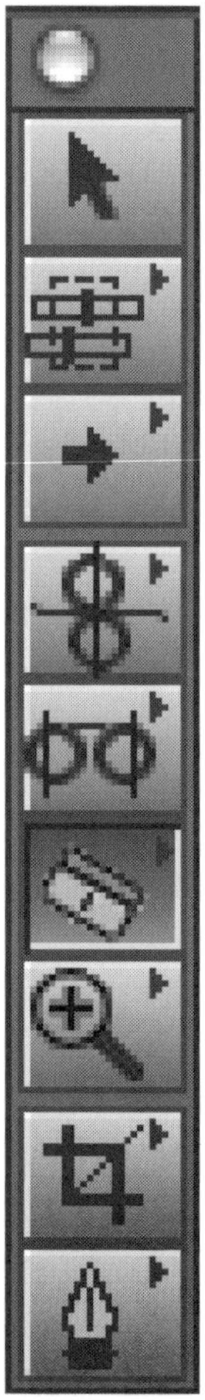

13.4

STEP 1: SELECT THE CLIP IN THE TIMELINE

- Open the file **superfastmodemo.fcp** in the Chapter 3 Projects folder.
- Select the movie clip in **Figure 13.3** in the timeline.

STEP 2: SLICE THE CLIP

- Using the **Blade** tool (**B**) in **Figure 13.4**, place a slice in the clip at the three-second mark in the clip.

TIP

You can easily move the play head to an exact location in the timeline by typing a time value into the time/frame field in the canvas window. Click the video clip in the timeline. Then, click once in the time/frame indicator field and type 3; (don't forget the ;) and then press return telling the play head to move to the position at exactly 3-seconds (and zero frames) into the timeline. Press Return and see the play head come to rest at the 3-second mark in the timeline.

13.5

The Blade tool slices the clip, dividing it into two adjacent clips, with no pause, break, or division between them.

STEP 3: SET THE SPEED

- Click to select the balance of the clip to the right of the slice you just made as shown in **Figure 13.5** and **Figure 13.6**.
- Choose **Modify ➢ Speed** in **Figure 13.7** and set the speed of the balance of the clip to the right of your cut to **200**, as shown **Figure 13.8.** Press Return to finalize the setting.

13.7

13.6

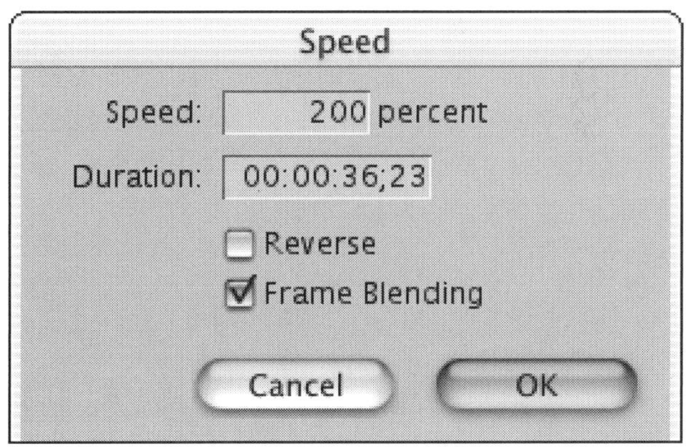

13.8

STEP 4: SLICE AGAIN

Set the play head two more seconds into the future by using the time/location field in the canvas window again. Set the play head location to five seconds by typing in **5;**, as shown in **Figure 13.9**.

■ With the Blade tool still selected, click to create another cut point in **Figure 13.10**.

■ Select the right-most clip to make the speed change in **Figure 13.11**.

■ Set the speed for this clip segment to 400. As shown in **Figure 13.12**, choose **Modify ➢ Speed** and then type **400** in the field.

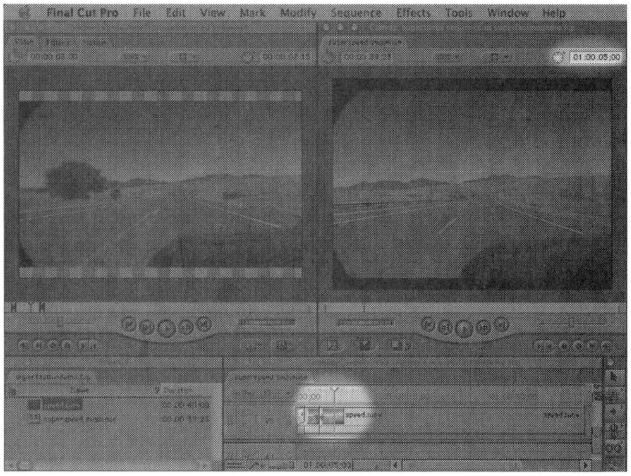

13.9

13.11

13.10

13.12

STEP 5: AND AGAIN AND AGAIN AND AGAIN

Repeat these steps four more times to create subsequently fast and faster clip segments.

- With the Blade tool still selected, click to create new cuts every two seconds for the balance of the clips.
- Select each clip segment and increase the speed of each by 200%. **Figure 13.13** shows the results of this process.

STEP 6: RENDER THE CLIP

- Render the clip in **Figure 13.14** and watch how the action progressively speeds up to 1200% of its original speed in 200% increments in the course of your quick Blade edits.

You can also see how the effect works ramping the video into progressively slower segments. Open the file **superslow.mov** in the Chapter 3 Projects folder.

13.13

13.14

TECHNIQUE **14**

REVERSE MOTION EFFECTS

14.1

14.2

Comedy lurks around every corner if you look for it and know how to use the tools to bring it out of everyday situations.

You can find one of the less obvious features of Final Cut Pro in the Clip Speed dialog box where you just set the playback speed for your clip. If you choose the Reverse check box in this dialog box, Final Cut Pro will reverse the playback order of all the frames in the clip selection.

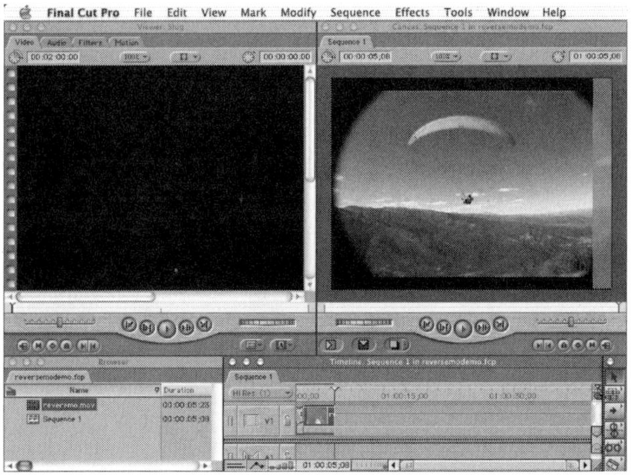

14.3

STEP 1: OPEN THE FILE

- Open the file **reversemodemo.fcp** in the Chapter 3 Projects folder.
- Select the video clip in the timeline as shown in **Figure 14.3**.

STEP 2: REVERSE THE PLAYBACK

- Choose **Modify ➢ Speed**.
- Select the **reverse** checkbox in the Speed dialog box in **Figure 14.4**.

STEP 3: RENDER THE CLIP

- Choose **Sequence ➢ Render All** (as shown in **Figure 14.5**).

Wasn't that just about the easiest technique you've learned so far? And the results are nothing short of amazing!

14.4

14.5

CHAPTER 4

LAYERS AND SUPERIMPOSITION

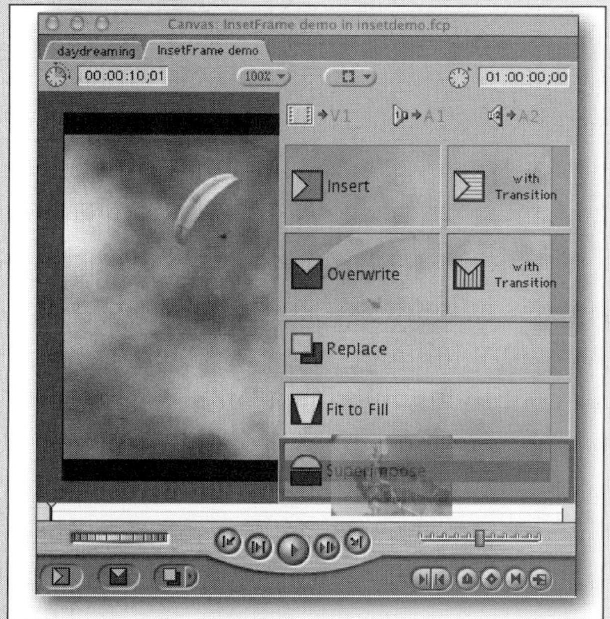

The technique of layering video clips is often used in instructional or news-related videos. In this technique, an additional frame of video displays a separate segment of video that can compliment the main subject matter. You typically see this technique every night on the evening news as the announcer is presenting the day's events, with an illustration or video clip playing in an inset frame just over the presenter's shoulder.

It's easy to add layers of video onto another track in order to achieve a number of interesting effects such as:

- An inset frame of video on top of another frame of video.
- An inset frame of video for an "over the shoulder" newscast-like effect.
- An inset frame of video that demonstrates a complimentary tutorial or additional instructions to the main video content.

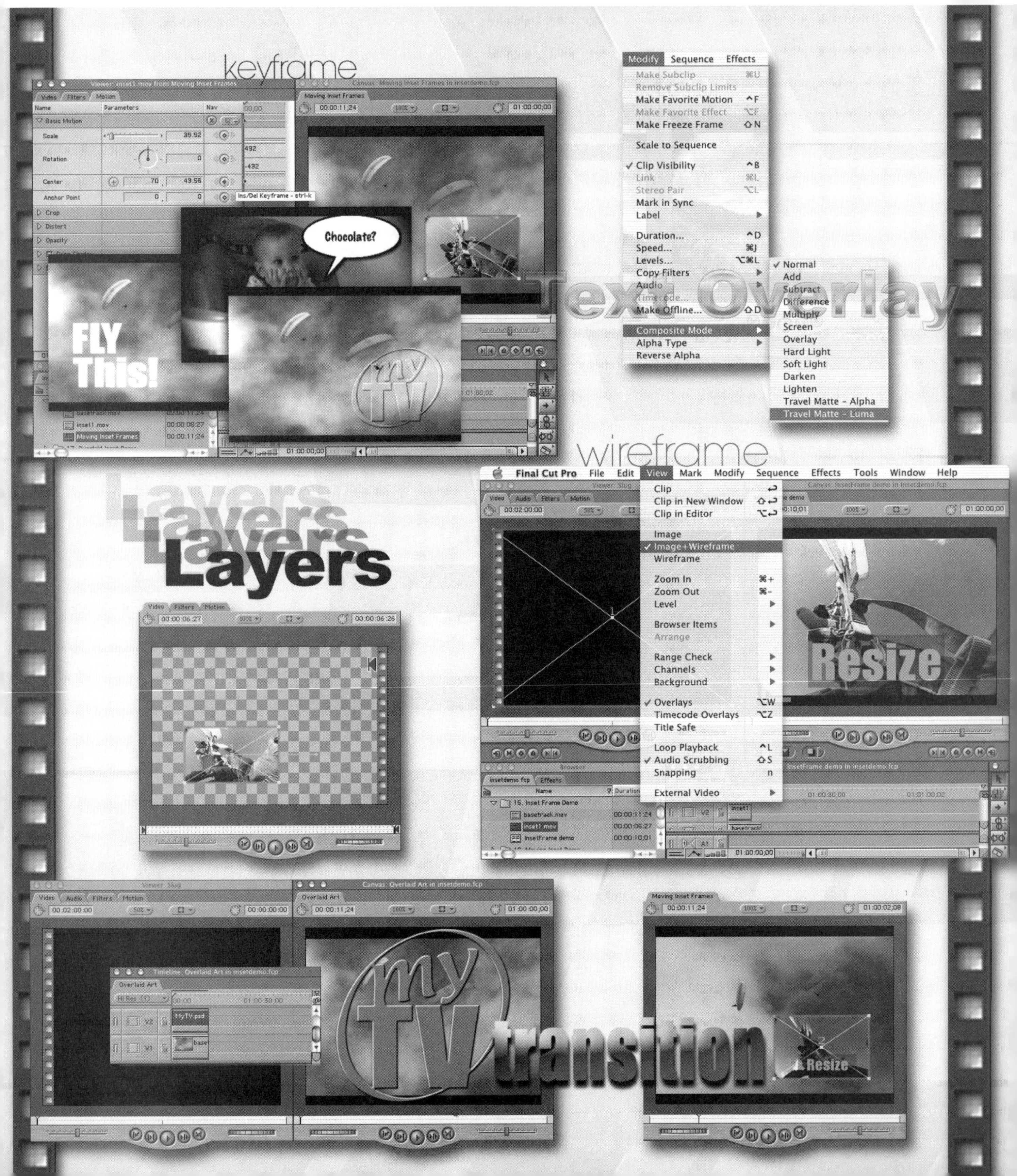
keyframe
Modify
Sequence
Effects
Make Subclip
Remove Subclip Limits
Make Favorite Motion
Make Favorite Effect
Make Freeze Frame
Scale to Sequence
Clip Visibility
Link
Stereo Pair
Mark in Sync
Label
Duration...
Speed...
Levels...
Copy Filters
Audio
Timecode...
Make Offline...
Composite Mode
Alpha Type
Reverse Alpha
Normal
Add
Subtract
Difference
Multiply
Screen
Overlay
Hard Light
Soft Light
Darken
Lighten
Travel Matte - Alpha
Travel Matte - Luma
Text Overlay
Chocolate?
FLY This!
wireframe
Final Cut Pro
File
Edit
View
Mark
Modify
Sequence
Effects
Tools
Window
Help
Clip
Clip in New Window
Clip in Editor
Image
Image+Wireframe
Wireframe
Zoom In
Zoom Out
Level
Browser Items
Arrange
Range Check
Channels
Background
Overlays
Timecode Overlays
Title Safe
Loop Playback
Audio Scrubbing
Snapping
External Video
Layers
Layers
Layers
Layers
Resize
my TV
transition
Resize

TECHNIQUE 15

ADDING AN INSET WINDOW WITH VIDEO

15.1 (CP5)

15.2 (CP6)

This technique shows you how to insert additional layers of video to any video clip.

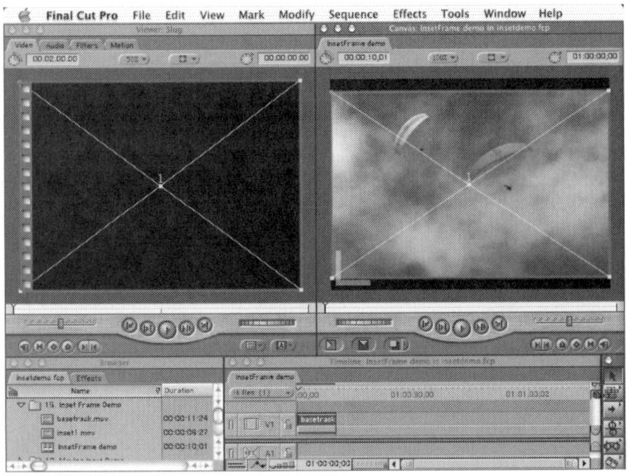

15.3

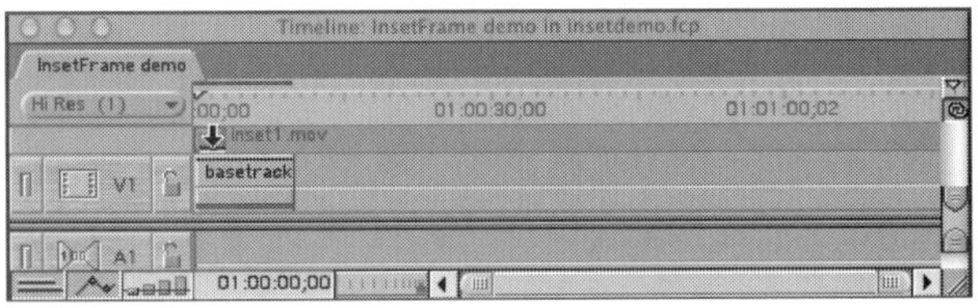

15.4

15.5

STEP 1: OPEN THE PROJECT MEDIA FILE

- Open the bin named **15. Inset Frame Demo** that you find in the Chapter 4 Project folder.
- Notice that in this demonstration an additional video clip is in the browser window entitled ***(inset1.mov)*** that will be added.

STEP 2: ADD THE CLIP TO THE TIMELINE

- Make sure your play head is at the beginning of the timeline as **Figure 15.3** shows.
- Drag the additional clip entitled **inset1.mov** into the region directly above the V1 video track. You will see in **Figure 15.4** that your cursor has turned into a down-pointing arrow indicating that the clip is ready to be added to your video.
- Release the mouse button after you see the cursor turn into a down-facing arrow. You'll see your second video track created directly above the clip in the V1 video track.

STEP 3: CHANGE VIEW TO WIRE FRAME

- Choose **View ➢ Image ➢ Wire Frame,** as shown in **Figure 15.5**. This menu allows you to see the wire frame on the inset track in the canvas window. Or, you can use the W key on your keyboard, which toggles you through the three wire frame view options.

One way to make sure that what you're seeing in the canvas or viewer window is what you're telling the program to place wireframes onto, is to first select the clip in the timeline by double-clicking it. This will load the media into the viewer window. Then choose the wireframe view you desire. Like many other computer applications, select the target first, then apply the command.

STEP 4: RESIZE THE VIDEO CLIP

- Resize the video clip by clicking one of the corner handles and dragging towards the center of the window. You will notice that the video clip always maintains its aspect ratio according to its original proportions. You don't have to worry about constraining the aspect ratio as you resize the clip.

STEP 5: PERFORM A TEST BEFORE RENDERING

Testing the changes that you have made before executing a complete rendering of your project is also helpful. This "pre-rendering" is not really a real-time rendering function, but a forced render, which doesn't take as long to preview the changes that you have made. This pre-rendering may not be helpful when multiple layers are present.

To execute this test render:

- Hold down the Option key.
- Drag the yellow playhead back and forth in the timeline to preview your changes.

In the example shown in **Figure 15.6**, your inset frame is riding right in the middle of the action and covering up important media in the base track. Move the inset frame to the lower-right corner of the image by clicking and dragging it into position, as shown in **Figure 15.7**.

15.6

NOTE

Final Cut Pro is smart enough to know what hardware configuration will produce the smoothest, most consistent user experience. For example, if you use a top-of-the-line desktop machine with plenty of RAM, a fast, dual-processor system using OSX, then Final Cut Pro allows you to view as many special effects and edits as possible in real-time. No rendering necessary.

Final Cut Pro is also smart enough to know if you are using a lower-end consumer system, disabling some of the real-time feedback and requiring you to render your edits before seeing them run smoothly. Using this approach, Apple includes everyone in the Final Cut Pro user experience. No one is excluded based on the speed or horsepower of their computer system.

TIP

The Option key forces the rendering of individual frames that aren't by default already rendered.

15.7

STEP 6: RENDER THE SEQUENCE

■ Choose **Sequence ➢ Render All** to see results of the changes you made.

You now see in **Figure 15.8** that you created a second video that is playing within your existing video segment.

15.8

TIP

You can enhance the effect of the inset frame by adding some additional enhancements to this technique that can add some interest to the clip. For example, you can add a soft drop shadow to the inset clip to give it some added dimension and special effect. Or you can move the inset frame while the sequence progresses over time. This enhancement would be useful for an intro clip that flies across the screen. If the clip is shorter than your base track, you can have it transition out of the frame by adding a dissolve transition to the end of the clip.

MOVING INSET WINDOW

16.1 (CP7)

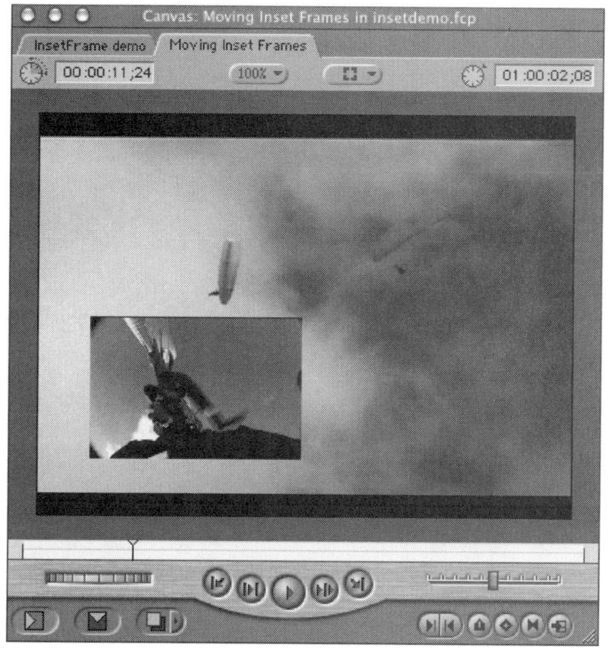

16.2 (CP8)

In addition to being able to have a window of data appearing on your background, you can move the inset window around by using key framing in Final Cut Pro to add some interest to your video clip. For example, you can have a video window with a frame and move that window from one side of the frame to another over the course of time.

The process of moving an object around on the frame is a fairly simple one that can be applied to any number of objects, such as moving still images, text, or filter effects. In this step, I show you how to move an inset window in order to accomplish this.

STEP 1: OPEN THE FILE

- Open the bin **Moving Inset Demo** that is found in the Chapter 4 Project folder.

Notice that this sample sequence looks a lot like the other video sample sequences, but as you see in **Figure 16.3**, a video clip has been placed into the V2 video timeline track, above the media clip in the V1 video track.

STEP 2: GO TO THE FIRST FRAME OF THE SEQUENCE

- Click to select the timeline window, then click to select the yellow play head marker and move it to the first frame of the sequence or use the up arrow to accomplish the same action in **Figure 16.4**.

STEP 3: SET THE KEYFRAME FOR THE FIRST LOCATION

Double-click the **inset1** clip in the timeline to display it in the viewer.

- In the viewer window, click the **Motion** tab.
- To the right of the fields defining the "Center" location of the selected clip, you'll see the round Keyframe button.
- Click the **Keyframe** button, marking this moment in the clip as a keyframe (shown in **Figure 16.5**).

STEP 4: GO TO THE LAST FRAME OF THE CLIP

- Click and drag the yellow play head marker and move it to the last frame of the clip in V2 or use the down arrow to accomplish the same action.

You may notice that moving the play head in the timeline window also moves it in the viewer window. This is normal. Move the play head in the timeline, watch the results in the canvas window, then see your setting for that location in the viewer window (where you can make changes to various settings).

16.3

16.4

16.5

STEP 5: SET THE KEYFRAME FOR THE SECOND LOCATION

- In the viewer window, click the **Motion** tab.
- Click the **Keyframe** centerpoint button on the right-hand side.

By performing this task, you tell Final Cut Pro to move from the location established in the first keyframe to the location in the second keyframe over these two seconds of time. Because the inset box occupies the same physical space, you now need to move the inset frame manually to a new location.

STEP 6: MOVE INSET BOX TO A NEW LOCATION

- Double-click on the object in the canvas window.
- The viewer window shows the inset with the wire frame within the canvas window.
- Click the **Motion** tab to display motion attributes, as shown in **Figure 16.6**.
- Choose the section marked **Center** and establish a new keyframe by clicking in the centerpoint button on the right-hand side (shown in **Figure 16.7**).
- Double-click on the **inset1** media clip in the timeline to display it in the viewer window in **Figure 16.8**.
- Drag the clip object in this window to the new location, as **Figure 16.9** shows.

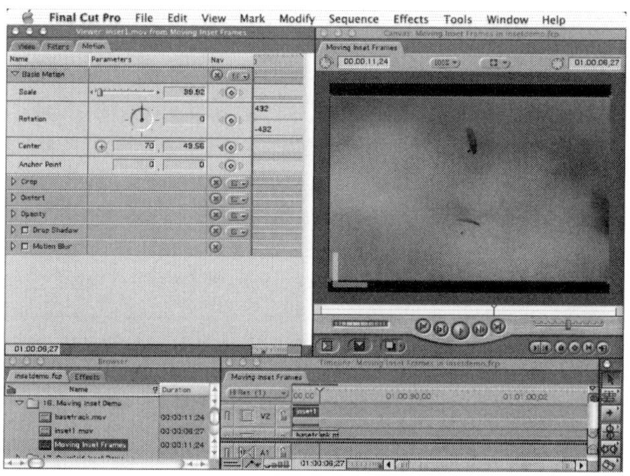

16.6

TIP

You can constrain the movement by holding down the Shift key as you drag the frame. When you perform this function, you see a line of dots that follow this move that resemble a series of knots on a rope from the origin point to the destination point. Each of these knots corresponds to an individual frame of video.

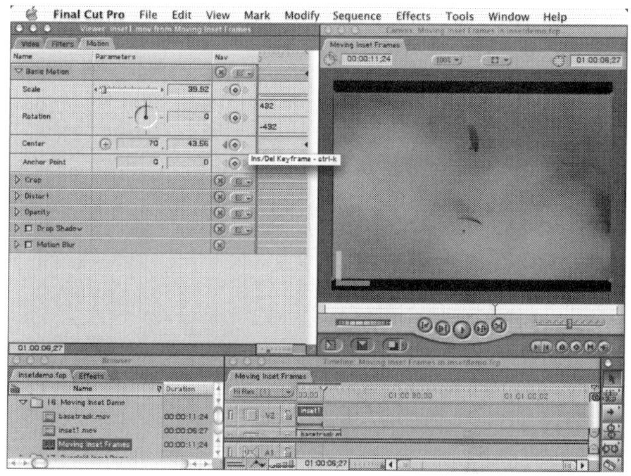

16.7

16.8

STEP 7: PERFORM A TEST BEFORE RENDERING

To execute this test render:

- Hold down the **Option** key.
- Drag the yellow play head back and forth in the timeline to preview your changes.

STEP 8: RENDER THE SEQUENCE

- Choose **Sequence ➢ Render All** (as shown in **Figure 16.10**) to see results of the changes you made.

STEP 9: SAVE PROJECT AS

- If you want to save the changes you made to this technique, choose **File ➢ Save Project As . . .** and give your file another name.
- Save your project.
- If you do not want to save your changes, close the file and do not save changes when prompted.

16.9

16.10

TECHNIQUE 17

THE OVERLAID INSET WINDOW

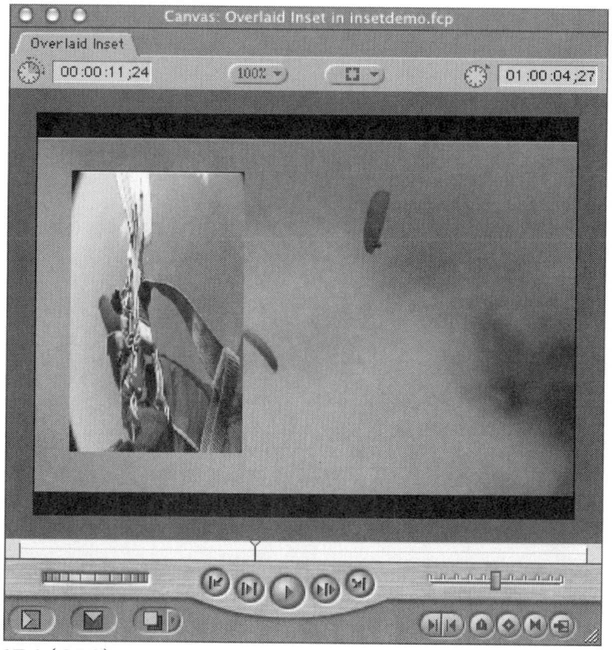

17.1 (CP9)

17.2 (CP10)

Inset or overlaid objects don't necessarily have to float as an overlaid object on a layer. Some very cool effects can be achieved layering objects by using different composite modes.

For example, instead of having a flat opaque window appear, float, or travel within your clip, you can have a window that composites against your background track differently. You can have it overlay, screen, or multiply just as you would choose a "Layer Mode" in a photo-editing program like Adobe's Photoshop. In Final Cut Pro, you choose a composite mode in order to accomplish a similar effect, but with full-motion video instead of a still image.

For this demonstration, use the same sample file you used in the previous techniques.

17.3

17.4

17.5

STEP 1: OPEN THE PROJECT MEDIA FILE

- Open the file named (**overlaid Inset demo**) that is found in the Chapter 4 Project folder. Your workspace should resemble **Figure 17.3**.

STEP 2: DRAG CLIP TO THE TIMELINE WINDOW

- Make sure your play head is at the beginning of the timeline.
- Drag the additional clip entitled **inset1** into the region directly above the V1 video track. You see that your cursor has turned into a down-pointing arrow indicating that the clip is ready to be added to your video like that shown in **Figure 17.4**.
- Release the mouse button when the cursor has changed to the down-facing arrow. This creates a new V2 video track with your newly added clip in it.

STEP 3: DISPROPORTIONATELY RESIZE INSET FRAME

- Select the video frame in the canvas window by clicking it.
- Hold down the Shift key while you drag and resize the video window to create a disproportionate size as shown in **Figure 17.5**. (This is an opposite effect to that of most programs that allow aspect ratios to be maintained while holding down the Shift key.)

TIP

Make sure that your wireframe + image view is still enabled to see your wire frame handles on the video image. If not, you can toggle the wire frame view with the 'w' keyboard shortcut.

STEP 4: CHANGE THE COMPOSITE MODE

- Select the video clip in the timeline.
- Choose **Modify ➢ Composite Mode** and choose the mode you want as shown in **Figure 17.6**.
- Try different modes, such as Screen, Multiply, or Overlay, to obtain the effect you want. **Figure 17.7** shows the Screen composite mode.

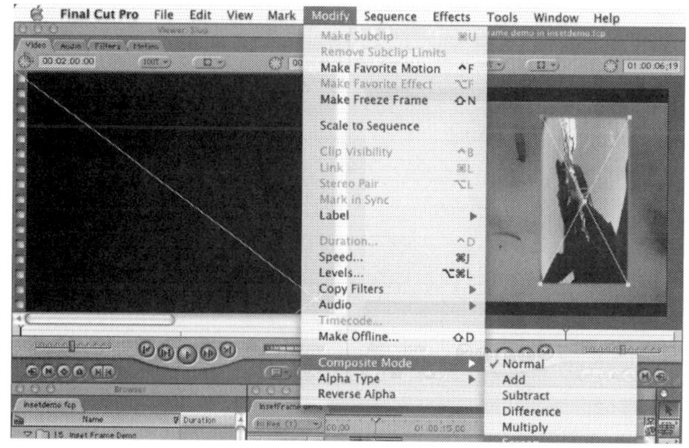

17.6

STEP 5: PERFORM A TEST BEFORE RENDERING

To execute this test render:

- Hold down the Option key.
- Drag the yellow play head back and forth in the timeline to preview your changes.

Remember that if your computer is powerful enough, you may not need to hold down the option key to force a render of the material. Final Cut Pro helps you by allowing you to view a preview of your work in real-time, if your machine configuration will support it. Otherwise, if your machine is not the most powerful box on the block, the preview is still available to you, using the option key enhancement to force a frame-by-frame render of the material.

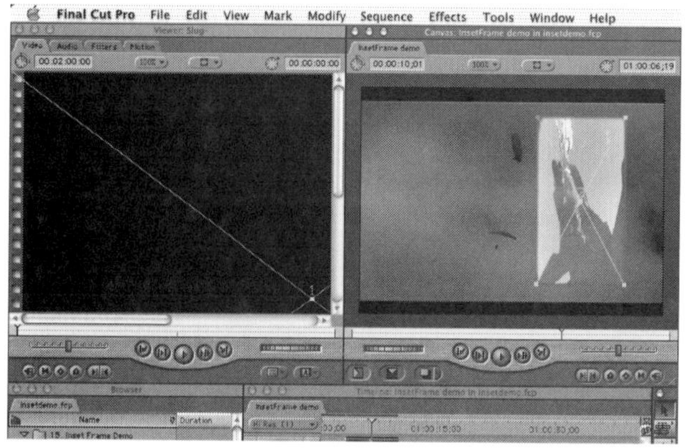

17.7

STEP 6: RENDER THE SEQUENCE

- From the Sequence menu, choose **Render All**, as you see in **Figure 17.8**, to see results of the changes that you made.

17.8

TECHNIQUE **18**

TEXT OVERLAYS

18.1

18.2 (CP12)

This technique shows you how to add text tracks to a video clip layer. Like other elements in Final Cut Pro, the layering model works similarly with text as it does with other video elements.

In this example, you add text to an existing clip and find out different ways to modify that text in order to accomplish specific functions, such as title tracks, credits, or item descriptions.

STEP 1: OPEN THE FILE

- Open the bin **Text Overlays Demo** that you find in the Chapter 4 Project folder.
- Make sure the yellow play head is at the first frame as shown in **Figure 18.3**.

18.3

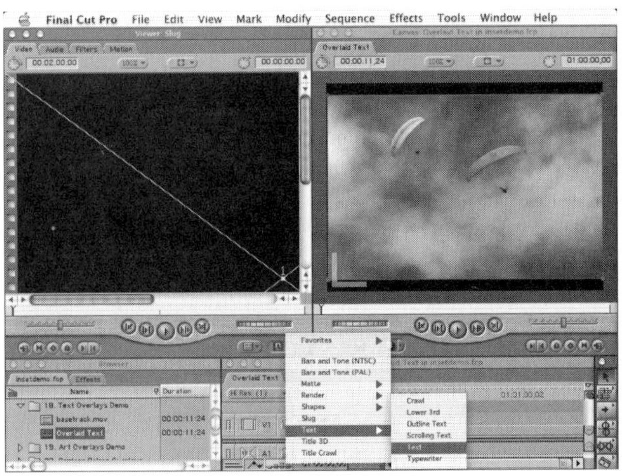

18.4

STEP 2: CREATE THE TEXT OBJECT

- Click the **Generator** button at the lower-right corner of the viewer window that looks like a piece of film with the letter A inside it.
- Hold down your mouse and select **Text** from the pop-up menu, as shown in **Figure 18.4**.
- Select **Text** again from the second pop-up submenu.

You see the viewer window now has the words Sample Text within it.

STEP 3: MODIFY THE TEXT ATTRIBUTES

- Click the **Controls** tab located at the top of the viewer window.
- Choose **Impact** from the **Font** pop-up selection menu.
- Highlight and type in the number **76** in the **Size** selection area.
- Change the **Alignment** setting to **Left**.
- Change the origin values to: **–222, 66**.
- Replace the words **Sample Text** with the words **FLY This!**
- Type a return between the words “Fly” and “This!” to force each onto its own line.
- Click the **Video** tab again to see the text changes that you made to the words **FLY This!** **Figure 18.5** shows these changes.

STEP 4: ADD TEXT TO CANVAS

- Toggle the view of this window so that it appears without wire frames (choose **View ➢ Image**).

- Click and drag the **FLY This!** text into the canvas window.
- As you perform this step, you see a series of insert options appear on the right-hand side of the canvas window.
- Drag your text selection into the purple area called **Superimpose**, as shown in **Figure 18.6**.
- After you release the mouse, you now see your **FLY This!** text appear in the canvas window and a text track is added to your time.

You now see that a text track is added to your timeline along within a new video track entitled **V2** in **Figure 18.7** and **Figure 18.8**.

18.6

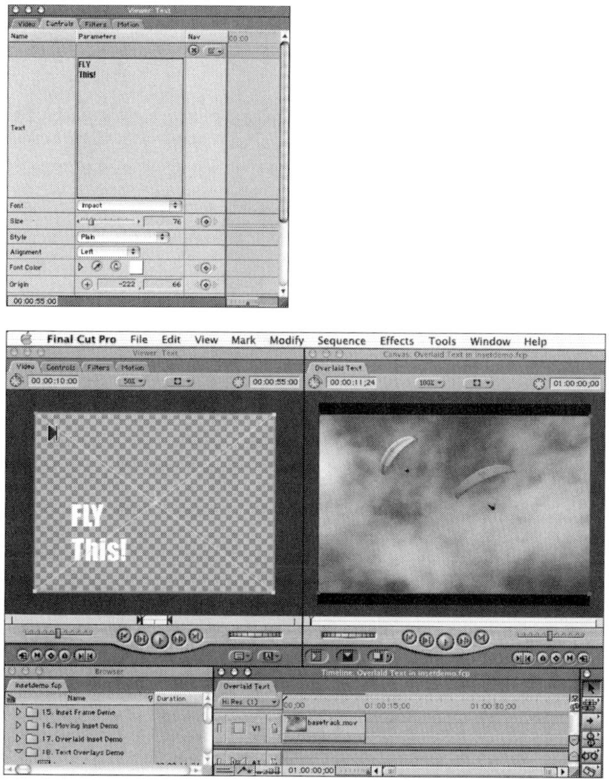

18.5 (CP11)

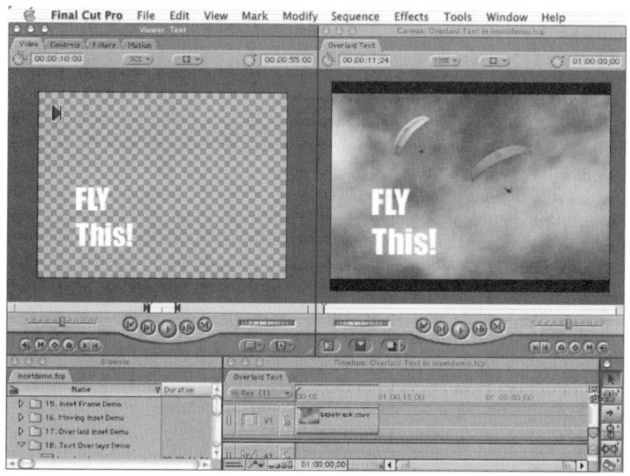

18.7

STEP 5: PERFORM A TEST BEFORE RENDERING

To execute this test render:

- Hold down the Option key.
- Drag the yellow play head back and forth in the timeline to preview your changes shown in **Figure 18.8.**

STEP 6: RENDER THE SEQUENCE

- From the **Sequence** menu, choose **Render All** (shown in **Figure 18.9**) to see results of the changes that you made.

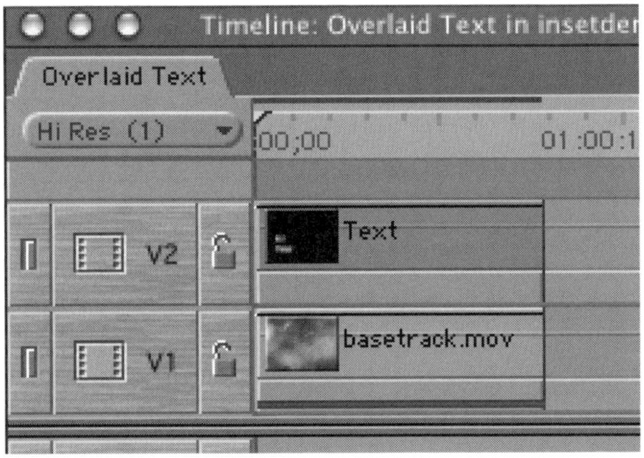

18.8

18.9

TECHNIQUE 19

ART OVERLAYS (LOGOS)

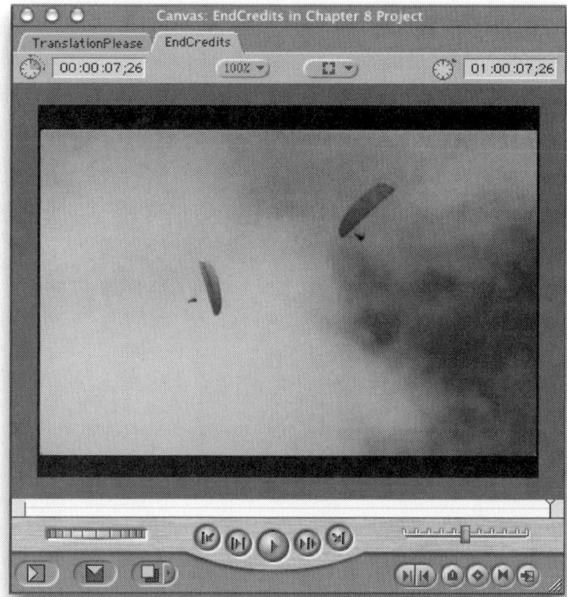

19.1

19.2 (CP14)

In addition to being able to lay text and video tracks onto your video clips, you can also add artwork. You may find art overlays useful for such elements as adding a company logo, a diagram, or picture that will reinforce the video content message.

The ability to control the composite mode for these art overlays is essential in order to make your video presentation both interesting and valuable to your audience. In this technique, I show you how to add art overlays to your existing video clip.

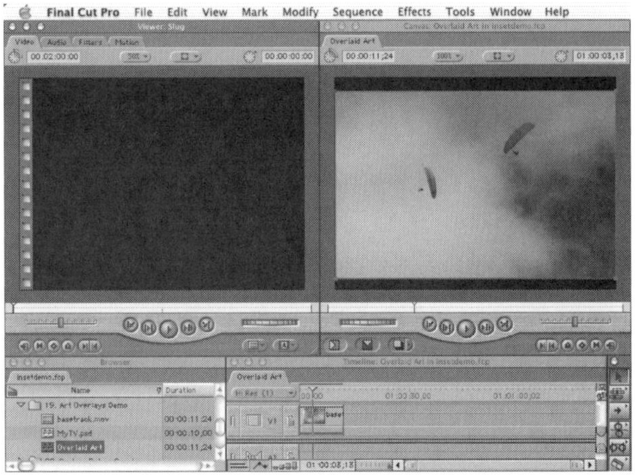

19.3

19.4

19.5

STEP 1: OPEN THE PROJECT MEDIA FILE

- Open the project file named **insetdemo.fcp** that you find in the Chapter 4 Project folder.
- Open the bin named **19. Art Overlays Demo** as shown in **Figure 19.3**.

STEP 2: ADD IMPORTED ART TO THE CANVAS WINDOW

- Make sure your play head is at the beginning of the timeline.
- Add the imported artwork by dragging the icon for the imported art clip named **MyTV.psd** from the browser window directly onto the canvas window.
- Choose the **Superimpose** overlay that appears in purple on your right-hand side as shown in **Figure 19.4**.
- Your canvas window should now look like **Figure 19.5**.

STEP 3: RESIZE AND REPOSITION THE ARTWORK

- Notice that an additional video track has been added to the timeline window for your clip. You now set the correct position for the artwork as **Figure 19.6** shows.
- Click the media clip item in the **V2** video track that holds the artwork in the timeline window.
- Go to the **View** menu. Choose **Image + Wireframe** (shown in **Figure 19.7**) or use the **W** key to toggle between the three wire frame settings that are available. You now see that your artwork has wire frame handles around the image.
- Resize the image by clicking one of the handles of the image and dragging it to the new desired size on the canvas, as **Figure 19.8** shows.

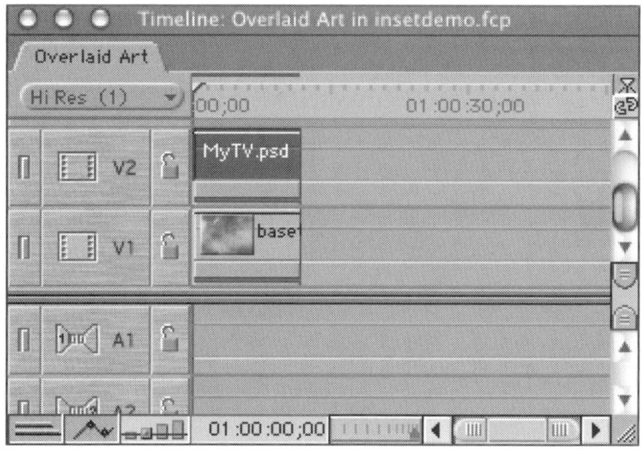

19.6

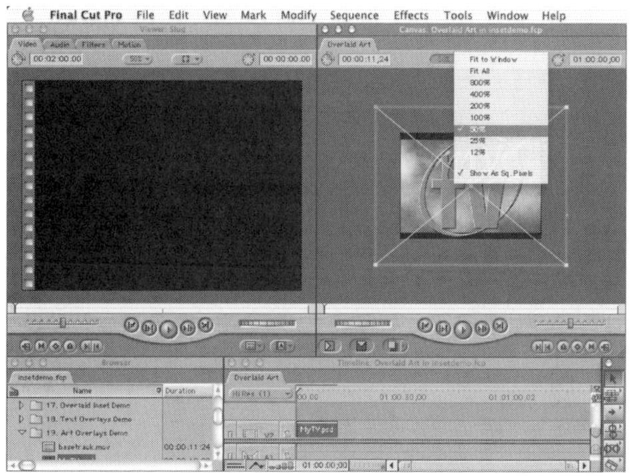

19.7

19.8

> **TIP**
>
> **You may need to reduce the view of the canvas window in order to see the handles of the wire frame in this demo. Do this by clicking the view percentage button at the top of the canvas window and choose a smaller view percentage from the pop-up menu that appears.**

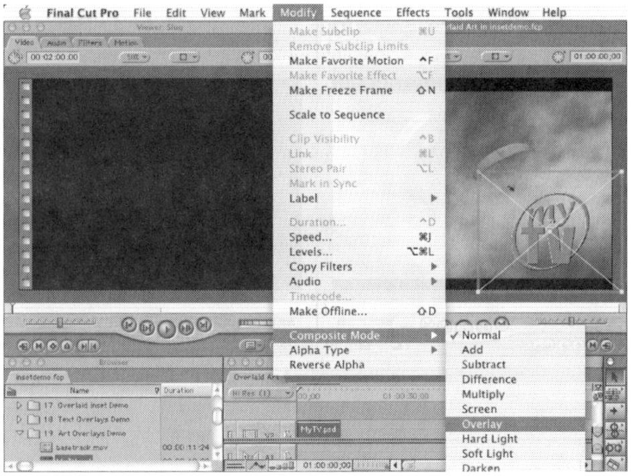

19.9 (CP13)

19.10

STEP 4: CHANGE COMPOSITE MODE

- Each of the different composite modes create a different effect dependent on the color and hue interaction and background combinations are either light or dark. Some applications (such as this one) require only a simple change to the Overlay composite mode.
- You may also consider changing the opacity when you want your video to appear through an imported graphics clip or appear somewhat transparent.
- Position the logo art in the lower-right quadrant of the video frame.
- Choose **Modify ➢ Composite Mode ➢ Overlay** as shown in **Figure 19.9**.

NOTE

You can change the opacity of any selected clip item by choosing the motion tab of the viewer window and setting a new value in the opacity field. However, in this demonstration, the actual "opacity" doesn't change, the composite mode does.

STEP 5: PERFORM A TEST BEFORE RENDERING

To execute this test render:

- Hold down the **Option** key.
- Drag the yellow play head back and forth in the timeline to preview your changes as shown in **Figure 19.10**.

> **TIP**
>
> Remember you can apply the same technique to move inset objects around the screen to move logo artwork around the screen, as well. Such techniques might include changing the position, color tint, and opacity, over time.

STEP 6: RENDER THE SEQUENCE

- From the **Sequence** menu, choose **Render All** (shown in **Figure 19.11**) to see results of the changes that you made.

19.11

TECHNIQUE 20

CARTOON BALLOONS

20.1 (CP15)

20.2 (CP16)

C*artoon balloons* allow you to add a cute pop-up effect where you need to inject a little humor to your video content. The pop-up can add visual commentary to a video clip.

In this technique, I show you how to add, modify, and manipulate cartoon balloons within your video presentation.

STEP 1: OPEN THE FILE

- In the Chapter 4 Projects folder, you find a bin entitled **Cartoon Balloon Overlays**, as shown in **Figure 20.3**, that contains the media clips that you add to the video track for this technique.
- Double-click to open the **Cartoon Balloons** sequence.

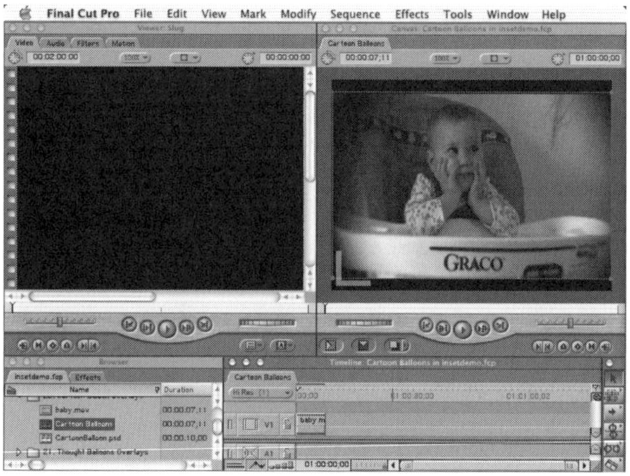

20.3

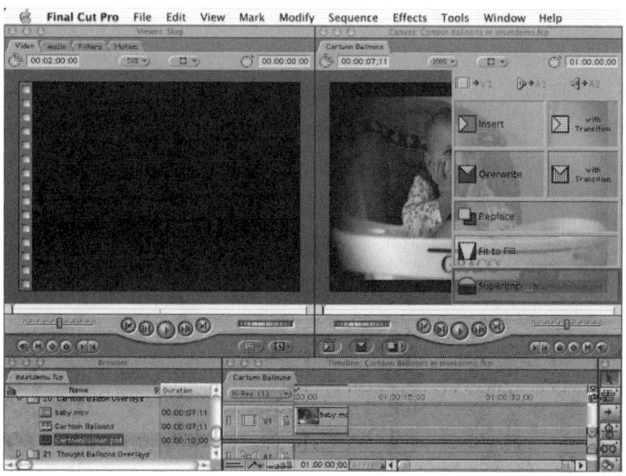

20.4

STEP 2: ADD THE CARTOON BALLOON ART TO THE TIMELINE

- Click and drag the artwork icon **CartoonBalloon.psd** from the browser window into the canvas window.
- Choose the **Superimpose** overlay from the choices on the right, as shown in **Figure 20.4**.
- You now see this element is added to the timeline window.
- Click to select the new clip in the **V2** video track. Toggle the display of wire frame handles with the **W** keyboard shortcut.
- Re-size and re-position the cartoon balloon to fit in the upper-right quadrant of your video frame.

STEP 3: ADD A SIMPLE DROP SHADOW EFFECT

- You can find some simple visual effects in the **Motion** tab of the viewer window. You can give the cartoon balloon a little more dimension and have it appear more natural inside the video clip. The effect you use is the **Drop Shadow**. You can see the results of this choice in **Figure 20.5**.

20.5

- Control-click the **Cartoon Balloon** element in the timeline in **Figure 20.6**, choosing the pop-up contextual menu item "Open Viewer" to load the clip element into the viewer window.
- Choose the **Motion** tab in the **viewer** window.
- Scroll down until you see the section marked **Drop Shadow** and select the check box to activate this feature.

STEP 4: CREATE AND MODIFY TEXT FOR THE CARTOON BALLOON

- In the **viewer** window, click the **Generator** button on the lower-right hand side.
- Choose **Text** in the pop-up menu and **Text** again the sub-menu option, as shown in **Figure 20.7**.
- Click the **Controls** tab at the top of the viewer window to reveal Text options.
- Select the sample text and type in **Chocolate?** where you see **Sample Text** in **Figure 20.8**.
- Set **Font** to **Sand**.
- Set the **Font size** to **24 point** as shown in **Figure 20.9**.
- Set the **Font Color** to **black** by clicking the square swatch revealing the HSV Color picker wheel, and slide the **value slider** located at the bottom to the left to the **zero** designation.

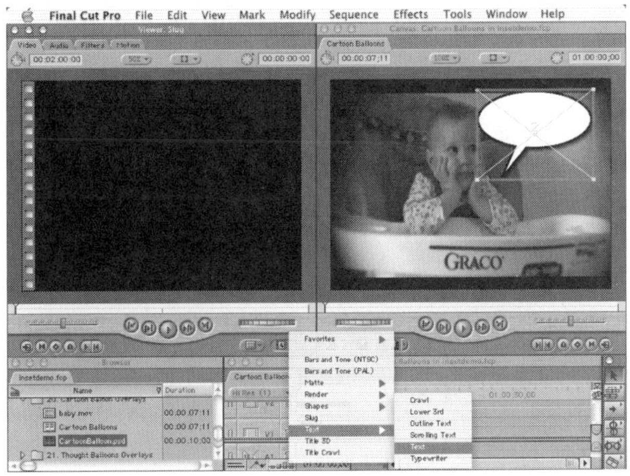

20.7

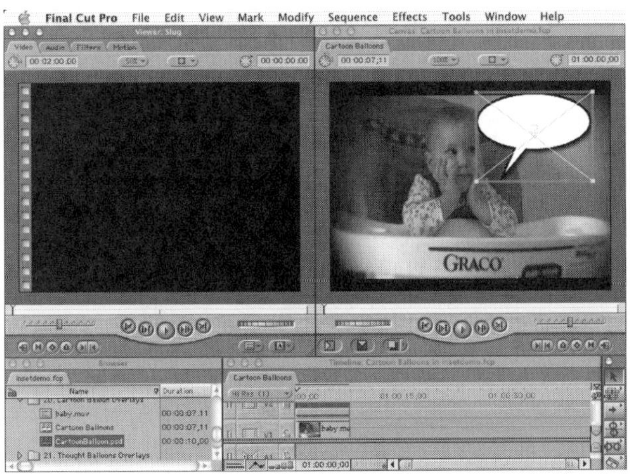

20.6

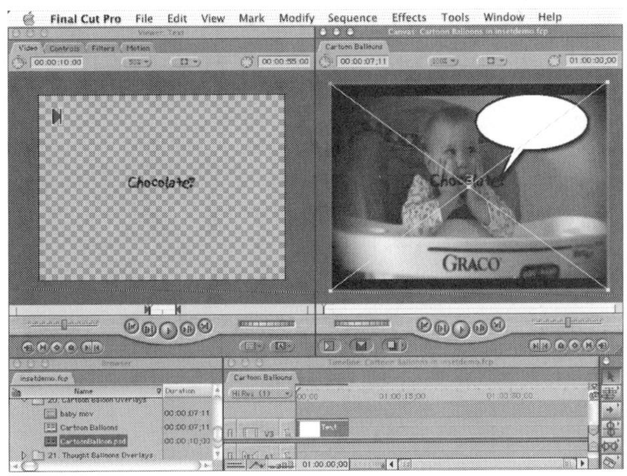

20.8

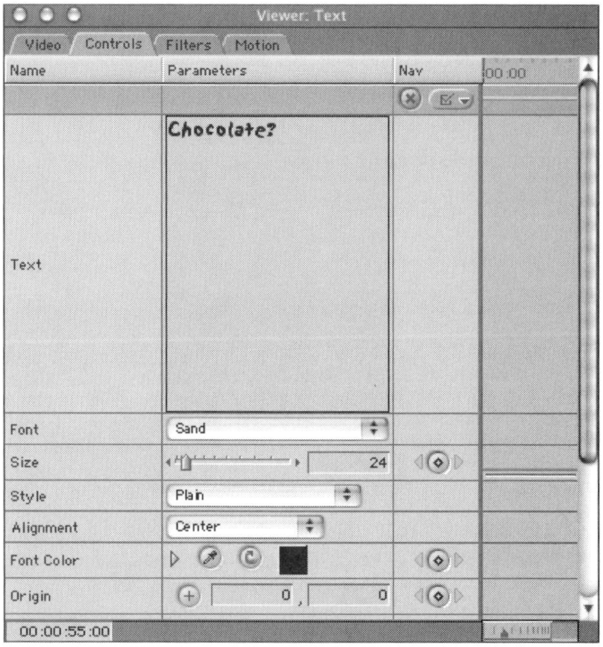

20.9

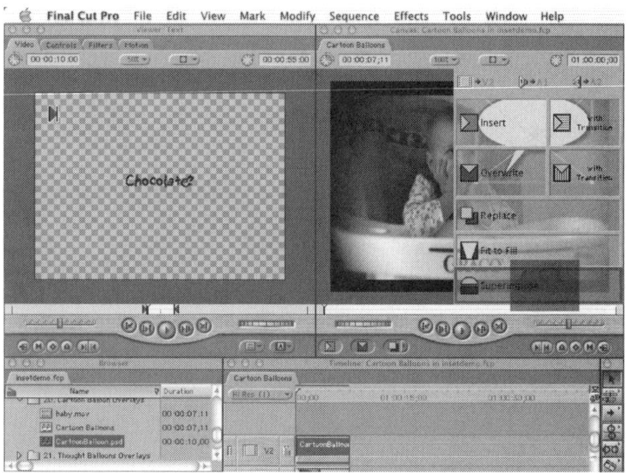

20.10

STEP 5: DRAG AND DROP THE TEXT ONTO THE CANVAS WINDOW

- In the timeline window, click the film clip icon next to the V2 video track. The track's color changes to yellow, which indicates that it is now the target track for any additions to the timeline.
- Click the **Video** tab in the viewer window to show the results of your text modifications.
- Drag the text you created from the viewer window into the canvas window and choose the **Superimpose** overlay, as shown in **Figure 20.10**. You see this text element is added to your timeline window.

STEP 6: REPOSITION THE TEXT IN THE VIDEO FRAME

In the timeline, select the clip item in the V3 video track. If you don't already see the wire frame handles surrounding it in the canvas window, toggle the display of the wire frame by using the keyboard shortcut W.

Click and drag the text item into position over the cartoon balloon in the upper-right quadrant of the video frame as shown in **Figure 20.11** and **Figure 20.12**.

> **TIP**
>
> **If you still have the wire frame option enabled in the video window, disable it so that the wire-frame and handles are no longer visible.**

STEP 7: LINK THE TEXT AND THE BALLOON ARTWORK

- Select both the **Text** elements and the **Cartoon Balloon** artwork by selecting them in your timeline window.
- Locate the link icon, located at the right of your timeline window, and click that icon to activate linking, as shown in **Figure 20.13**.
- Your text and cartoon balloon are now linked together as one element. Any movement that you create now applies to both the text and the cartoon balloon.

STEP 8: PERFORM A TEST BEFORE RENDERING

To execute this test render:

- Hold down the Option key.
- Drag the yellow play head back and forth in the timeline to preview your changes.

> **TIP**
>
> **When elements are linked or nested within each other, you can apply transition or video effects to them as a group.**

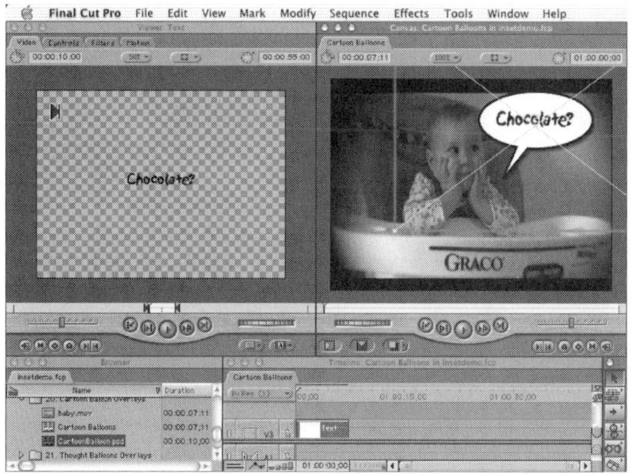

20.12

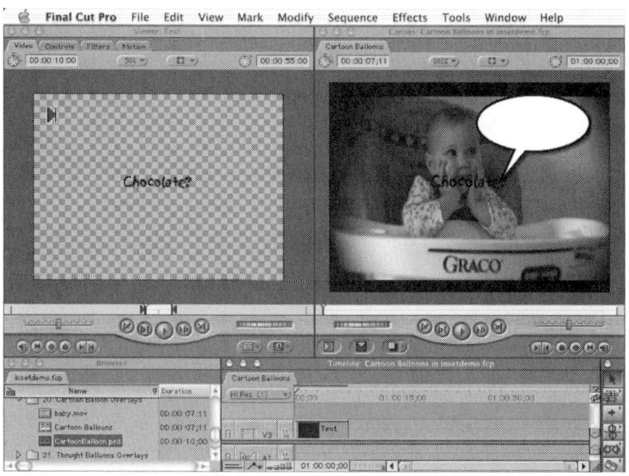

20.11

20.13

20.14

STEP 9: RENDER THE SEQUENCE

- Choose **Sequence ➢ Render All** as seen in **Figure 20.14** to see results of the changes that you made.

TIP

The link button is a little hard to find the first time you go looking for it. You can also use the keyboard shortcut Shift+L to link selected clip elements together.

IMAGINATION BALLOONS

21.1

21.2 (CP18)

Imagination balloons performs the same effect as the cartoon balloon, only the imagination balloon contains a video clip that promotes the concept of imaginary thought.

This technique is good where you have a long shot with a subject that has a thought over his head indicating what he is thinking about.

In this technique, I show you how to add, modify, and manipulate imaginary balloons within your video presentation.

Figure 21.1 and **Figure 21.2** show the effect you'll be exploring with this technique.

STEP 1: OPEN THE FILE

- Open the Chapter 4 Project folder. Inside the browser window, you find a bin entitled **Thought Balloon Overlays** that contains the files you need for this technique.
- Double-click to open the sequence called **Daydreaming**.
- Make sure your yellow play head is at the beginning of your timeline window as **Figure 21.3** shows.

STEP 2: ADD THOUGHT BALLOON ARTWORK

The "Thought Balloons Overlays" bin contains a native Photoshop file titled "thoughtballoon.psd."

- Drag the **thoughtballoon.psd** artwork from the bin onto the canvas window and choose the **Superimpose** overlay, as shown in **Figure 21.4**.
- This media clip item is now added to your timeline. In a new V2 video track above the target video track as **Figure 21.5** shows.

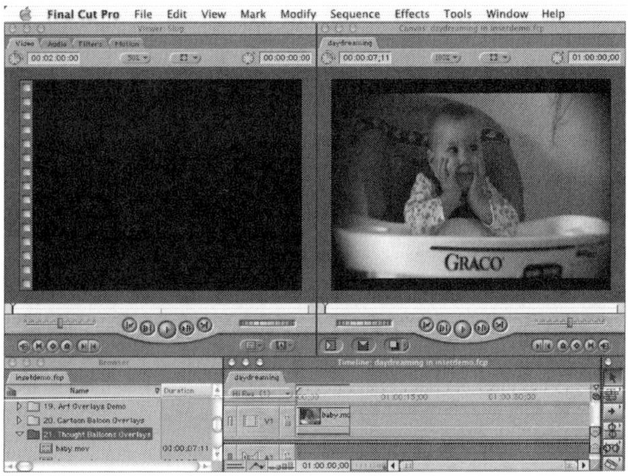

21.3

21.5

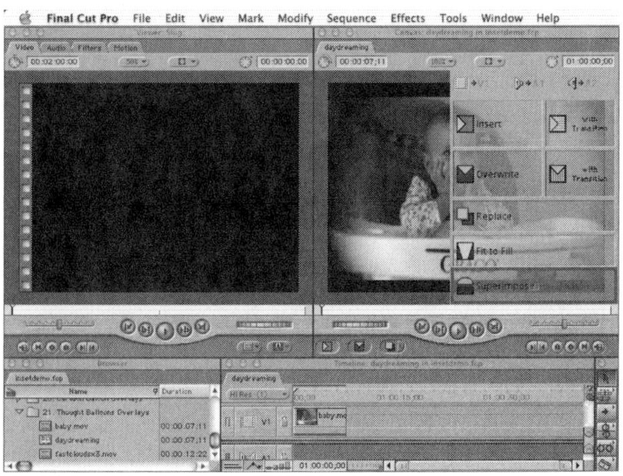

21.4

21.6

STEP 3: ADD A VIDEO CLIP TO ARTWORK

- Click the film clip icon in the **V2** video track to establish this as the target video track.
- Drag the video clip item named **fastcloudsx3.mov** onto the canvas window.
- Choose the **Superimpose** overlay, as shown in **Figure 21.6**.
- Three tracks are in your timeline window: the **basic** track, the **artwork** track, and the **inset video** track, in that order, as shown in **Figure 21.7**.

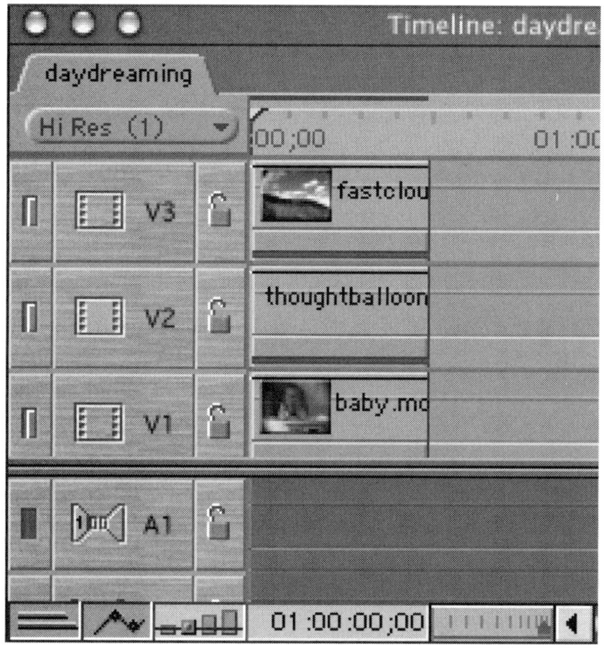

21.7

STEP 4: CHANGE THE COMPOSITE MODE

- Select the new clip at the top of the video track hierarchy containing the fastclouds video data in the timeline and double-click on it to load it into the viewer window.
- Choose **Modify ➢ Composite Mode ➢ Travel Matte-Luma** as shown in **Figure 21.8**.

21.8

NOTE

By performing this task, you create an area to accommodate a window through which a video can play. This concept is opposite from the normal process of working with mattes in graphic programs, which traditionally treat mattes as the top layer of a multi-layered environment.

This effect demonstrates the concept of "luminance" where the mask or travel matte creates a window through which you can see your video image. Opacity or transparency of the matte window is determined by the brightness of the pixels in the mask or matte element.

STEP 5: RESIZE AND REPOSITION THE THOUGHT BALLOON PICTURE MASK

- Click to select the **thoughtballoon.psd** clip item in the timeline.
- If the wire frame handles are not already visible, toggle their display with the **W** keyboard shortcut.
- Re-size and re-position the matte mask artwork so that only the clouds are visible, as **Figure 21.9** shows.
- Select both the **V2** and **V3** tracks in the time line as you did in the previous exercise and click the **Link** icon in the timeline window to link these two media clips together. Now, if one is moved, so is the other.

STEP 6: PERFORM A TEST BEFORE RENDERING

To test render:

- Hold down the Option key.
- Drag the yellow play head back and forth in the timeline to preview your changes.

STEP 7: RENDER THE SEQUENCE

- Choose **Sequence ➢ Render All** (shown in **Figure 21.10**) to see results of the changes that you made.
- In this technique, you learned how to create a matte mask for objects that appear in the timeline.

21.9 (CP17)

21.10

CHAPTER 5

SUPERIMPOSING SPECIAL EFFECTS

The open area in the sky provides us with a canvas on which to paint any ornaments we can envision ominous clouds, planets, and moons in the distance, and elements such as streaking meteors or comets. The choice is yours.

In this chapter, you take a look at several of these kinds of special effects and how you can enhance and alter your video content to include these different aspects.

Overcast Clouds
Divine Inspiration
Comets and Meteors
Planets and Moons
Monster Eyes

TECHNIQUE 22

PLANETS AND MOONS

22.1 (CP19)

22.2 (CP20)

Perhaps the easiest of the techniques presented in this chapter, adding a planet or an moon to any video clip, is as easy as dropping the artwork onto a new video track and changing its composite mode.

In this demonstration, you add two mysterious and mystical looking moons to the sky, giving us an otherworldly feeling to the video.

PIXEL ASPECT RATIO

It's a good time now to touch on a new concept of pixel aspect ratio. Simply put, pixels in a graphics program and pixels in the video world are differently proportioned. Pixels in the graphics world are square and video pixels are not. Be prepared for your scanned, painted, or rendered pixels from the graphics world to appear distorted when imported to Final Cut Pro.

So, how do you make sure your imported graphics are the correct aspect ratio to fit the frame sizes in Final Cut Pro? The current version of Adobe Photoshop has video frame size presets as available document sizes when you create a new document. Check your frame size and aspect ratio in Final Cut Pro when you start a new project, then when you create a new graphic to import in Photoshop, you can choose the appropriate document size to match your target frame size proportions.

22.3

STEP 1: OPEN THE PROJECT MEDIA FILE

- Make sure that you close any previous project tabs.
- Open the **Chapter 5 Projects** folder and open the **Planets and Moons** bin.
- You see the base video track **V1** is already in place.

Make sure that the play head is at the very beginning of the clip, as shown in **Figure 22.3**. You can press the up arrow key on your keyboard as a shortcut.

STEP 2: ADD THE GRAPHICS

Drag the graphics file **moon3.tif** into the canvas window (shown in **Figure 22.4**) and choose the superimpose overlay when presented.

22.4

■ Notice that the graphic addition creates a new video track called **V2** that has automatically filled the timeline to the length of the original base V1 video clip in the timeline window, as seen in **Figure 22.5**.

STEP 3: CHANGE THE OPACITY AND COMPOSITE MODE

■ Click to select the **moon3.tif** clip in the V2 track of the timeline.
■ From the menu, choose **Modify ➢ Composite Mode ➢ Screen**, as seen in **Figure 22.6**.
■ Double-click in the **moon3.tif** clip in the timeline window to load it into the viewer window.
■ Click the **Motion** tab in the viewer window.
■ Click the **delta** next to the Opacity option to view the opacity settings for the selection. Set the opacity for this clip to **66**.
Figure 22.7 shows how the opacity setting should appear on your screen.

NOTE

Wherever you see a triangle beside a menu command or in a floating palette window, it indicates that more information is available about that command or palette when you click the triangle. To differentiate between the triangle in a floating palette window and the triangle found in a menu command, the triangles seen in floating windows and palettes will be referred to as a delta.

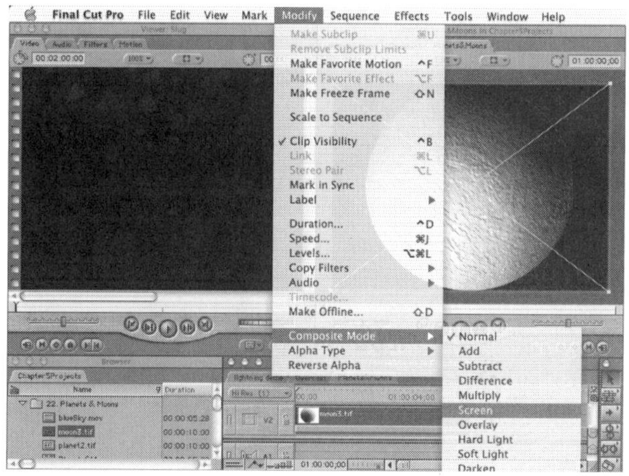

22.6

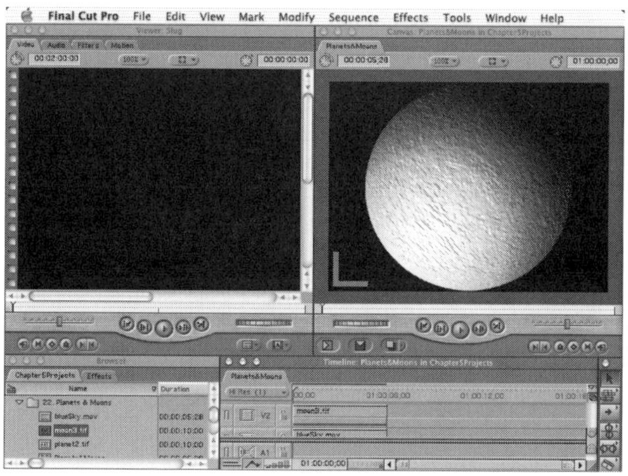

22.5

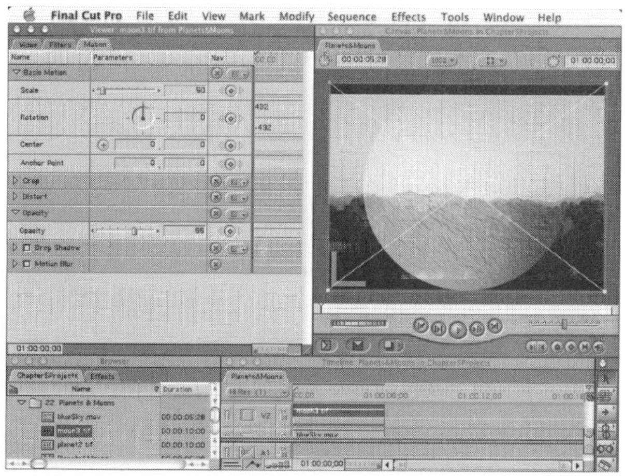

22.7

22.8

22.9

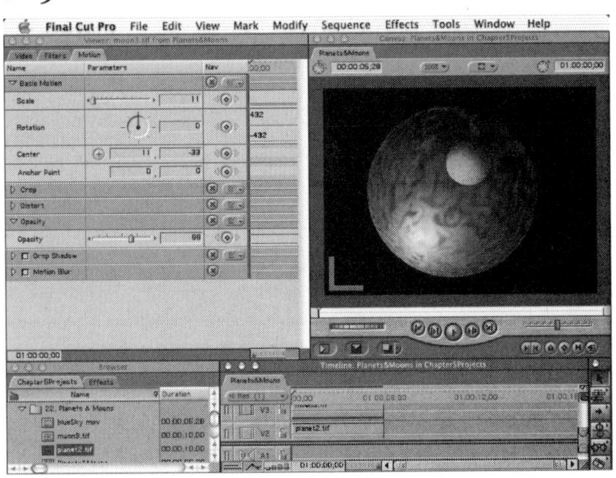

22.10

STEP 4: CHANGE THE SIZE OF THE MOON

- From the menu, choose **View ➢ Image+Wireframe.**
- Click to select one of the corner handles of the wire frame and re-size the moon and then adjust the location of the moon by dragging it above the horizon line to hang comfortably in the sky.
- To set a numeric value to the position, choose the **Motion** tab in the viewer window and set the **Scale** setting to **11** and the **Center** setting to **11, –33. Figure 22.8** shows the results of these settings.

STEP 5: ADD ANOTHER PLANET

The new digital video capabilities afford you the freedom to live on any world and create any reality you care to. Go ahead and add another celestial body to your magical off-world sky.

- Click and drag the graphic file **planet2.tif** in the canvas window and choose the **Superimpose** overlay when presented, as seen in **Figure 22.9**.

Figure 22.10 shows the new graphic media added to a new track in the timeline. Note that the yellow film-icon next to the V1 video track indicates that this track is the "target" track. Anything added to the timeline will appear in a track above the "target" track.

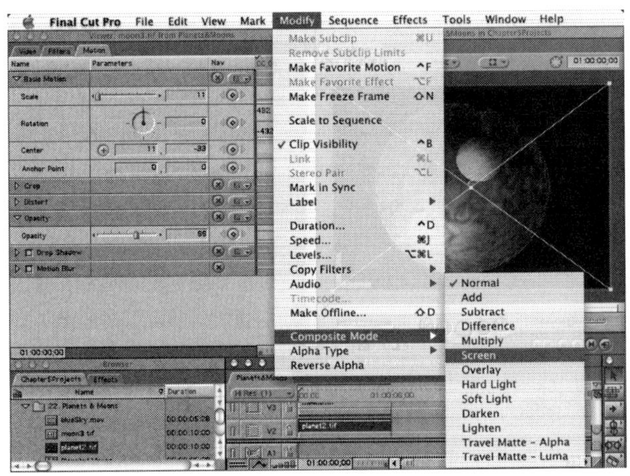

22.11

STEP 6: CHANGE THE COMPOSITE MODE

- Select the **planet2.tif** clip in the timeline window as shown in **Figure 22.11**.
- From the menu, choose **Modify ➢ Composite Mode ➢ Screen**.

STEP 7: CHANGE THE SIZE AND POSITION

- Your view of the track should still be showing the wire frame handles on the currently selected clip.
- Enlarge the clip by dragging one of the corner handles out and away from the center of the clip. Then move the clip up into the sky so that it appears that the new planet is hanging from outside the frame.
- Double-click on the **planet2.tif** clip item in the timeline window to display it in the viewer window.
- You can apply a numeric value to the position by clicking the **Motion** tab in the viewer window and setting the **center** value to **–55** and **–111**, respectively. See how the changes result in **Figure 22.12**.

STEP 8: RENDER THE SEQUENCE

- Choose **Sequence ➢ Render All** in **Figure 22.13** to see the changes you made.
- After you finish, close this Project tab by Control-clicking on the tab name and choosing "Close Tab" or use the keyboard shortcut Command-W.

Now you created a very striking effect with something as simple as an overlaid graphic object. Because both imported graphic objects are screened against the background, they have the appearance of a realistic atmosphere between the objects and our home planet.

TIP

Note that the illustration was carefully crafted to show the apparent light source for each celestial object is oriented in the same direction, adding a level of realism to your surreal scene.

22.12

22.13

TECHNIQUE 23

LIGHTNING BOLTS

23.1

23.2 (CP22)

Using simple layer effects, you can create your own lightning bolts striking any object in your video project. The technique takes advantage of the Final Cut Pro advanced layer and composition mode effects.

This project uses sample files, created by using Adobe Photoshop, provided here for your use. These art samples are included and pre-arranged in the project folder for this technique.

STEP 1: OPEN THE PROJECT MEDIA FILE

- Make sure you close any previous Project tabs.
- Open the **Chapter 5 Projects** folder. You find the bins for each technique that you work with in this chapter.
- In the Lightning bin, double-click the sequence named **lightning demo** to see it appear in the timeline window as you see in **Figure 23.3**.

23.3

23.4

STEP 2: ADD THE LIGHTNING FILE TO THE TIMELINE

- Make sure the play head in the timeline is at the very beginning of the clip. You can use the up-arrow keyboard shortcut for this if the timeline window is selected.
- Add the **lightning** file to the timeline on top of the base track.
- Drag and drop the image file named **lightning.tif** from the browser window onto the canvas window and choose the superimpose overlay as seen in **Figure 23.4**.
- Notice that the lightning graphic appears in its own new video track above the V1 clouds track in the timeline as shown in **Figure 23.5**.

STEP 3: ESTABLISH THE STARTING POINT

- Select the **current time code field** in the canvas window to set the insertion point at the **2-second** mark into the clip. Type in the number **2**, the **semicolon** key, and then press **Return**.

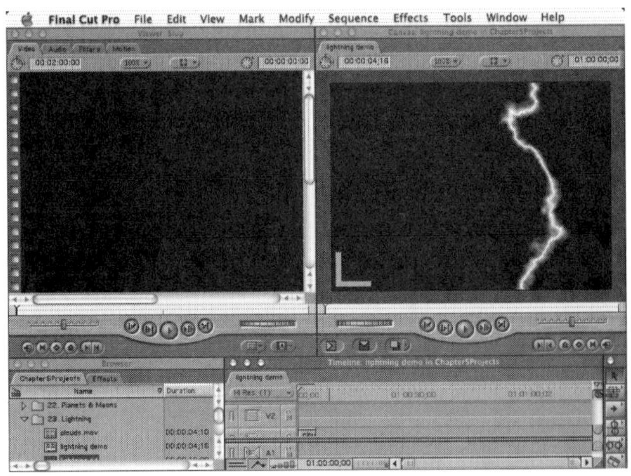

23.5

■ Notice that the play head moves to the 2-second position in the timeline window as seen in **Figure 23.6**.

STEP 4: CHANGE THE LIGHTNING'S STARTING POINT

■ Turn the snapping function on by choosing **View ➢ Snapping** or by using the keyboard shortcut "n" (the "n" key toggles the snapping feature in Final Cut Pro).

■ Click the insertion point of the lightning clip in the V2 track in the timeline window and drag the left edge of the lightning clip to the right until it snaps into position at the 2-second marker as you see in **Figure 23.7**.

TIP

You can mark this point allowing you to return to it easily later on by using the keyboard shortcut key "M". This timeline has it marked and labeled for you to easily navigate to the beginning point of your lightning clip.

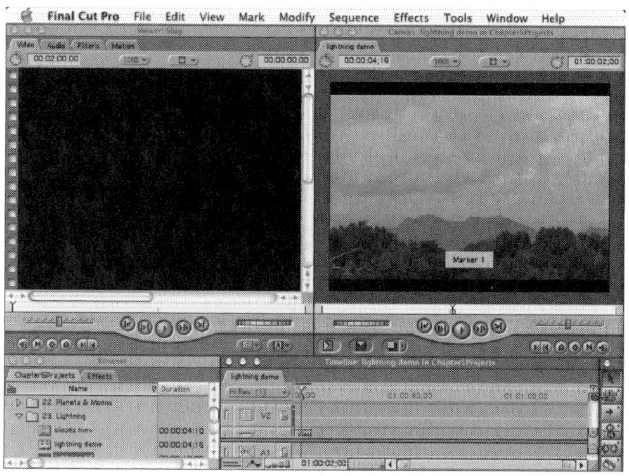

23.6

STEP 5: CHANGE THE COMPOSITE MODE

■ Select the **lightning** clip in the timeline by clicking on it.

■ Choose **Modify ➢ Composition Mode ➢ Screen** as shown in **Figure 23.8**.

NOTE

Composite screen mode allows lighter and white pixels to show up against a background, while darker pixels are ignored and appear transparent.

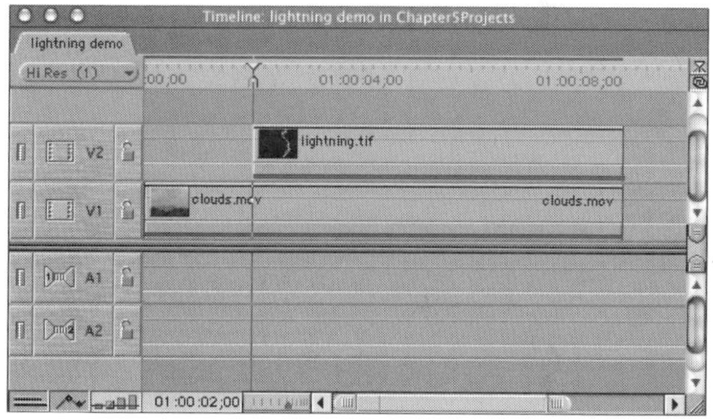

23.7

23.8 (CP21)

23.9

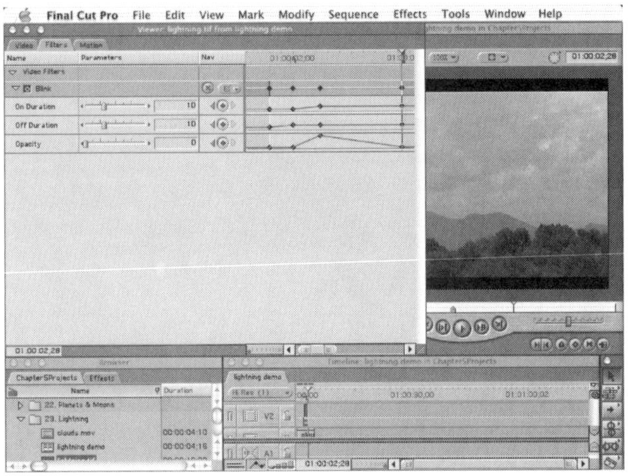

23.10

STEP 6: MAKING IT "FLASH"

- Double-click the **lightning** clip in the timeline to display it in the viewer window.
- Choose **Effects ➢ Video Filters ➢ Video ➢ Blink** as shown in **Figure 23.9**. This sets up the process of keyframing positions in the timeline so that the lightning flashes.

In the viewer window, click the **Filters** tab to see the blink settings. You may want to stretch the viewer window out a bit in order to see the timeline along side of the blink settings. **Figure 23.10** shows this.

- Click the keyframe button beside each of the duration and visibility settings. This sets a starting point that defines the values of those settings at this moment in time.

STEP 7: CHANGE THE FLASH FREQUENCY

- Move the play head about **2-seconds** later in the timeline by dragging the play head in the filters timeline to about 2-seconds further down to establish its position.
- Click the **keyframe** marker in the **nav** column of the video filters window to set another keyframe.
- Change the Off Duration to **10**, which makes the time between the lightning flashes longer.
- Move the play head to **2-seconds** later in the timeline and establish another keyframe by clicking the **keyframe** marker in the **nav** column of the video filters window.
- Set the **on and off duration** to **10**, which makes the lightning bolts flash more frequently when you render the clip.

For an added hint of reality, change the opacity of the lightning bolt from 100 to 0 percent over the remaining two seconds in the clip. See the Opacity setting trailing off from 100-percent to 0-percent in **Figure 23.10**.

STEP 8: RENDER THE SEQUENCE

- Choose **Sequence ➢ Render All** (shown in **Figure 23.11**)to see results of the changes that you made.
- After you finish, close this project tab by Control-clicking on the tab name or use the keyboard shortcut Control-W.

You can now see how easy it is to add a still graphic element to a video track as an active element of your project. By experimenting with the keyframes and blink settings with the blink filter, you can achieve very realistic simulations of your lightning bolt effects.

Be prepared to experiment with the settings to get the best results. Half the fun of composing special effects in Final Cut Pro is experimenting with the settings to get the most believable results.

23.11

DIVINE INSPIRATION

24.1

24.2 (CP24)

Use this technique to present the concept of divine inspiration. It's easy to create and fun to play with as you shine a heavenly beam of light onto any subject. It works well with people and objects and can create a feeling of inspiration. In this demonstration, you indicate some kind of divine inspiration affecting the windows of this middle-class suburban home.

NOTE

You can import any Photoshop file you create into final Cut Pro 3. Make sure that the art you create conforms to your project's frame size and proportions. In this example a simple grayscale single-layer image was created using a variety of simple blur and distortion filters in Photoshop, then saved as a .tif image and imported into Final Cut Pro 3.

24.3

24.4

STEP 1: OPEN THE PROJECT MEDIA FILE

- Make sure to close any previous project tabs. An easy shortcut to remember for this is to hold down the control key as you click any open sequence tab, and then choose Close Tab from the pop-up contextual menu that appears.
- In the Chapter 5 Projects folder, find the bin entitled **Divine Inspiration** and open it as shown in **Figure 24.3.**
- Double-click the sequence titled **inspiration** to see it in the timeline window.
- The base video track should already have the movie clip **roofline.mov** imported to it.
- Move your yellow play head in the timeline window to the beginning of the clip if it is not already there. A shortcut to do this is to press the up arrow key.

STEP 2: ADD THE HEAVENLY BEAMS OF LIGHT

The artwork shown here was created from scratch by using Adobe Photoshop. Creating artwork like this is relatively easy. In case you don't have Photoshop, you can use the file supplied with this project.

- Drag the **rays.psd** artwork from the browser window into the canvas window and choose the superimpose overlay when it appears on the right-hand side as shown in **Figure 24.4.**
- You should now see a second video track containing the static artwork images of the beams of light as shown in **Figure 24.5.**

STEP 3: CHANGE THE COMPOSITE MODE

- Select the artwork that you have just added by clicking it in the timeline window.
- Choose **Modify ➢ Composite Mode ➢ Screen** as you see in **Figure 24.6.**

- You now see your heavenly beams of light are raining down from the sky onto the suburban family home in **Figure 24.7**.

STEP 4: CHANGE THE TRANSPARENCY

Some applications of this screened image may look better if the video art layer is less than 100 percent opaque. You can change this by adjusting the transparency of the layer.

- Double-click the **rays.psd** video track to show it in the viewer window.

24.5 (CP23)

24.6

- Choose the **Motion** tab.
- Click the delta next to the Opacity item to expose the opacity value setting.
- Drag the opacity value slider to the left to reduce the opacity value setting of this image on the video track to **50%** as shown in **Figure 24.8**.

24.7

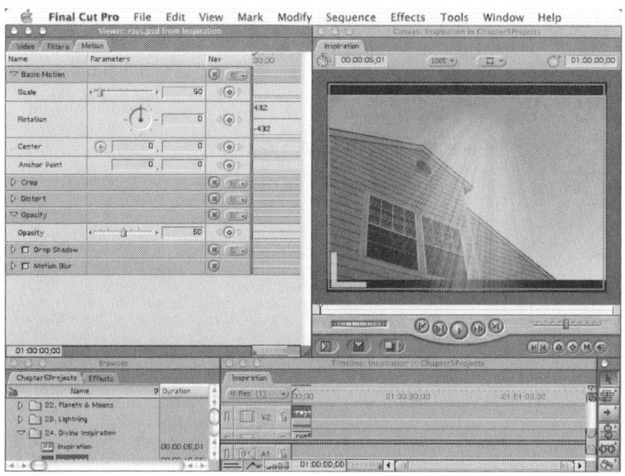

24.8

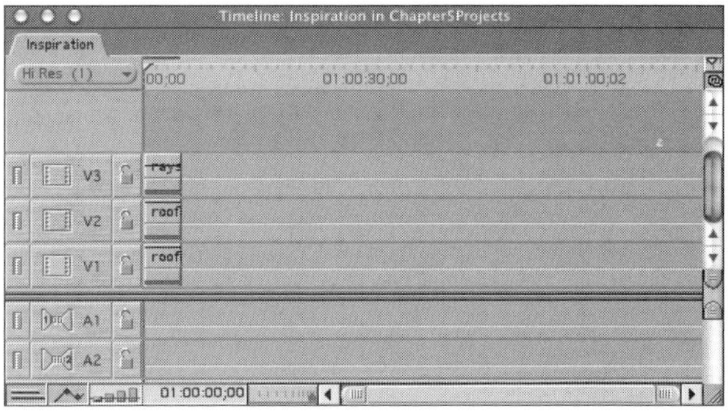

24.9

24.10

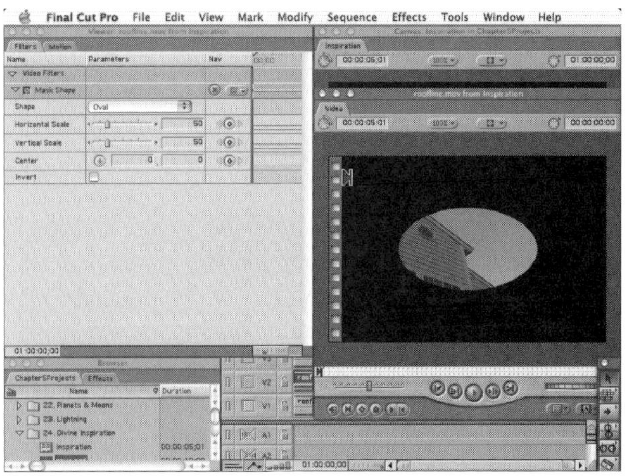

24.11

STEP 5: DUPLICATE AND REORGANIZE YOUR VIDEO TRACKS

This step shows how to simulate a projected light source by changing the brightness and contrast of a feathered matte window area.

- Select media in both the V1 and V2 video tracks by holding down the shift key while you select both tracks.
- Duplicate the **roofline.mov** video track by holding down the Option and Shift keys while you click and drag video tracks upwards one level above the V2 track. Watch for the insertion cursor to change to a down-facing arrow before you let go of the mouse button.
- **Figure 24.9** shows that you created a duplicate video track entitled **V3**.

STEP 6: CREATE A HIGHLIGHT AROUND YOUR SUBJECT AREA

The changes that you make to the shape of the matte window filter occur in the Filters tab window. This change creates a window shape that more closely reflects the shape of our newly created projected light.

- Select the **V2** video track from the timeline window and double-click on it to load it in the viewer window.
- Choose **Effects ➢ Video Filters ➢ Matte ➢ Mask** Shape as you see in **Figure 24.10**.

- Click the **Filters** tab and in the area marked Mask Shape. Select Oval from the **Shape** menu.
- Preview the changes to the Mask shape by clicking and dragging the video tab in this window away and to the right to create a new and separate window. **Figure 24.11** shows a workable screen layout showing the Filters tab and the Video tab side by side.

STEP 7: CHANGE THE ATTRIBUTES OF THE FILTER

In the Filters tab, set the horizontal scale to **33** and the vertical scale to **77**.

- Move the center point of the mask shape to a point near the center of the two windows on the house. Set the value for this demonstration to **–71** and 82 as shown in **Figure 24.12**.

STEP 8: CHANGE THE FEATHER ATTRIBUTES FOR THE MASK AREA

Now create a soft-blurred edge to our matte selection to replace the hard edge that is present in the default setting.

- Choose **Effects ➢ Video Filters ➢ Matte ➢ Mask feather** as shown in **Figure 24.13** to apply a feathered edge to the matte selection.
- Change the softness level of the mask feather to 22 as shown in **Figure 24.14**.

> **TIP**
>
> **You can rotate the heavenly beams of light to create other striking effects, such as a broadcast or projected light source from almost any source.**
>
> **You can also distort the beams of light to match almost any use, in any orientation on your video clip.**

24.12

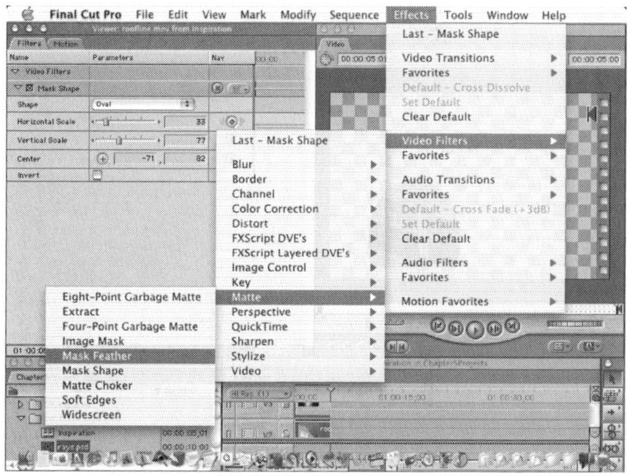

24.13

24.14

24.15

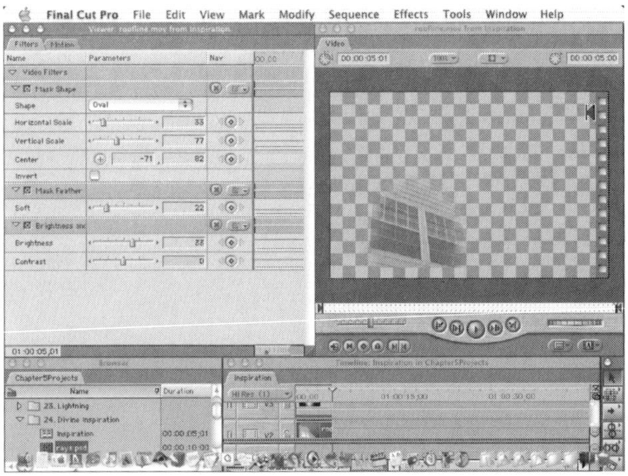

24.16

24.17

- Now choose **Effects ➢ Video Filters ➢ Image Control ➢ Brightness and Contrast (Bezier)** as shown in **Figure 24.15** to change the contents of the video window so that it appears brighter than the surrounding video track in V1.
- Set the brightness slider to **33** to brighten up the area in the masked shape as you see in **Figure 24.16**.

Now you created a nice feathered and brighter inset that lays on top of our video. In the main canvas window, you can see the effects of the changes that you made.

Click the canvas window to preview the effect and see the results of your work. Your window should appear as shown in **Figure 24.17.**

STEP 9: RENDER THE SEQUENCE

- From the Sequence menu, choose **Render All** as shown in **Figure 24.18** to see results of the changes that you made.
- After you finish, close this Project tab by Control-clicking on the tab name or use the keyboard shortcut Command-W.

Here you learned some valuable techniques for adding a screened video element to any clip and then use a matte mask to create a brighter area in the video image to help our simulation.

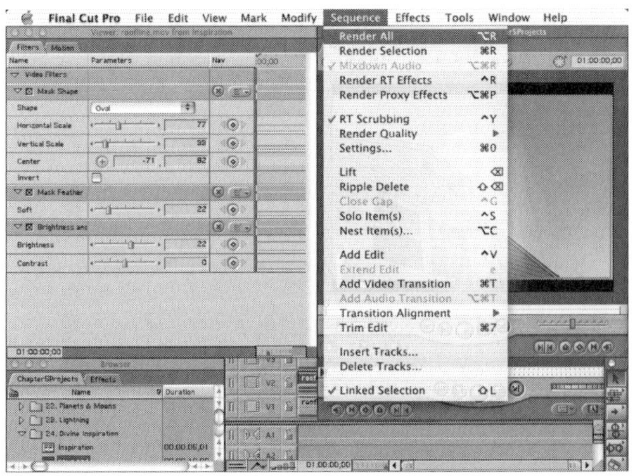

24.18

TECHNIQUE 25

COMETS AND METEORS

25.1 (CP25)

25.2 (CP26)

This trick is great for adding a surreal but recognizable special effect to almost any video clip. Imagine adding a comet or meteor to any night (or day for that matter) sky. The meteor effect is a simple superimposition of art over a clear space in your sky shot. It changes shape over time and moves across the sky.

The base video track for this timeline is simply a daytime clip that has been altered by using the brightness and contrast filter to make it appear as early-evening dusk.

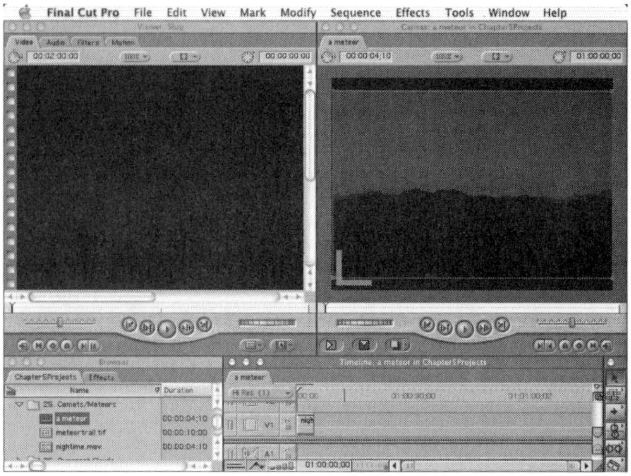

25.3

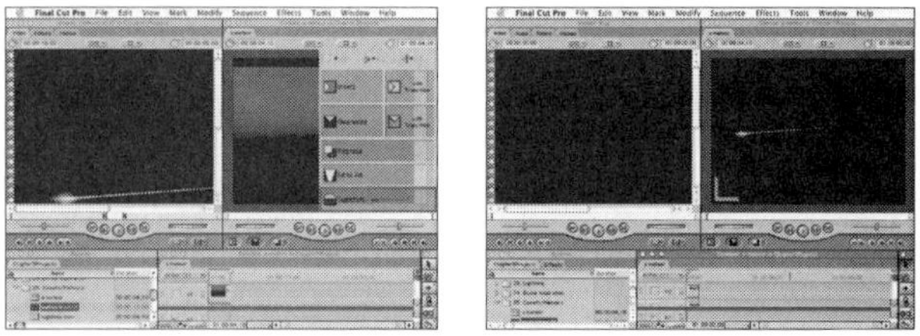

25.4

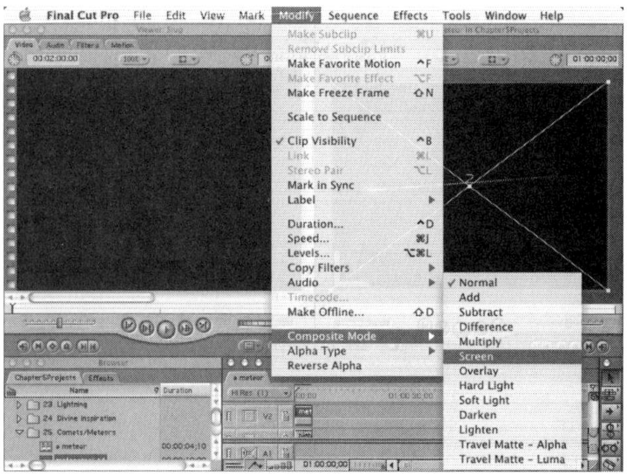

25.5

STEP 1: OPEN THE PROJECT MEDIA FILE

- Make sure you close any open previous project tabs.
- In your Chapter 5 Projects folder, you find a bin labeled **26, Comets and Meteors.**
- Open the bin and make sure that your play head is at the very beginning of the clip in the timeline window as you see in **Figure 25.3.**

STEP 2: ADD THE ART TO THE TIMELINE

- Drag and drop the **meteortrail.tif** art file onto the canvas window and choose the superimpose overlay when presented as you see in **Figure 25.4.**

STEP 3: CHANGE THE COMPOSITE MODE

- Select the **meteortrail.tif** video track in the timeline window as shown in **Figure 25.5.**
- From the menu, choose **Modify ➢ Composite Mode ➢ Screen**. This allows only the lighter pixels in the **meteortrail.tif** art to show up on top of the video track.

STEP 4: CHANGE THE GEOMETRY

- Click in the canvas window to activate it.
- From the menu, choose **View ➢ Image+ Wireframe.** You can also use the keyboard shortcut "w" to cycle through the wireframe view options.
- Click and drag the corner handles on the wire frame overlay to re-size the graphic element to about 50% of its original size.
- Move the cursor to one of the boundaries of the wire frame. Notice how the cursor changes to the circular arrow and change the angle of the meteor trail by rotating it counter-clockwise about 33 degrees. For an example, see **Figure 25.6.**

STEP 5: REPOSITION THE ARTWORK

- Make sure the play head is at the beginning of the clip in the timeline.
- Click the center of the wire frame guides for the graphic image and drag it up and out of the frame.

You will still be able to see the wire frame guide, but the graphic element is just outside of the video frame as shown in **Figure 25.7**.

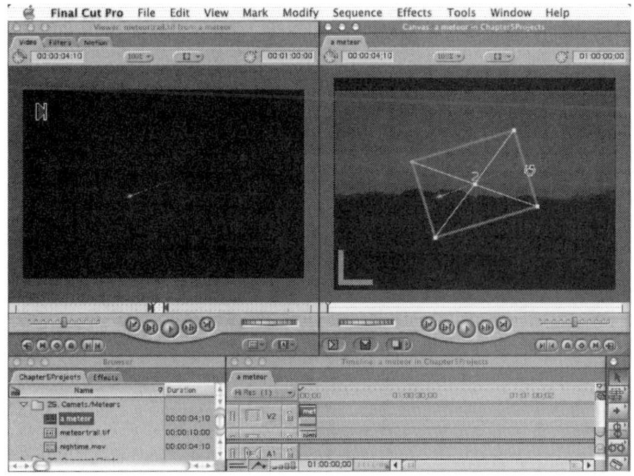

25.6

STEP 6: KEYFRAME THE LOCATION AND SIZE ATTRIBUTES

- Double-click on the **meteortrail.tif** graphic in the timeline to load it into the viewer window.
- Click the **Motion** tab to expose all of the motion attributes for this clip element.
- Set a keyframe by clicking each of the keyframe marker buttons, **Scale**, **Rotation**, **Center**, and **Anchor Points** in the **nav** column, as you see in **Figure 25.8**.

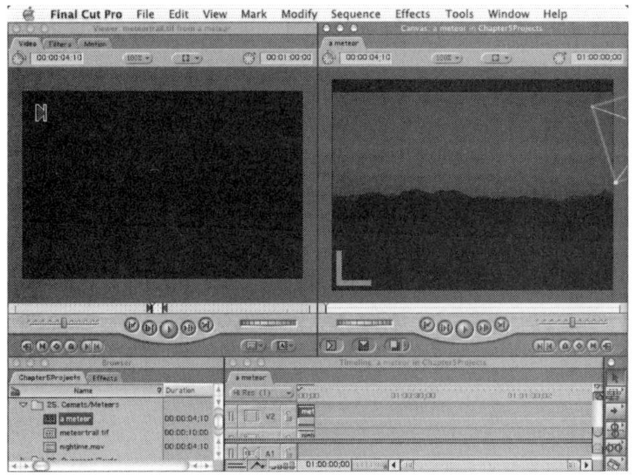

25.7

STEP 7: MOVE AND RESCALE THE GRAPHIC ELEMENT

- Press the down-arrow key on your keyboard to move the play head to the next edit point at the end of the clip.
- In the **Motion** tab of the viewer window, click to set a keyframe for each of the nav definitions in the **nav** column, **Scale**, **Rotation**, **Center**, and **Anchor Points**.

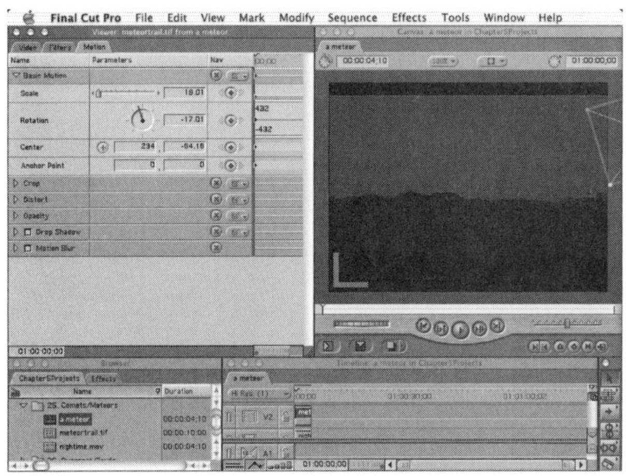

25.8

TIP

Unlike most other graphic programs, holding down the shift key while dragging the image corner handles does not constrain the image proportions. In Final Cut Pro, it allows you to resize the element disproportionately.

TIP

No matter what size and angle you change your meteor graphic to, you can make sure that the meteor travels in an straight line by watching the "knots-on-a-rope" motion indicator, as seen in the wire frame view. Make sure that the line of the meteor trail artwork is as parallel as possible to the motion guide that is created when you drag the graphic image to the center of the window.

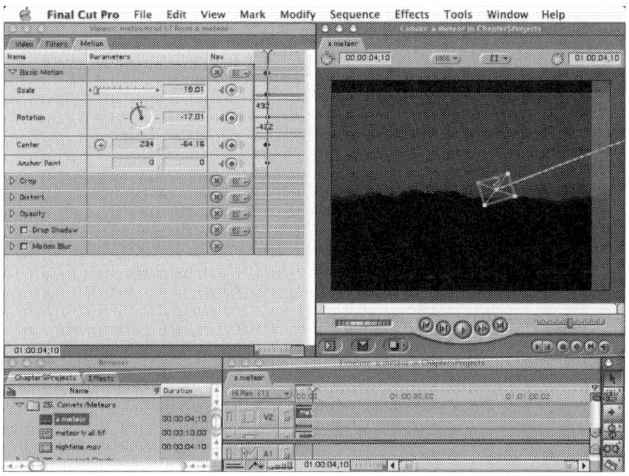

25.9

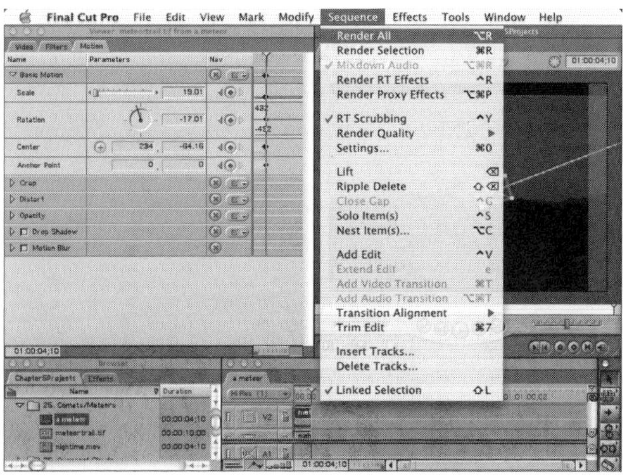

25.10

- Move the graphic element to the center area of the picture.
- Drag the wire frame handles to resize the **meteortrail.tif** graphic. **Figure 25.9** shows where your wire framed object should end up after these changes have been made.

STEP 8: RENDER THE SEQUENCE

- Choose **Sequence > Render All** to see results of the changes you made as shown in **Figure 25.10**.
- After you finish, close this Project tab by Control-clicking on the tab name or use the keyboard shortcut Control-W.

STEP 9: REMEMBER TO SAVE YOUR WORK

- Remember to save your changes whenever possible.
- After you finish, close this Project tab by Control-clicking on the tab name as shown in **Figure 25.11**, or use the keyboard shortcut Command-W.

There you have it. A perfectly believable and natural-looking meteor passing through the atmosphere directly over your head. Don't forget to make a wish . . .

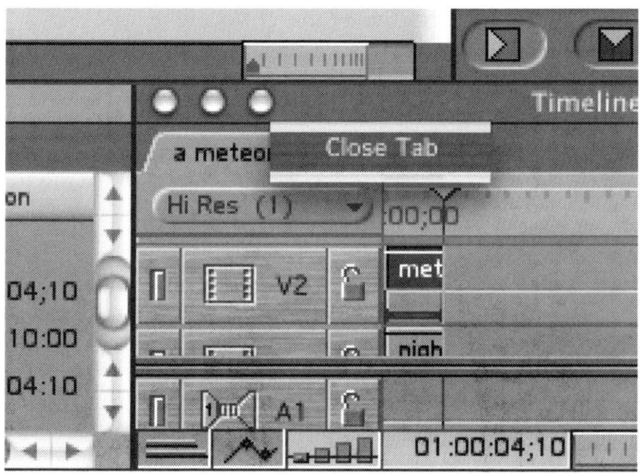

25.11

TECHNIQUE **26**

OVERCAST CLOUDS

26.1 (CP27)

26.2 (CP28)

Another easily achieved effect using imported art as an overlaid effect. This technique demonstrates the use of color keys to create a matte window through which to see the effect.

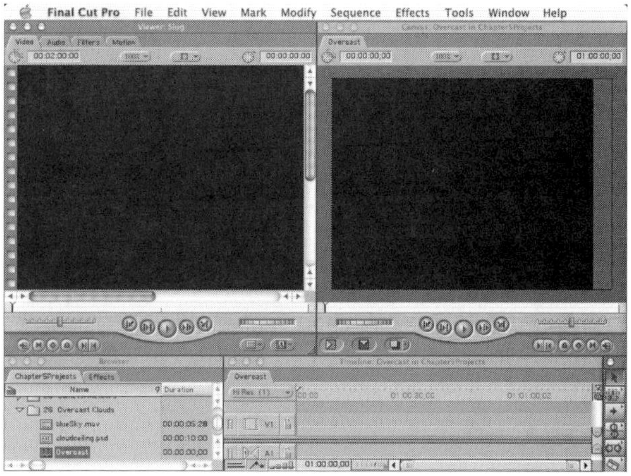

26.3

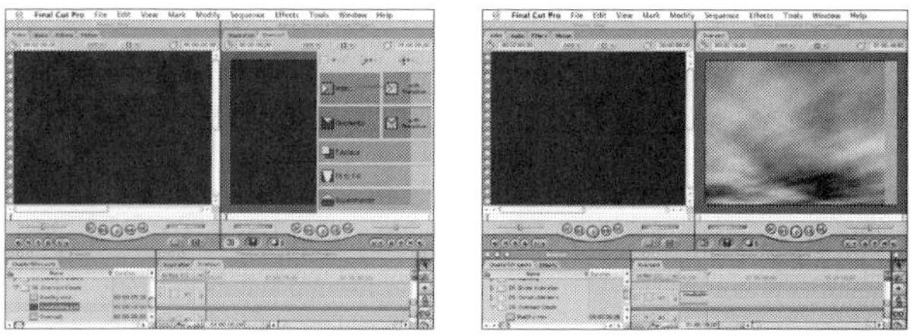

26.4

26.5

STEP 1: OPEN THE PROJECT MEDIA FILE

- Make sure you close any previously opened projects.
- In your **Chapter 5 Projects** folder, look for the document named **Overcast clouds**.
- Double-click and open the sequence **Overcast**. Your screen should appear as shown in **Figure 26.3**.

STEP 2: ADD THE WEATHER BACKGROUND

- Drag the graphic file **cloudceiling.psd** onto the canvas window.
- Choose the Insert overlay when presented as shown in **Figure 26.4**.

STEP 3: ADD THE SUNNY DAY

- Make sure your play head is at the beginning of the clip in the timeline window.
- Drag the movie **bluesky.mov** into the timeline window and watch for the cursor to turn into a downward-pointing arrow before you release the mouse button.
- Notice that a new track entitled **V2** is added to the timeline window.
- Click to select the new V2 track clip and drag it to the left until it snaps into place at the beginning of the timeline as shown in **Figure 26.5.**

STEP 4: SHORTEN THE CLOUD CLIP

- Click to select the right edge of the **cloud ceiling.psd** clip and watch for the cursor to change into a pair of vertical lines representing the clip-edge handle.
- Drag the right edge of the **cloudceiling.psd** clip to the left until it snaps into position at the end of the video clip in track V2.
- Notice that the still image is 10-seconds long, and the video clip you added in V2 is only 6-seconds long. You want both clips to be the same length. **Figure 26.6** shows how your result should appear.

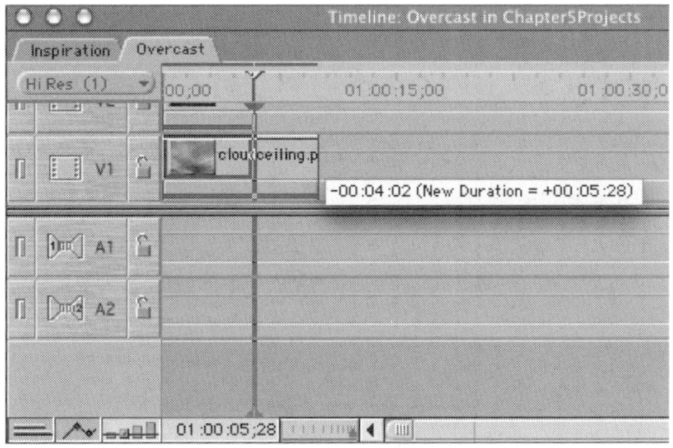

26.6

STEP 5: CREATE THE COLOR KEY MASK

Ideally, you want to see the dark and menacing clouds showing only in the sky, and Final Cut Pro provides a handy but very advanced tool for accomplishing this.

- Select the video clip in the V2 channel of the timeline window.
- Double-click on the V2 track in the timeline window to load it into the viewer window.
- From the menu, choose **Effects ➢ Video Filters ➢ Key ➢ Color Key** as shown in **Figure 26.7**.
- Select the **Filters** tab in the viewer window, make sure the pop-up menu is set to **Final**, and see the results of your color key work appear in the canvas window as shown in **Figure 26.8**.

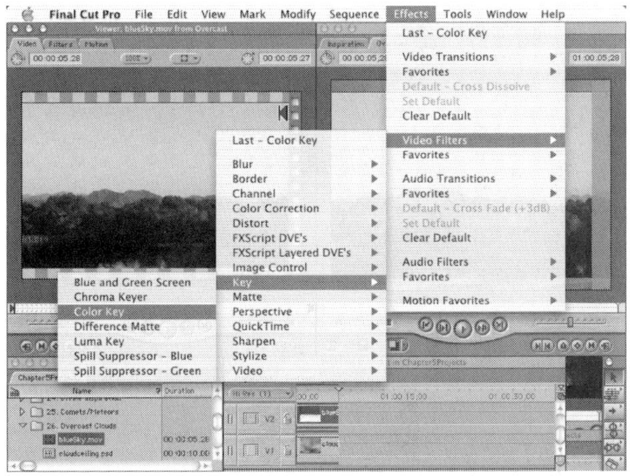

26.7

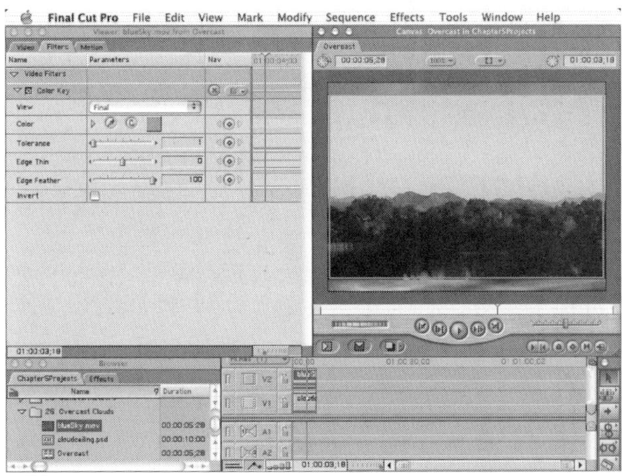

26.8

> **TIP**
>
> **Step 4 can be made easier if the "snap" command is toggled on. Press the "n" key on your keyboard to toggle the snapping attribute.**

STEP 6: SET THE TOLERANCES

- Use the **eyedropper** tool in the **Filters** tab to select an initial color shade in the canvas window. Click near the center of the sky, between the horizon line and the top of the frame. You may not see any immediate change in the canvas window because the default settings for the color key filter are pretty broad.
- In the color key section of the **Filters** tab, try dragging the tolerance, edge thin, and edge feather sliders back and forth to see what effects they have on the key matte you're creating.
- Set the following setting values: **tolerance** to **33**, **edge thin** to **–22**, **edge feather** to **1** (to soften the transition between the matte and the background image.) Your results should be close to what you see in **Figure 26.9**.

Of course these generic values approach this technique without much finesse. Remember, sometimes a little experimentation with filter parameters can yield some intriguing differences in the effects. Another way to adjust the values represented by these sliders is to click the arrows at either end of the sliders to increment or decrement the values a little more precisely.

STEP 7: CHANGE THE PERSPECTIVE

Because our background image is as large as the overlaid video track, and the horizon line is closer to the center of the frame, you can adjust the size of the base track containing the **cloudceiling.psd** image.

- Double-click to select the **cloudceiling.psd** clip in the V1 track of the timeline and notice it now displays in the viewer window.
- Toggle the display options of the wire frame outline and use the keyboard shortcut W to display the image with the wire frame outline indicator. You'll see the wire frame handles appear as shown in **Figure 26.10**.
- In the viewer window, click the **Motion** tab to display the physical attributes of the clip's geometry.
- Hold down the Shift key as you drag the corner handle of the wire frame indicator up to re-size and re-proportion the graphic image clip.

TIP

By default, resizing always happens around the anchor in the center of the wire frame, so you may have to reposition the clip after resizing.

26.9

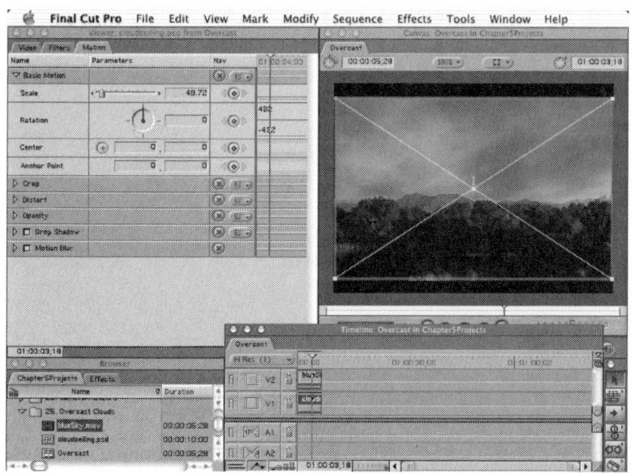

26.10

STEP 8: SET THE NUMERIC VALUE POSITIONS

- Make sure that the top-edge of the clip aligns with the top-edge of the frame, and the bottom-edge of the clip extends below the horizon line.
- In the **Motion** tab, find the settings labeled **Distort**.
- Specify numeric values for the position and proportions of the selected clip as follows, and as shown in **Figure 26.11**:

  Upper Left: –360, –270
  Upper Right: 360, –270
  Lower Right: 360, 270
  Lower Left: –360, 270
  Aspect Ratio: –77

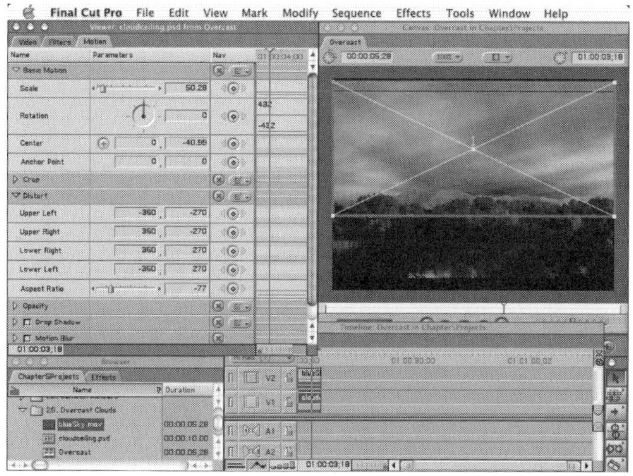

26.11

STEP 9: RENDER THE SEQUENCE

- Choose **Sequence ➢ Render All** as shown in **Figure 26.12** to see results of the changes you made.
  - After you finish, close this Project tab by Control-clicking on the tab name and choosing "Close Tab" from the pop-up menu that appears or use the keyboard shortcut Command-W.

26.12

TECHNIQUE **27**

MONSTER EYES

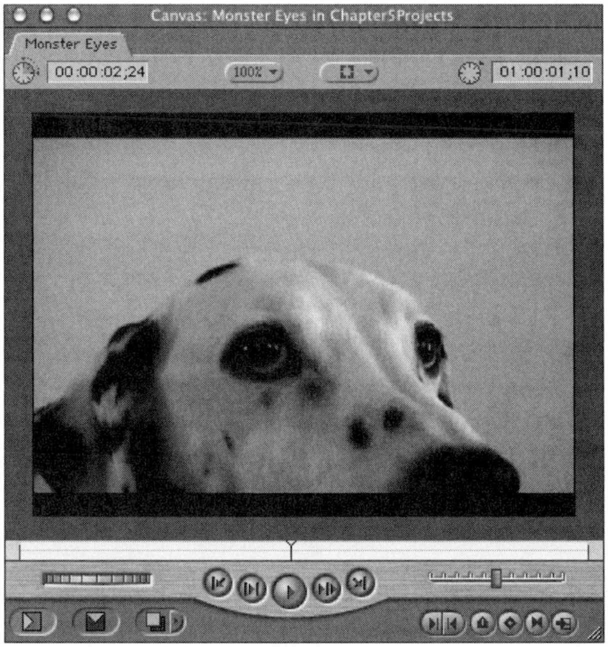

27.1 (CP29)

27.2 (CP30)

This technique is sure to be one of your favorites because it is so easy to accomplish in Final Cut Pro 3. No artwork imports are required and all the steps are performed using native Final Cut Pro effects.

Your objective here is to simulate glowing monster eyes in any subject, indicating a hint of evil lying just beneath the surface of even the most innocent character, such as the family dog.

STEP 1: OPEN THE PROJECT MEDIA FILE

- Look for the project file called **Monster Eyes** in the Chapter 5 Projects folder.
- Double-click to open the **Monster Eyes** timeline as shown in **Figure 27.3**.

STEP 2: NOTE THE MARKER

- Locate the file **rayeyes.mov** and notice the marker in the browser window indented under the media clip.

27.3

27.4

- Double-click the **rayeyes.mov** media clip ***in the timeline***, which loads it into the viewer window. Notice that the marker is shown about two-thirds of the way into the movie file as shown in **Figure 27.4**.

STEP 3: GO TO THE MARKER

- Force the play head to move directly to the marker by using the keyboard shortcut Shift-M as shown in **Figure 27.5**.
- Use this mark as your insertion point for the effect.

STEP 4: DUPLICATE THE VIDEO TRACK IN THE TIMELINE

This technique works by stacking matte windows on top of the video track, and then colorizing the contents of these matte windows.

- Start by duplicating the video track in V1. Do this by holding down Shift+Option while you click and drag the clip into the space directly above it.

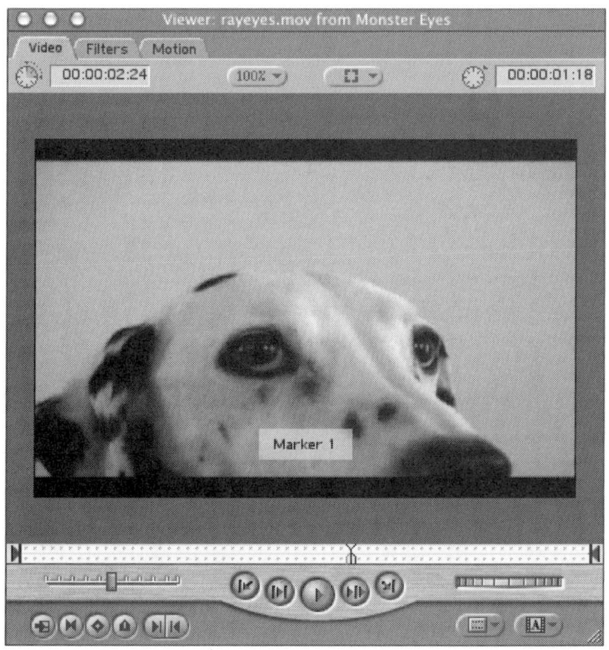

27.5

You'll see your duplicate track appear in the V2 video track, including the placed marker as shown in **Figure 27.6**.

STEP 5: CREATE A NEW MATTE WINDOW

- Move the play head back to marker indicator. An easy shortcut for this step is to press the up arrow, and then Shift+M.
- Double-click the V2 video track media clip in the timeline window to load it into the viewer window
- From the menu, choose **Effects ➢ Video Filters ➢ Matte ➢ Mask Shape** as shown in **Figure 27.7A**.
- Notice that a rectangular window has appeared around the subject's eyes in the center of the video image as you see in **Figure 27.7B**.

STEP 6: CHANGE THE SHAPE AND LOCATION OF THE MATTE WINDOW

- Separate the **Video** tab by dragging it away from the viewer window so that you can see both the video image and the Filters tab window.
- In the filters window, notice the Mask shape video filter that is indicated with an "x" in the check box next to the delta symbol. This indicates that the video filter is applied to the video clip.
- Select **Oval** from the Shape pop-up menu.
- Resize and reposition the oval by first clicking on the crosshairs button in the Center feature in the Filter tab under Mask Shape. When depressed, this button permits you to manually drag the mask to a precise location in the video tab window.

You can also precisely adjust position and other values by manually defining values in the Filters tab. Try setting the following values, as shown in **Figure 27.8**.

27.7A

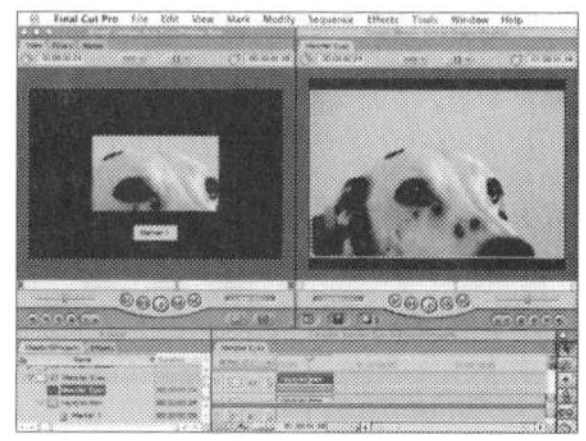

27.7B

27.6

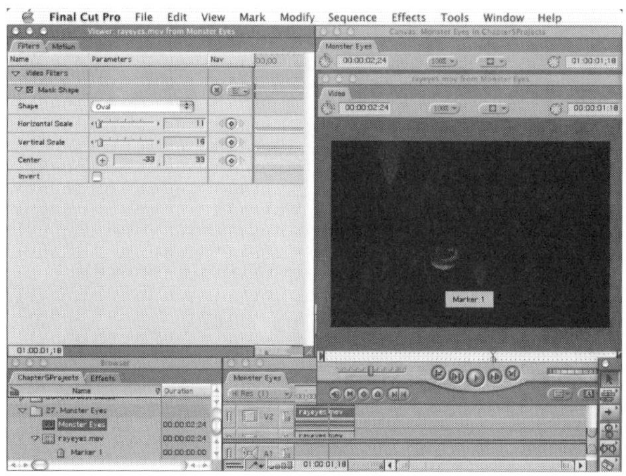

27.8

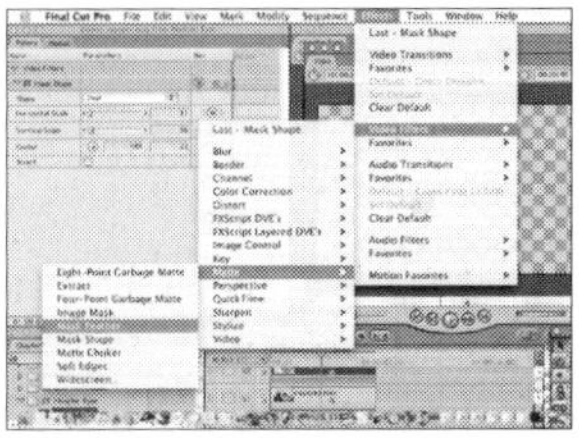

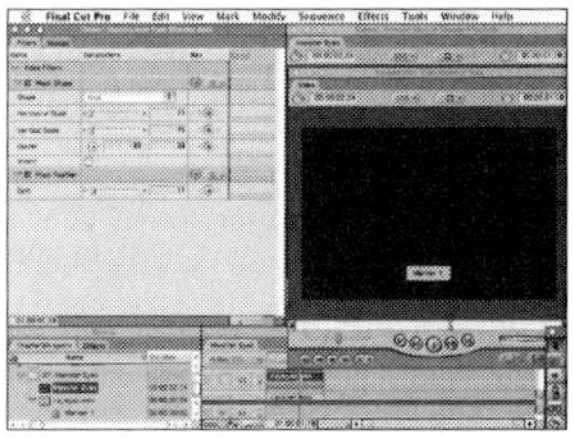

27.9

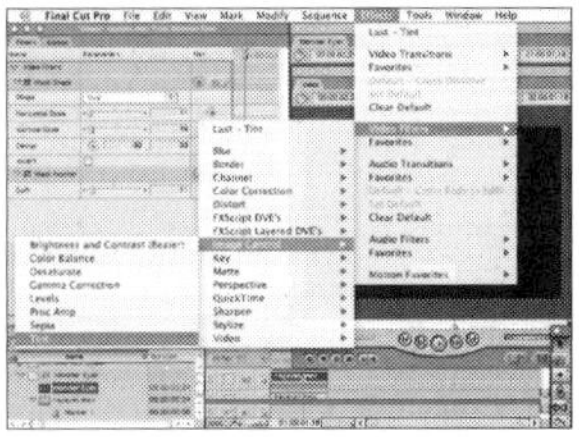

27.10A

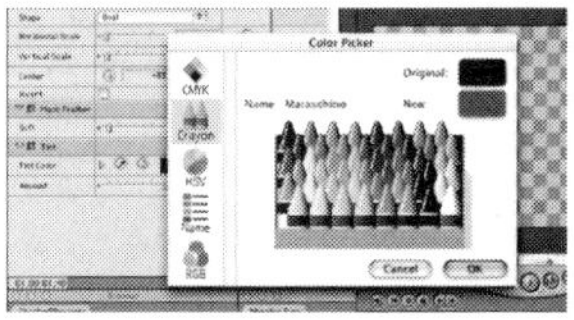

27.10B

27.11

NOTE

Be aware that the sample files provided here are compressed and sized considerably to allow for all of them to be included in the CDROM that ships with the book. When you are adjusting the feather value for the effect in full-resolution digital video, your feather setting will likely be higher than the one shown here. Remember to experiment.

- In the **Filters** tab area, change the horizontal scale to **11**, the vertical scale to **16**, and the center location to **–33** and **33** respectively. This filter positions a nearly round matte window directly over the right eye of the subject.

STEP 7: ADD A FUZZY EDGE TO THE MATTE WINDOW

- From the menu, choose **Effects ➢ Video Filters ➢ Matte ➢ Mask Feather** as shown in **Figure 27.9**.
- In the filters window, change the Mask Feather to a fuzzy edge by setting the soft value to **11** and dragging the slider bar to the right, or by typing **11** in the field.

STEP 8: COLORIZE THE CONTENTS OF THE MATTE WINDOW

- Choose **Effects ➢ Video Filters ➢ Image Control ➢ Tint** as shown in **Figure 27.10A**.
- Locate the **Tint Filter Control** in the **Filters** tab window. Click the square color swatch and choose a brilliant red color from the color picker as shown in **Figure 27.10B.**

STEP 9: PREVIEW YOUR WORK

- Preview your progress so far by checking the canvas window to see the dog with one brilliant red eye. **Figure 27.11** shows this preview.

TIP

You can use any color model in the color picker window to choose your favorite color. In this case, the simplest, most direct method is to choose the crayons and click Maraschino red.

STEP 10: CHANGE THE OPACITY

- In the viewer window, click the **Motion** tab to expose the opacity settings for the clip.
- Click the delta next to the Opacity setting.
- Click the keyframe button to establish a keyframe at the moment in time.
- Set the opacity level to 0 by dragging the slider bar all the way to the left as you see in **Figure 27.12.**

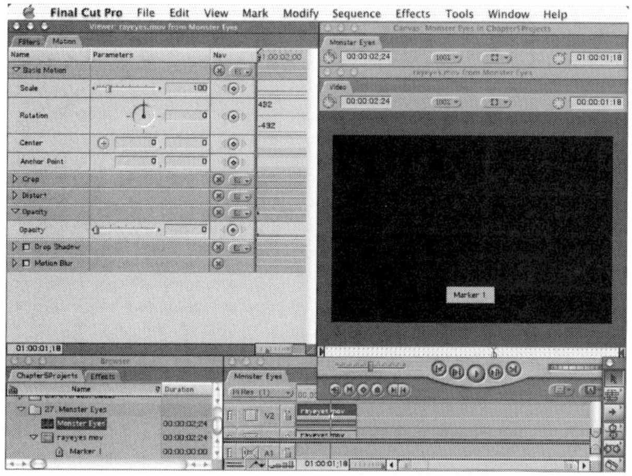

27.12

STEP 11: SET ANOTHER KEYFRAME AND ITS OPACITY

- Press the down-arrow key and move the play head to the last frame in the clip.
- In the **Motion** tab window, click the opacity keyframe button to create another keyframe.
- Set the opacity for this keyframe to **100** as shown in **Figure 27.13**.

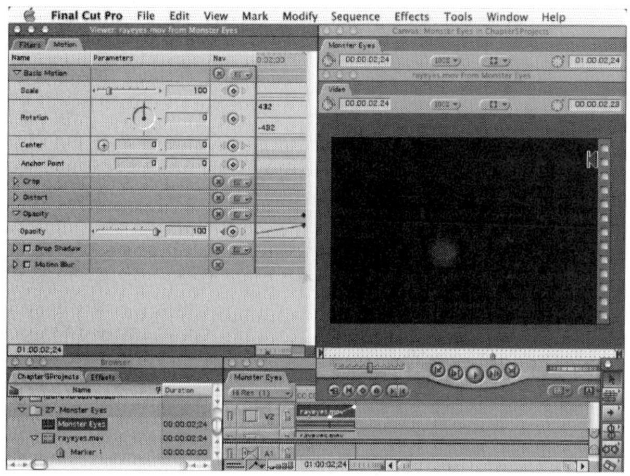

27.13

STEP 12: DUPLICATE THIS MEDIA CLIP FOR THE SECOND EYE

- To create the second eye, go to the timeline window, hold down the Option and Shift keys together, and then click and drag the V2 clip upward to create a third video track, which is automatically duplicated and labeled V3 as you see in **Figure 27.14**.

STEP 13: CHANGE THE LOCATION OF THE NEW MATTE WINDOW

- Double-click on the media clip in the V3 track to display it in the viewer window.
- Choose the **Filters** tab to show the Mask shape filter settings.

27.14

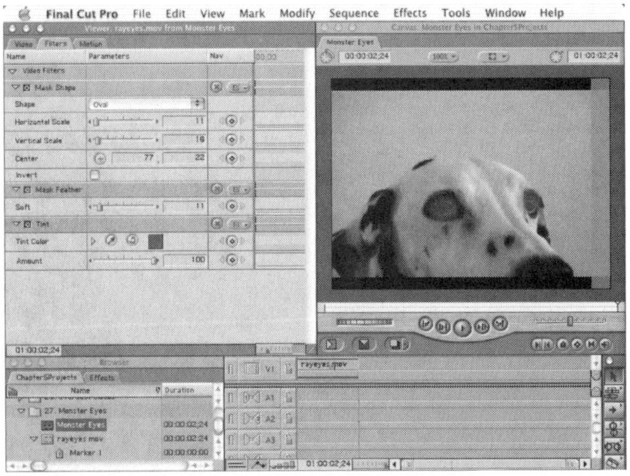

27.15

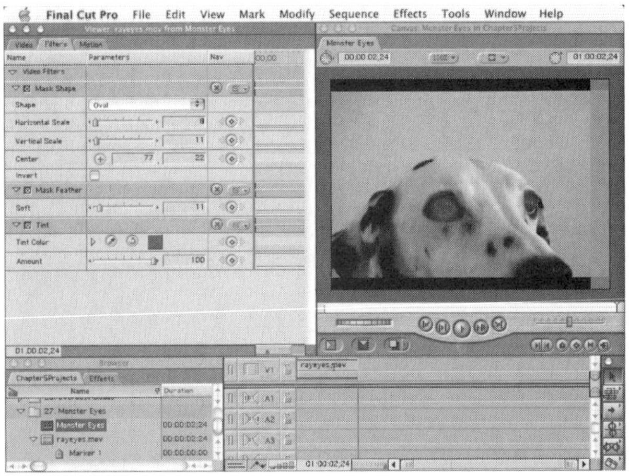

27.16

27.17

■ Click the **center crosshair** button in the Filters tab, and then click the **dog's left eye**, positioning the second matte window. This applies all of the attributes to the selected area.

■ For a more precise positioning in the matte window, go to the Center field settings and type in the numeric values of **77** and **22**, respectively, as shown in **Figure 27.15**.

STEP 14: CHANGE THE SIZE OF THE SECOND GLOWING EYE

To add an additional hint of realism, you can change the size of the matte window of the second glowing eye.

■ In the mask shape settings area, change the horizontal scale to **8** and the vertical scale to **11**.

■ Notice that the second glowing eye, furthest from the camera, is now smaller and gives the clip a subtle but greater degree of realism. It might not be as evident in print, as you see in **Figure 27.16**.

STEP 15: RENDER THE SEQUENCE

■ Choose **Sequence ➢ Render All** as shown in **Figure 27.17** to see results of the changes you made.

■ After you finish, close this Project tab by Control-clicking on the tab name or use the keyboard shortcut Command-W.

TECHNIQUE 28

GREEN FACES

28.1 (CP31)

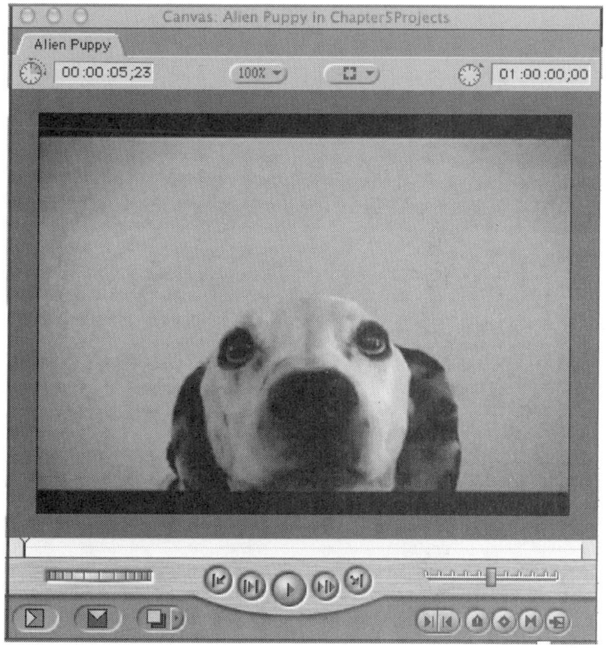

28.2 (CP32)

This fun and mischievous Final Cut Pro effect employs a simple technique, similar to your glowing monster eyes. You use a feathered mask shape to define a colorized area in your video to create the illusion of any color skin tone on your subject.

Isn't there someone in your immediate workspace that you're sure is an alien being? Do you have any videotape of their face? Using this technique, you can expose them for what they really are.

28.3

28.4

28.5

STEP 1: OPEN THE PROJECT MEDIA FILE

- Open the Project file named **Green Faces** in the Chapter 5 Projects folder.
- Double-click on the **Alien Puppy** sequence to load it into the timeline window as you see in **Figure 28.3**.
- Make sure you close any previously opened Project tabs.

STEP 2: CREATE A MATTE WINDOW

- Make sure the play head is positioned at the beginning of the media clip.
- Double-click the media clip in the timeline to display it in the viewer window.

Your workspace should resemble that shown in **Figure 28.4**.

STEP 3: DUPLICATE THE V1 VIDEO TRACK

- In the timeline window, hold down the Option and Shift keys together, and then click and drag the V1 video clip upward to create a second video track that is automatically duplicated and labeled V2 as shown in **Figure 28.5**.
- Click to select the media clip in the new video track retitled V2.

STEP 4: CREATE A MATTE WINDOW FOR THE NEW TRACK

- From the menu, choose **Effect ➢ Video Filters ➢ Matte ➢ Mask Shape** as shown in **Figure 28.6**.

HALF PRICE BOOKS®

Half Price Books
1835 Forms Drive
Carrollton, TX 75006
OFS OrderID 39482935

Thank you for your order, Main Address!

Thank you for shopping with Half Price Books! Please contact Support@hpb.com. if you have any questions, comments or concerns about your order (113-7330623-7187415)

Visit our stores to sell your books, music, movies games for cash.

SKU	ISBN/UPC	Title & Author/Artist	Shelf ID	Qty	OrderSKU
S444131962	9780764524462	50 Fast Final Cut Pro 3 Techniques (50 Fas... Meehan, Tim	12--18--2	1	

SHIPPED STANDARD TO:
Main Address
800 Avondale Ave
1033834-1-0102
Grandview Heights OH 43212
j1gg094j97htty5@marketplace.amazon.com

ORDER# **113-7330623-7187415**
AmazonMarketplaceUS

STEP 5: CHANGE THE SHAPE, LOCATION, AND EDGES OF THE MATTE

■ Separate the Video tab window from the viewer window by clicking the tab and dragging it to the right, so that you can see both the contents of the Filter tab and the video at the same time.
■ From the pop-up menu in the shape section, choose the **Oval** setting.
■ You can drag the sliders, experimenting with the settings to create an elliptical matte window about the size and shape of the dog's head.
■ If you prefer, you can manually make the setting in the position values area by typing in the following settings:

Horizontal scale: 44
Vertical Scale: 66
Center: 3, 72

■ From the menu, choose **Effects ➢ Video Filters ➢ Matte ➢ Mask Feather.**
■ In the Filters tab, set the softness value to 22 as you see in **Figure 28.7.**

28.6

STEP 6: COLORIZE THE CONTENTS OF THE MATTE WINDOW

■ From the menu, choose **Effects ➢ Video Filters ➢ Image Control ➢ Color Balance.**
■ In the Filters tab window of the viewer, adjust the green value for the Midtones-only setting to 88 as you see in **Figure 28.8.**

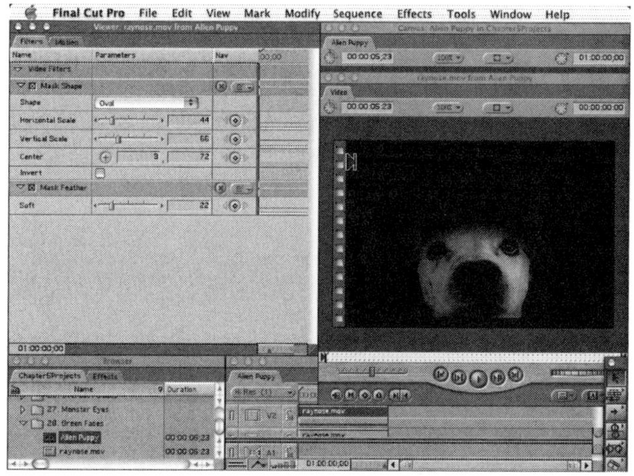

28.7

28.8

28.9

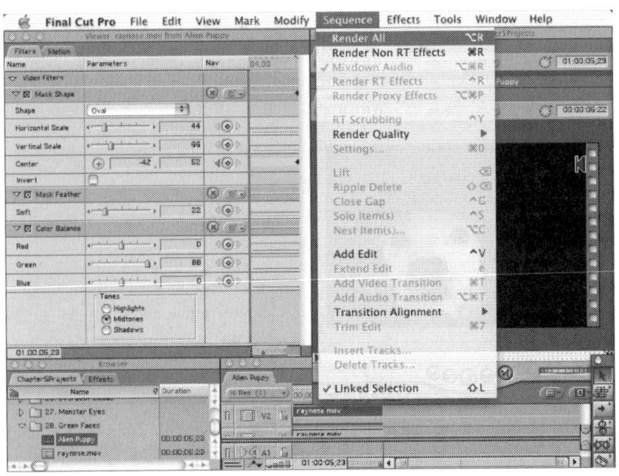

28.10

STEP 7: KEYFRAME THE LOCATION OF THE MATTE WINDOW

- Click the keyframe button next to the Center setting to mark the position of the matte window at this particular moment in time.
- Move the play head to the end of the clip by pressing the down-arrow key on your keyboard or by clicking the Next keyframe button on the viewer window.
- Notice that in the video window, the dog's head has moved while the green field has not.
- Click the keyframe button for the center attribute in the mask shape filters window.
- Change the Centerpoint settings to **–42, 52**, respectively, as shown in **Figure 28.9**.
- You now see the green field has now moved its location to the area occupied by the dog's head.

STEP 8: RENDER THE SEQUENCE

- Choose **Sequence ➢ Render All** as shown in **Figure 28.10** to see results of the changes you made.
- After you finish, close this Project tab by Control-clicking on the tab name or use the keyboard shortcut Command-W.

Final Cut Pro automatically "tweens" the location of the matte window over the length of the clip to move with the dog's head. *Tweening*, also known as "in-betweening," is a term used to refer to calculating the intermediate frames between two keyframes to simulate smooth motion. You can establish as many keyframes for as many attributes of the matte window as you want, making the matte window able to follow your subject as closely as you want to across the timeline.

CHAPTER 6

ADVANCED MATTE EFFECTS

Until now, your special effects work in Final Cut Pro has involved relatively simple one-step filter effects and overlaid video tracks. This chapter adds to your expertise by leading you down the path of multiple layers and compound video effects applied to your video media content.

Follow along carefully with the steps in this chapter as the techniques and procedures become progressively more complex. As you finish the techniques, expect your render times to increase as the complexity and breadth and depth of the filter effects increase.

A note of thanks here to the good folks at ArtBeats who provided the exciting flames and explosions clips for your use in the techniques.

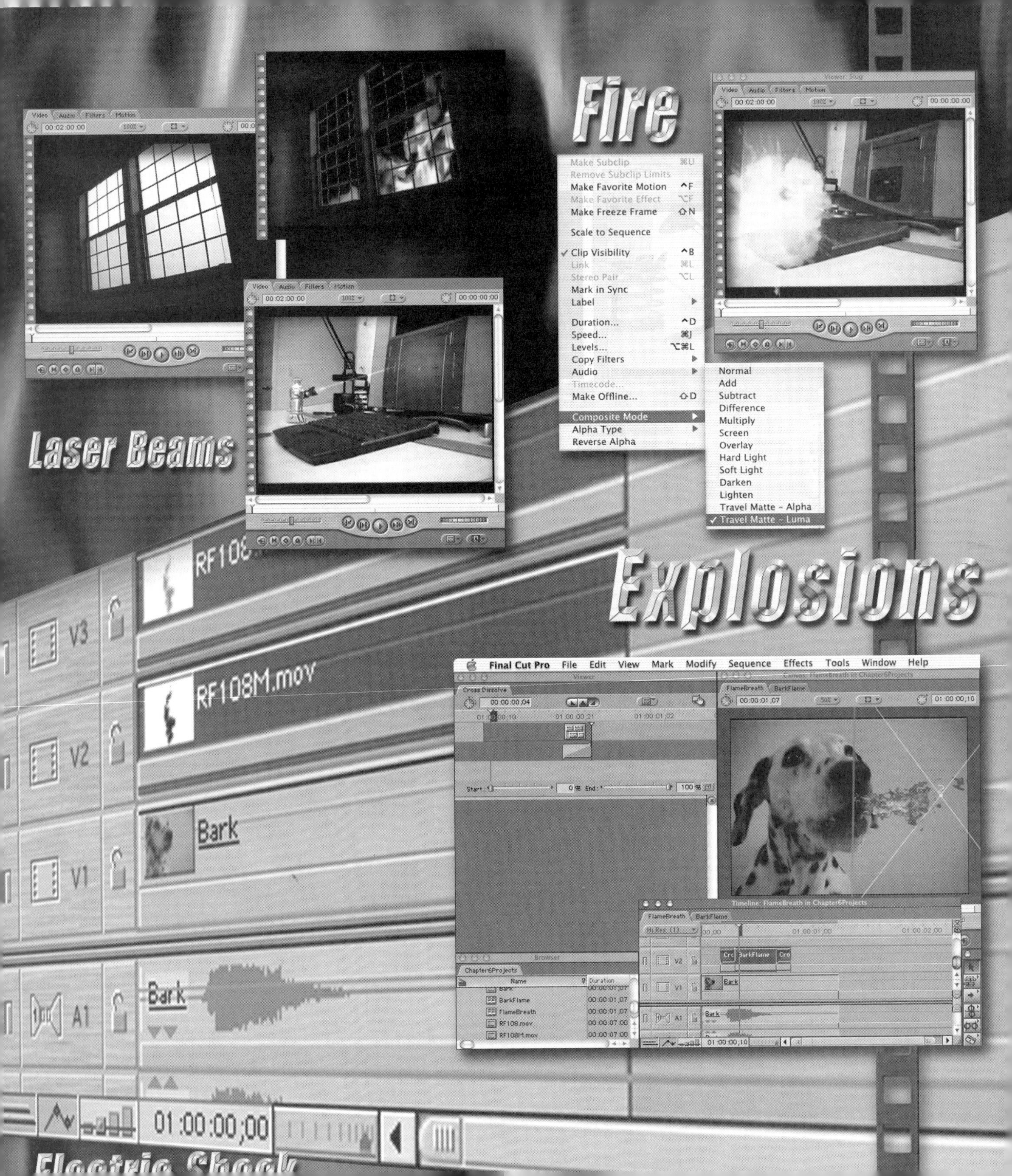
Fire
Laser Beams
Explosions
Electric Shock
Make Subclip ⌘U
Remove Subclip Limits
Make Favorite Motion ^F
Make Favorite Effect ⌥F
Make Freeze Frame ⇧N
Scale to Sequence
✓ Clip Visibility ^B
Link ⌘L
Stereo Pair ⌥L
Mark in Sync
Label
Duration... ^D
Speed... ⌘J
Levels... ⌥⌘L
Copy Filters
Audio
Timecode...
Make Offline... ⇧D
Composite Mode
Alpha Type
Reverse Alpha
Normal
Add
Subtract
Difference
Multiply
Screen
Overlay
Hard Light
Soft Light
Darken
Lighten
Travel Matte - Alpha
✓ Travel Matte - Luma
Final Cut Pro File Edit View Mark Modify Sequence Effects Tools Window Help
RF108M.mov
Bark
V3
V2
V1
A1
01:00:00;00

TECHNIQUE 29

LASER BEAMS

29.1

29.2 (CP34)

Laser Beams is a fun track composition technique that you can easily apply to almost any video clip. The secret here is in planning your shots to accommodate the destruction of your subjects realistically (without actually documenting the destruction of actual subjects). This is a good example of pre-planning shots by using simple storyboarding and thumbnail techniques.

This demonstration leads you through the steps of simulating a laser beam discharge against a simple desktop object, including a special effects enhancement.

STEP 1: OPEN THE SEQUENCE

- Make sure you close any previously opened project tabs.
- In your Chapter 6 Projects folder, find and open the bin labeled **Laser Beams.** Note that this file now includes a timeline and all the imported art and video necessary to complete this effect.
- Double-click to open the sequence timeline **Lasers.** Your workspace should look like the one shown in **Figure 29.3.**

29.3

STEP 2: PREVIEW THE RAW VIDEO CLIP

- Double-click the **robotclip.mov** media import in the timeline window to see it in the viewer window.
- Play the clip to see the action.

Note that two markers are already in place to help guide you in placing the action that you'll add to the clip, as shown in **Figure 29.4.**

STEP 3: PLACE THE LASER BEAM ART

- Drag the **LaserBeam.tif** art icon from the bin onto the canvas window and choose the **Superimpose** overlay after it appears.
- This overlay creates a new video track in the timeline window labeled **V2** that contains the laser beam art.
- You now see in **Figure 29.5** that the still image has expanded to fill the entire length of the video track.

29.4

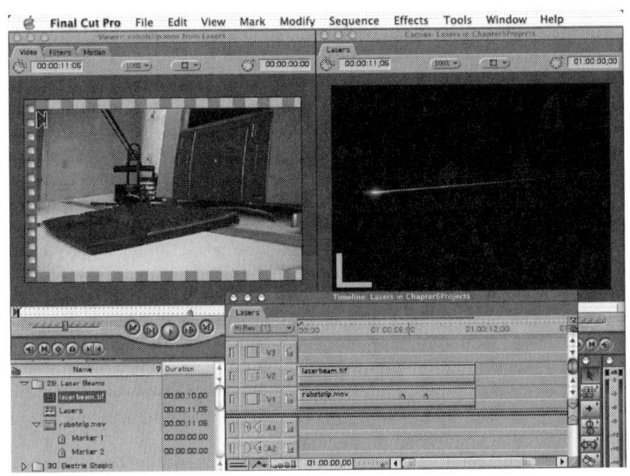

29.5 (CP33)

STEP 4: SET THE BEGINNING POINT OF THE LASER BEAM

- Drag the left edge of the media clip in V2 to the right edge, matching up the left margin of the **laserbeam.tif** image with the first marker in the **robotclip** media clip in the timeline as shown in **Figure 29.6**.

STEP 5: SHORTEN THE LASER CLIP

The laser clip only needs to extend for a couple of seconds, so that in this step, you can shorten its duration in the timeline.

- Drag the right edge of the **laserbeam.tif** image to the second marker point as shown in **Figure 29.7**. If snapping is enabled, it will easily snap into place at the second marker.

TIP

The keyboard shortcut "n" toggles the snapping feature.

NOTE

If the laserbeam.tif clip looks short and may be too small to comfortably manipulate in the timeline, you can enlarge the thumbnails by pressing the ⌘ and the + sign when the timeline window is selected. Final Cut Pro allows you to instantly enlarge and reduce your views in any window with either Command+ or Command-.

29.6

29.7

STEP 6: CHANGE THE COMPOSITE MODE OF THE IMPORTED ART

- Select the **laserbeam.tif** media clip in the timeline and then choose **Modify ➢ Composite Mode ➢ Screen** as you see in **Figure 29.8**.
- You've now changed the appearance of the artwork, making the black pixels in the V2 track transparent and the white pixels overprint on our video background.

STEP 7: CHANGE THE BEAM LOCATION

Changing the location and shape of any overlaid video track is easy by using the wire frame handles.

- Click to select the **laserbeam.tif** clip in the timeline.
- Toggle the display of the overlaid V2 track so that the image and the wire frame are both visible. You can also use keyboard shortcut "w" to toggle through your options.
- Change the size and angle of the V2 track content by dragging the corner handles and wire frame edges to make the ends of the laserbeam extend between the robot and the computer.
- If you want to set the location numerically and match yours to the one shown here, double-click the **laserbeam.tif** clip in the timeline and then define the following values in the Motion tab of the viewer window: **Scale: 33, Rotation: –11, Center: –8, –33** as shown in **Figure 29.9**.

STEP 8: WHAT COLOR IS YOUR LASER BEAM?

You can adjust the color of the overlaid laserbeam art by using a simple filter effect.

- Double-click on the **laserbeam.tif** media clip in the V2 video track. You see the image appear in the viewer window.
- From the menu, choose **Effects ➢ Video Filters ➢ Color Correction ➢ RGB Balance**.
- Click the Filters tab in the viewer window.
- Set the values in the **RGB Balance filter** options section to:
  - **RED: 509, 155, 0**
  - **GREEN: 64, 0, 0**
  - **BLUE: 64, 0, 0**

29.8

29.9

The canvas window now displays your newly created red laser beam, as you can see in **Figure 29.10**.

STEP 9: PREVIEW YOUR LASER ATTACK

Now is a good time to preview your composited video sequence. Here are two methods to preview your clips:

- Drag the play head back and forth in the canvas window. This is known as "scrubbing."
- Render the sequence by choosing **Sequence ➢ Render All** as shown in **Figure 29.11** and play the clip.

> **NOTE**
>
> **Depending on the type of machine you're using, the effects may not automatically render on the fly. You may need to hold down the option key while scrubbing to see your rendered results.**

STEP 10: ADD THE FLASH

What laser beam attack would be complete without some form of explosion or glowing flash?

- In the viewer window, choose the **Video** tab.
- Look for the little film clip icon on the lower-right bottom corner of the window. This film clip icon is the video "generator" button.
- From the pop-up menu, choose **Shapes ➢ Circle.** You'll see the new media item appear in the viewer window, a circle.
- Add the circle shape to the Project bin by clicking in the video window and dragging it straight down into the bin. Release the mouse button when the Laser Beams bin highlights.
- Click the new icon that appears in the bin to select it and to rename it: **laserflash**.
- Double-click on the new clip icon in the bin to display it in the Viewer, and then click the **Controls** tab in the viewer window. Click the **color swatch** next to the color setting. When the color picker is presented, choose the **crayons** option and pick the bright **red crayon**. (After you've chosen it, its name will appear in the color picker window. It's named **maraschino**.)

29.10

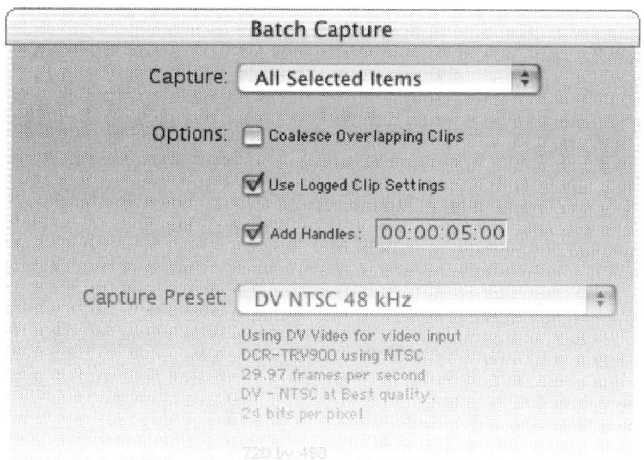

29.11

■ Click the Video tab again in the viewer window and then drag the laserflash media clip onto the canvas window. Choose the **Superimpose** overlay after it's presented.
■ Drag the edge boundaries of the laserflash still clip to match the In and Out points of the laser beam in the timeline. This will be a little easier if the snapping option is active. Remember, the keyboard shortcut "n" toggles the snapping attribute.
■ Set the same exit point of the laser flash as the laser beam to set the same Out points for this clip as **Figure 29.12** shows.

NOTE

You see that the view in the canvas window changes to a black frame with a red laser beam with a red flash. The circle shape appears on top of the clip between video tracks V1 and V3 because V1 is the target track indicated by the yellow color in the V1 Track Control film clip icon.

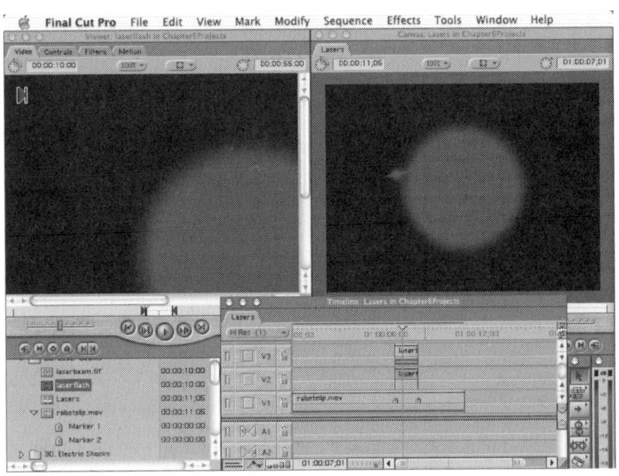

29.12

STEP 11: CHANGE THE FLASH ATTRIBUTES

This step enables you to match the amount of time that the laserflash and laserbeam both take up within this clip. One of the objectives here is to create a glow and flash that changes over time.

■ Move the play head to the beginning of the laser beam clip.
■ Enable wire frame view by pressing the "w" key on your keyboard.
■ Move the flash clip to the tip of the beam to where it intersects the right-hand edge of the laserbeam in the canvas window. You accomplish this by clicking the wire frame indicator and dragging it to where the laserbeam ends in the canvas window.
■ Double-click on the laser flash art in the canvas window, which displays it in the viewer window.
■ Click the Controls tab in the viewer window and set the **Size** of this item to **1%**, and the **Softness** to **4%**.
■ Click the **Keyframe** button for the softness setting to mark the point in time.
■ Now click the **Motion** tab and set the **Center** location to **72** and **–53** respectively.

TIP

Depending on the size of your monitor and the workspace layout you've chosen, the nav column of your controls tab might be too small in the Controls tab to navigate easily. Drag the bottom right corner of that tab window to enlarge it and expose more of the nav column. When you're finished, if the Controls tab is taking up too much of your workspace area, Final Cut Pro makes resetting your workspace screen layout as easy as a keyboard shortcut. Try Control-U to reset all the windows to their default positions.

NOTE

If you follow the numeric formula correctly for the location of the laserbeam, you see that this new tiny flash appears exactly at the endpoint of the laserbeam in our canvas window.

- Move the play head in the timeline to the end of the beam clip.
- Expose the keyframe controls again by double-clicking on the laserflash clip and loading it into the viewer window.
- Click the **Controls** tab and set the new **Size** and **Softness** values at **11%** and **22%** respectively.
- Click the keyframe button to set this as a keyframe. **Figure 29.13** shows how your screen should appear.

STEP 12: SET THE COMPOSITE MODE

- Click to select the laserflash clip in the timeline window.
- From the menu, choose **Modify ➢ Composite Mode ➢ Screen** as you see in **Figure 29.14**.

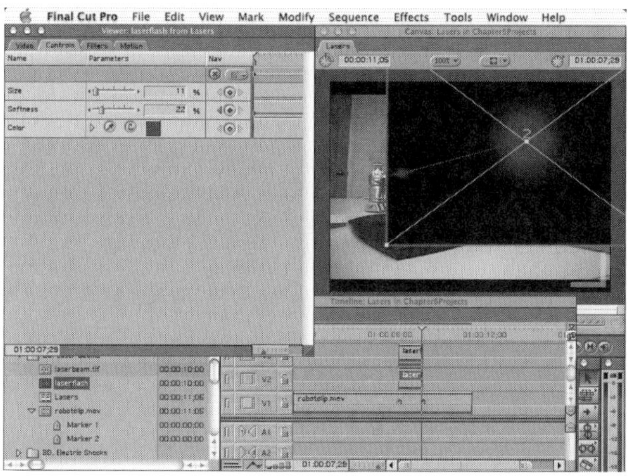

29.13

STEP 13: RENDER THE CLIP

- Choose Sequence ➢ Render All (as shown in **Figure 29.15**) to see results of the changes you made.
- After you finish, close this Project tab by Control-clicking on the tab name or use the keyboard shortcut **Control-W**.

After you view the rendered clip, you see the little toy robot enter the scene, stop and fire the laser beam at the computer, which initiates a glowing red flash and the computer response of opening its CD-ROM hatch.

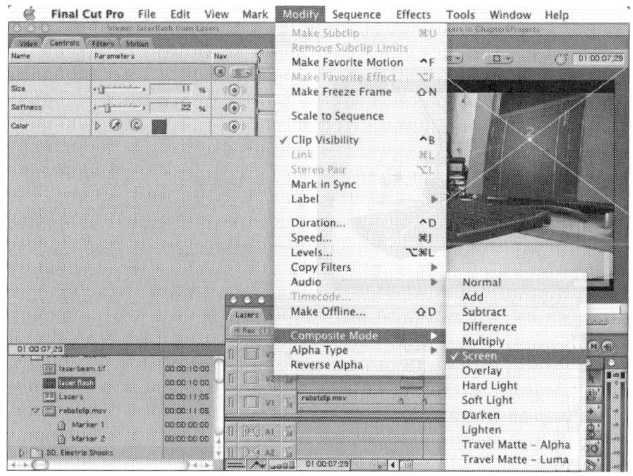

29.14

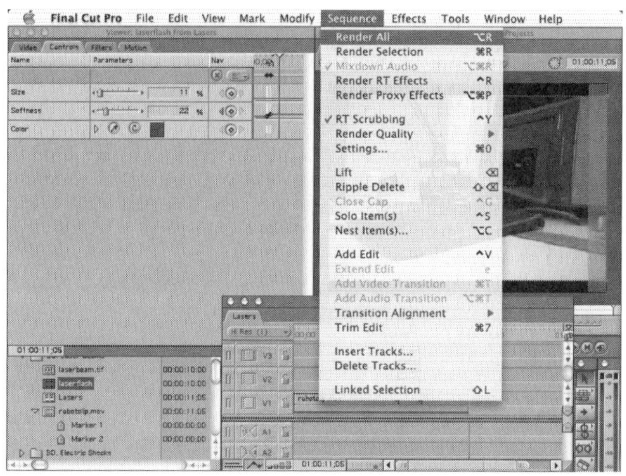

29.15

TECHNIQUE **30**

ELECTRIC SHOCKS

30.1 (CP35)

30.2 (CP36)

This is another fun clip overlay superimposition technique, which creates electric shocks. The electric shocks can be a fun effect to add to almost any video clip. This technique also introduces you to the concept of "nesting" an animation within a clip.

Nested clips can be controlled and filtered as separate media clip items. This technique shows us how to control a nested clip as an object.

STEP 1: OPEN THE PROJECT

Make sure you close any previously opened Project tabs.

- Open the Chapter 6 Projects folder.
- Locate and open the bin called **electric shocks**.
- Double-click to open the sequence **shocking**. Your workspace should look like the one shown in **Figure 30.3**.

STEP 2: COMPOSE A CLIP SEQUENCE USING STILLS

This clip sequence is composed of a series of still images that were created in Adobe Photoshop. They're labeled **spark1.tif**, **spark2.tif**, **spark3.tif**, and **spark4.tif**. Each has been constrained to two frames in length.

Depending on your thumbnail view of the timeline, these clips may seem very small and hard to manipulate. If this is the case, click the timeline window and use the keyboard shortcut Command+ to enlarge your view to a more comfortable size.

- Click and drag the clip media item **spark1.tif** into the V2 video track. Be very careful to drag the clip onto the timeline and not release the mouse button until you see the cursor change to a down-pointing arrow icon. This allows you to add the media clip to the timeline without inserting it and disrupting the base V1 track.
- Click and drag the media clip item **spark2.tif** onto the timeline, adjacent to the clip media item **spark1.tif**. Be careful to drop it in the same way and watch to make sure that the insertion cursor is a downward-facing arrow.
- Click and drag **spark3.tif** into the timeline in **V2** while watching out for the same cursor change as before.
- Repeat the preceding steps a few more times, placing the same clip media item in a different order to enhance the random feeling of an electric shock as shown in **Figure 30.4**.
- Make sure that each cell of the random electric shocks is only two frames in length by setting the duration in the timecode field to two frames.

The Timecode and duration fields are convenient places to define specific locations and duration in a clip's timeline. Both have a little stopwatch icon next to them, the Duration field has a graphic representation meant to indicate time passage. See **Figure 30.5** for a look at the Duration field.

30.3

30.4

STEP 3: REPOSITION THE SPARKS

Now, for each of the sparks, set the Location, Size, Angle, and Composite mode to match the media in the V1 track.

- Select each of the **spark.tif** import files by holding down the shift key while you select each with a mouseclick. Set the Composite mode to screen by choosing **Modify ➢ Composite Mode ➢ Screen** from the menu.
- Enable the wire frame by using the "w" shortcut on your keyboard.
- Rotate, reposition, and resize the sparks to extend between the lens of the CD-ROM drive in the center of the open hatch and the robot. Repeat this procedure for each of the **spark.tif** files that you imported into your project so far. **Figure 30.6** shows one clip already in place.

STEP 4: NEST THE CLIPS

- Select all six clip media items in the V2 video track by clicking and dragging across them with your mouse cursor.
- Choose **Sequence ➢ Nest Item(s)**.

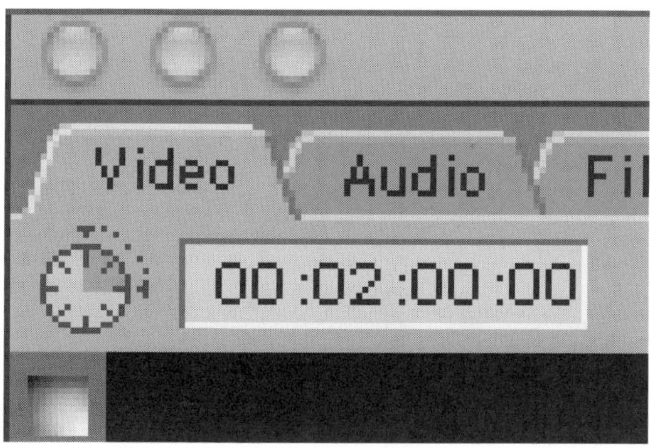

30.5

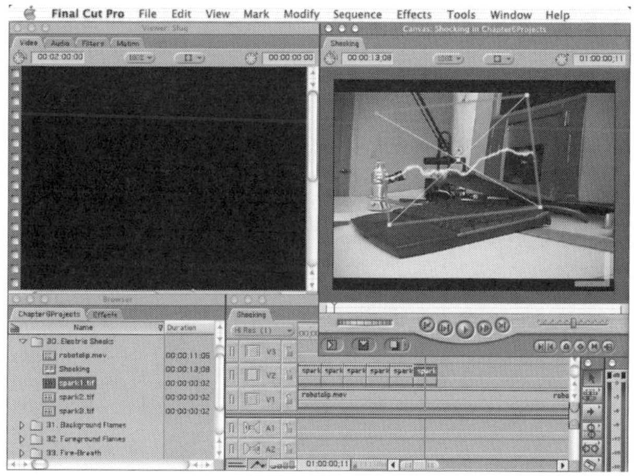

30.6

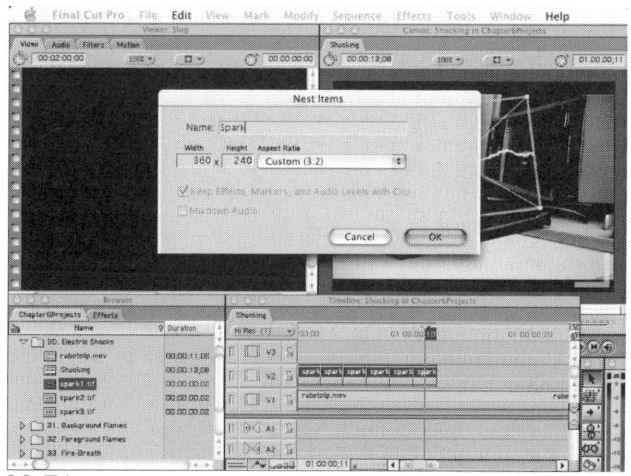

30.7A

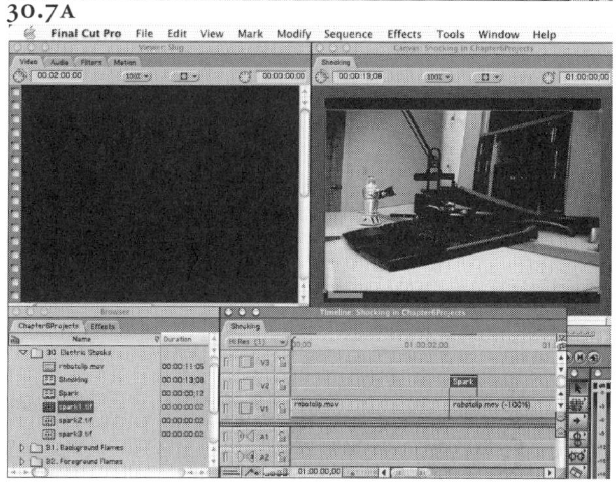

30.7B

- When presented with a dialog box, set the name of new nested clip to **Spark.** This groups the sparks into a media clip that can be controlled as a single object. You also notice that a new sequence has appeared in the bin named **Spark**, as shown in **Figure 30.7A** and **30.7B**.

STEP 5: REPOSITION THE NESTED CLIP

- Click to select the nested clip in V2 and drag it to a new position in V2 so that the nested clip begins at the division between the two pre-positioned clips in V1 as illustrated in **Figure 30.8.**

30.8

STEP 6: DUPLICATE THE NESTED CLIP ITEMS

This is a great sill image clip sequence, but it's a little short. Let's double the length by duplicating it and adding the duplicate to the timeline.This step shows how easy it is to duplicate a nested clip.

- Duplicate the nested clip items by first selecting them with your mouse cursor.
- Hold down the Option and Shift key, drag the selected items above the V2 track in your timeline window, and release the mouse, which creates a new video track labeled **V3**.
- Drag and reposition these clip items in the V3 video track to the point in the timeline where the V2 video track ends, as shown in **Figure 30.9.**

30.9

STEP 7: RENDER THE CLIP

- Choose **Sequence ➢ Render All** as in **Figure 30.10** to see results of the changes you made.
- After you finish, close this Project tab by Control-clicking on the tab name or use the keyboard shortcut Control-W.

See how easy it is to add an electric shock to any video clip sequence!

30.10

TECHNIQUE 31

BACKGROUND FLAMES

31.1 (CP37)

31.2 (CP38)

A saying in the firefighting business is "Everything is flammable, given enough heat." With Final Cut Pro 3, you can test this theory, at least digitally, and easily set any environment on fire.

As in any artistic endeavor, there's a threshold where the technique or the effect can be overapplied, hitting your viewer over the head with an image, when all along, a subtler, less-obvious application can be a more effective approach.

This demonstration shows you a more measured and subtle application of this technique.

STEP 1: OPEN THE FILE

- Make sure you close any previously opened Project tabs.
- Open the Chapter 6 Projects folder.
- Locate the timeline sequence called **background flames**.
- Double-click to open the sequence and load it into your timeline window as you see in **Figure 31.3**.

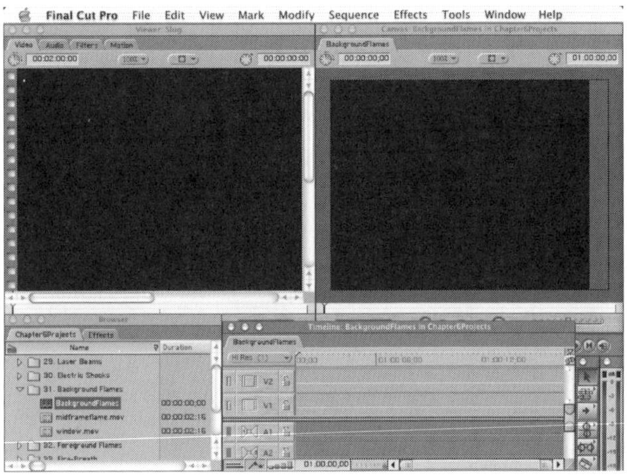

31.3

31.4

STEP 2: CUE THE FLAMES AND THE WINDOW

- Drag and drop the media clip **midframeflame.mov** onto the canvas window and choose the insert overlay option after it appears. This lays down a base video track of flames in the background on which you will place a mask window.
- Place the play head at the very beginning of the timeline and drag and drop the media clip **window.mov** onto the canvas window by choosing the **Superimpose** overlay option when it appears. See **Figure 31.4**. This puts a window scene on top of the flames ultimately allowing you to show flames through the window.

STEP 3: COLOR KEY THE WINDOW

- Double-click the **window.mov** media clip in the timeline to load it into the viewer window.
- From the menu, choose **Effects ➢ Video Filters ➢ Key ➢ Color Key**.
- Click to expose the **Filters** tab in the viewer window.
- Click to select the **Eyedropper** tool and then click to select **Color** in a windowpane in the canvas window as **Figure 31.5** shows.

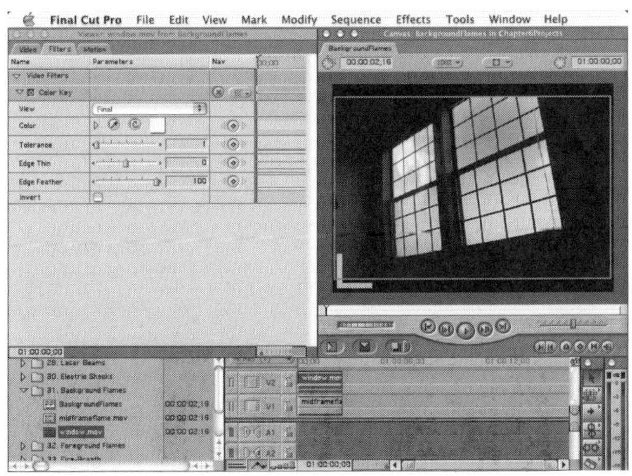

31.5

STEP 4: ADJUST THE KEY

The image appears as if nothing has changed in the canvas window at this point, even though you applied a color key effect and chose a viable key color, that's because the settings for color key are still too broadly defined.

- Drag the sliders for **Tolerance**, **Edge Thin**, and **Edge Feather** until you see the flames burning outside the window.
- A good range of values (yours may vary depending on where your initial color selection is made) is: **Tolerance: 55**, **Edge Thin: –55**, and **Edge Feather: 0** as you see in **Figure 31.6**.

STEP 5: PREVIEW THE EFFECT

- As always, you can preview your effect prior to rendering if you hold down the Option key while you drag the play head back and forth in the timeline window. Remember, some machines have enough processing horsepower and memory to render the clip on the fly.

STEP 6: RENDER THE CLIP

- Choose **Sequence ➢ Render All** as shown in **Figure 31.7** to save your movie with the new effect applied.
- After you finish, close this Project tab by Control-clicking on the tab name or use the keyboard shortcut Control-W.

As you've seen in previous techniques, you can use any video image with a plain and consistent background color as a color key matte window through which any video media can be played.

In this instance, you used windows through which a very homogenous background color can be seen and therefore easily selectable as a key window. This technique is easily applied to almost any subject matter and can create some striking and believable effects from some relatively common media.

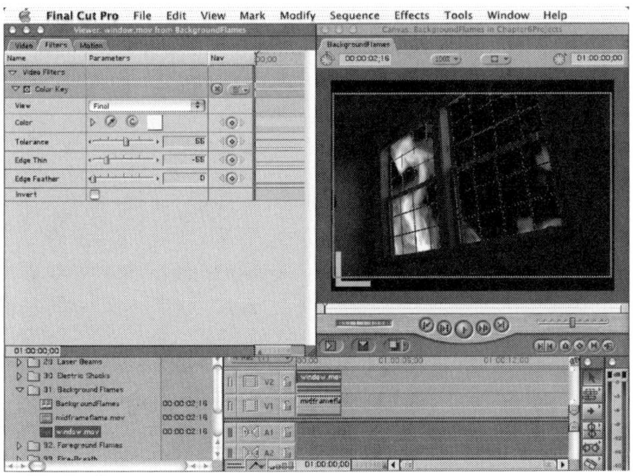

31.6

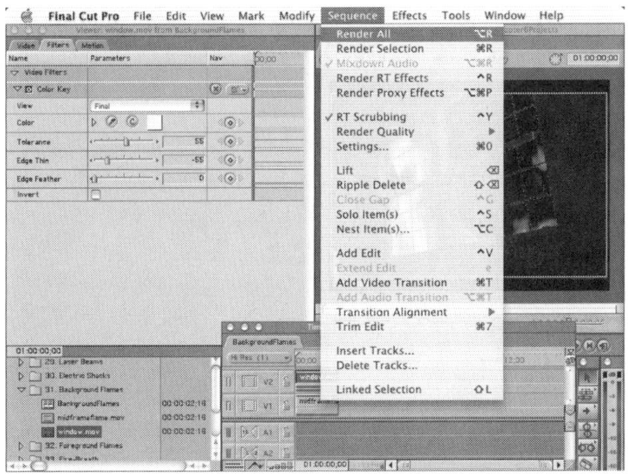

31.7

TECHNIQUE **32**

FOREGROUND FLAMES

32.1 (CP39)

32.2 (CP40)

The previous technique shows that keying out a color in a video image to expose a background image is a fairly easy one-step process that uses the foreground window image made for a relatively easy color key mask because it has straight lines and hard edges.

How many times in your film making career have you needed to set something on fire outdoors, but your mom wouldn't let you do it? Here's a technique that let's you set fire to anything in your camera's field of view, safely and effectively.

In this technique, I demonstrate how to use your imported effect footage to create a travel matte to more realistically add moving flames to the foreground of your video footage.

The more literal objective with this technique is to create the appearance of flames emanating from the inkbottle on the desk.

STEP 1: OPEN THE FILE

Make sure you close any other previously opened Project tabs.

- Open the timeline sequence **Foreground Flames** in the Chapter 6 Projects folder. In **Figure 32.3**, you find a 10-second video clip already in the V1 video track.

STEP 2: LIGHT THE FIRE

- Drag the video clip **RF108M.mov** onto the V2 video track and make sure it snaps to the very beginning of the sequence. You can see the flames through the mask in the RF108.mov media that you import next.
- Now drag the **RF108.mov** media clip into your timeline to create a new video track named V3 and snap the beginning of this clip to the beginning of the sequence as well. **Figure 32.4** shows how this should look at this point.

32.3

STEP 3: SET THE COMPOSITE MODE

- With the V3 video track clip selected, choose **Modify ➢ Composite Mode ➢ Travel Matte – Luma** as shown in **Figure 32.5**.

> **NOTE**
>
> **This menu setting makes the V2 video track into a mask window around which the background image may be seen, and creates a matte window through which the flames are visible. This works because these two video tracks are perfectly synchronized frame by frame.**

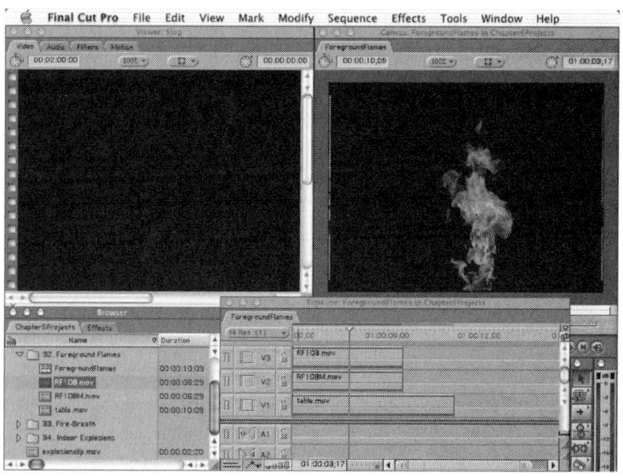

32.4

32.5

STEP 4: NEST THE CLIPS

- Select both the V3 and V2 video track media items.
- From the menu, choose **Sequence ➢ Nest Items** (shown in **Figure 32.6**). You can use the keyboard shortcut Option-C.
- Name the nested clip **Flames**.

STEP 5: REPOSITION THE NESTED CLIP MEDIA

Notice that your flames appear brilliantly in the very foreground of your image, but the intension is to have the flames appear to emanate from the inkbottle in the middle of the image.

- Expose the wire frame handles by choosing **View ➢ Image + Wireframe** from the menu.
- Reposition the flames over the top of the inkbottle by dragging the center point of the wire frame into position above the inkbottle. See **Figure 32.7**.

STEP 6: RENDER THE CLIP

- Render All (shown in **Figure 32.8**) to save your movie with the new effect applied.

32.6

NOTE

Because the pixel resolution of the sample media clip is different from the resolution of the base video clip, the nested sequence may appear to have shrunken in size as Final Cut Pro 3 tries to match up the pixel resolution. This is okay as you need to resize the scale of the nested clip anyway.

32.7

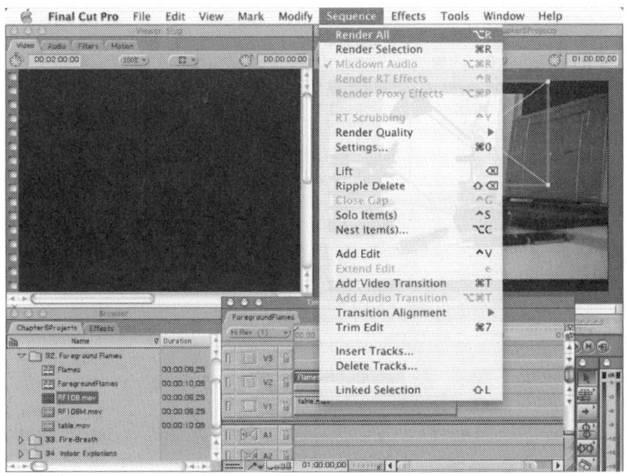

32.8

Not bad. Now, add one more step to this already cool technique.

STEP 7: ADD A TRANSITION EFFECT

- From the menu, choose **Window ➢ Effects** or use the keyboard shortcut F5 to expose the Floating Effects palette.
- Double-click the V2 video track items to load them into the timeline. To see the individual clip elements, double-click them to display them individually in the viewer window.
- From the Floating Effects palette, open the Video Transitions bin and then open the Wipe bin.
- Click and drag the Random Edge Wipe icon from the bin onto the beginning of the video clip in V2 of the timeline window, as shown in **Figure 32.9.** The transition should snap to the left edge of the clip.
- Double-click the transition icon in the clip to load the transition into the viewer window where you can edit its attributes.
- The only attribute you need to set is the angle at which the wipe occurs. Set that to 0 degrees so that the wipe occurs vertically.

32.9

STEP 8: RENDER THE CLIP

- Choose **Sequence ➢ Render All** as shown in **Figure 32.10** to save your movie with the new effect applied.
- This rendering may take awhile considering all the nesting, masking, and transition effects that you added. But the results are striking.

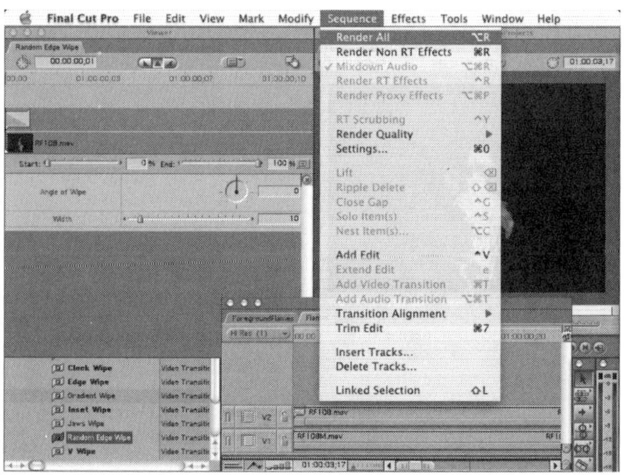

32.10

Click back on the foreground sequence in the timeline to see the effects of your work in progress.

> **NOTE**
>
> **Double-clicking the nested clip opens the nested clip in its own timeline, which has its own tab in the timeline window.**

> **NOTE**
>
> **Sometimes clips can appear pretty small in the timeline. You can get a better view of small clips in the timeline by using the Command-+ keyboard shortcut to enlarge the timeline clip icons.**

TECHNIQUE **33**

FIRE BREATH

33.1 (CP41)

33.2 (CP42)

Unless you grew up in the circus or descended from mythical dragons, fire-breathing relatives are probably a statistical rarity. This technique teaches you how to effectively create a burst of flame in almost any environment, from almost any mouth, even your boss at work!

Because the boss was unavailable for this technique, we are going to make use of the family pet in order to create the illusion that he has eaten some high-octane chili peppers prior to a short bark. Feel free to substitute any house pet or family member, and any yawn, cough, sneeze, or belch for any of the previous details in your own video.

The secret to this technique is in how deftly you handle the dissolution of the flame effect!

STEP 1: OPEN THE FILE

- Play the clip **bark.mov**.
- Note the movement of the dog's head. Over the course of our one-second of video time, the position of the dog's nose changes. Later on, the dog's nose will be key in your position of the flames.

Figure 33.3 shows the play head at the end of the inserted clip.

33.3

STEP 2: ADD THE FLAMES CLIP AND THE FLAMES MASK

Move the play head to the beginning of the timeline. Because no edits are in the imported clip, you can use the up-arrow keyboard shortcut.

- First drag the media clip item **RF108.mov** onto the canvas window.
- Choose the **Superimpose Overlay** option as shown in **Figure 33.4**.
- Repeat this procedure by using the **RF108M.mov** clip item in order to make the second flames clip the mask layer.

Because the V1 video track is the "target track"(see the yellow clip icon on the left-side column), the new clip and track are added immediately above the target track. **Figure 33.5** shows the layer order of the imported clips

STEP 3: SET THE COMPOSITE MODE

- Select the media clip item in V3.
- Choose **Modify ➢ Composite Mode ➢ Travel Matte – Luma** as you see in **Figure 33.6**.

33.4

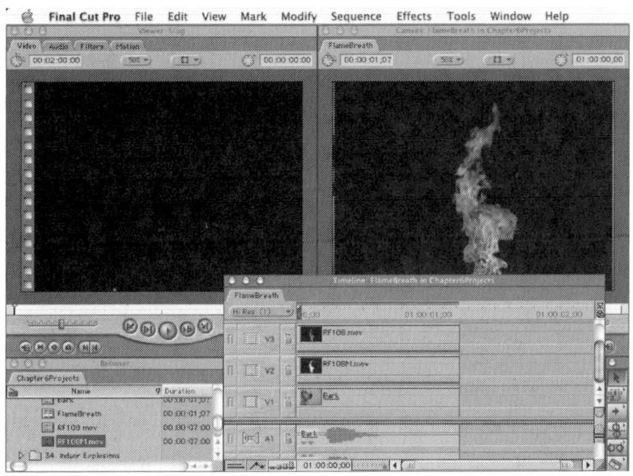

33.5

Because the flame's clip and the flame's mask are perfectly aligned and synchronized, the mask creates a window through which the flames data can be seen. The effect is seamless and natural looking, leaving the flames opaque against the background. This is shown in **Figure 33.7**.

STEP 4: NEST THE FLAMES

This effect requires making multiple modifications to the flames, including position, size, location, and transitions. To make this task easier, nesting the two clips together is a good idea so that any changes that are made apply to both media clip items simultaneously.

- Select clips in the **V2** and **V3** tracks by clicking and dragging around both until they are highlighted.
- Choose **Sequence ➢ Nest Items** or use the keyboard shortcut Option-C as shown in **Figure 33.8**.
- A dialog box appears that requires you to name the newly nested clip. Name this clip Barkflame, as **Figure 33.9** shows.

33.6

33.7

33.8

33.9

■ Because the flames don't need to persist through the entire clip, shorten the duration of nested clip by dragging the right edge of the media clip in the V2 track to the left.
■ Make the duration of the clip about two-thirds of a second, or 20-frames long as you can see in **Figure 33.10**.

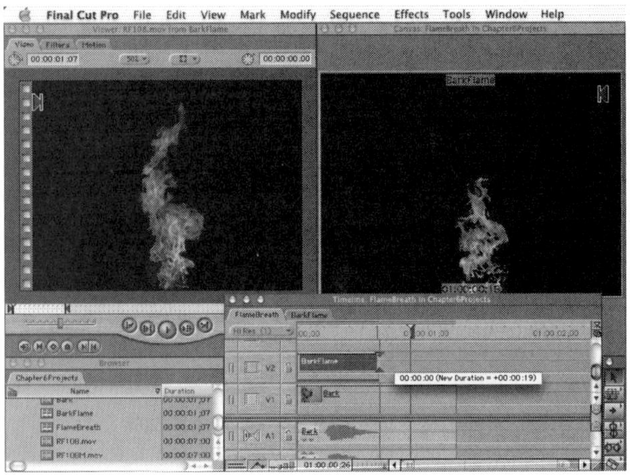

33.10

STEP 5: ADD TRANSITION TO THE NESTED CLIP

■ From the Window menu, choose Effects to see all of the separate transition effects that are available in a floating palette.
■ Click to open the bin titled **Video Transitions** and then open the bin titled **Dissolve**.
■ Click and drag the **cross dissolve** icon onto the nested flamebreath clip. Snap the edge of the transition to the left edge of the clip as shown in **Figure 33.11**.

STEP 6: CHECK THE TRANSITION

■ Double-click the transition in the clip in the timeline to preview it in the viewer window.
■ You can adjust the length of the transition by dragging the right edge of the transition icon left while watching the pop-up yellow field to see the duration of the transition. Adjust this one to just four frames in duration as seen in **Figure 33.12**.
■ If you are comfortable adding the cross-dissolve transition to the clip, add another cross-dissolve transition to the end of the V2 clip and establish the same short four-frame duration to it.

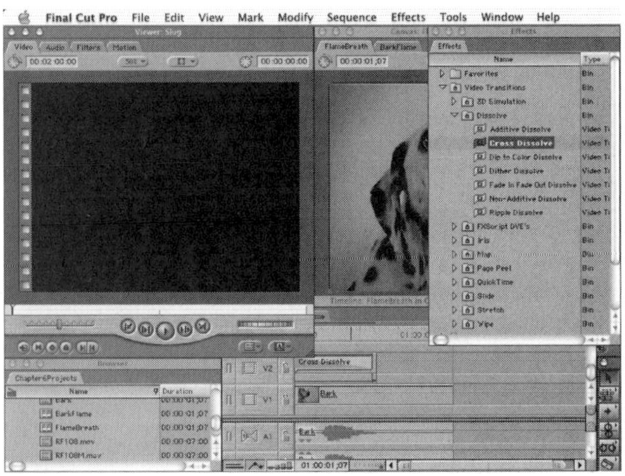

33.11

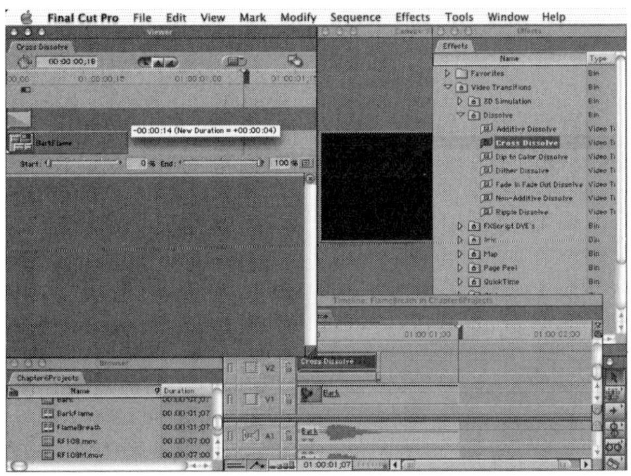

33.12

STEP 7: MOVE AND ROTATE THE CLIP

The duration of this flame clip is short, approximately ½ of a second. The clip appears and disappears in almost no time at all. Nonetheless, you want to make the clip appear as natural as possible.

First order of business is to move the nested clip into the appropriate position in the timeline.

- In the **timeline** window, move the play head to **5-frames** into the sequence. An easy way to do this is to type a **5** into the **Timecode** field at the top left corner of the canvas window.
- Click and drag the nested clip over to the right until it snaps into position with its left edge at the play head position as shown in **Figure 33.14**.
- Enable the **image + wireframe** view in the View menu or use the keyboard shortcut "w".
- Note that as you move the cursor near a corner handle of the wire frame, the cursor changes into a cross hair, allowing you to resize the object as shown in **Figure 33.15**. If on the other hand, you move the cursor over the edge of the wire frame, it becomes a rotation arrow.
- Using the rotation arrow symbol, click and rotate the clip about 90 degrees clockwise.

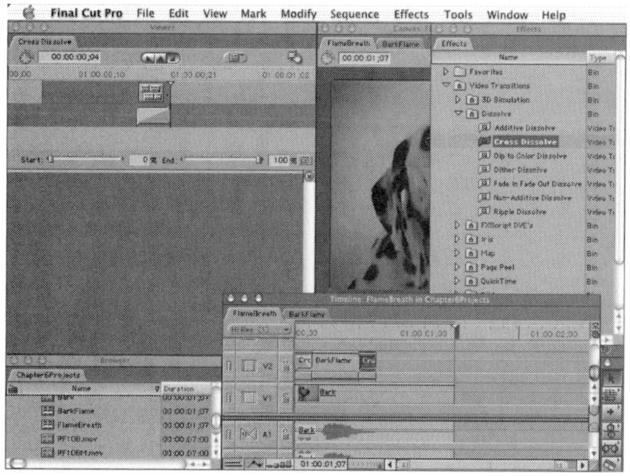

33.13

33.14

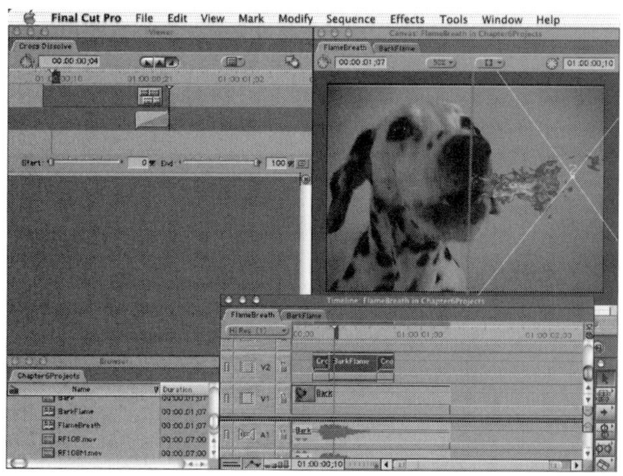

33.15

STEP 8: TEST AND MOVE THE LOCATION OF THE NESTED CLIP

- Test your work by Option-scrubbing by holding down the Option key as you move the play head back and forth. Close, but no cigar just yet. You still need to move the position of the nested clip.
- Click and drag the location of the (now sideways-blowing) flame, down and to the right of the dog's nose. You see in **Figure 33.16** that this position is more logical as it will appear that the flames are emanating from the dog's mouth when she barks.

STEP 9: RENDER THE CLIP

- As shown in **Figure 33.17**, choose **Sequence ➢ Render All** to save your movie with the new effect applied.

Now you can make any family member or house pet have explosive, caustic breath in any video situation, which is suitable for producing your own home antacid commercials.

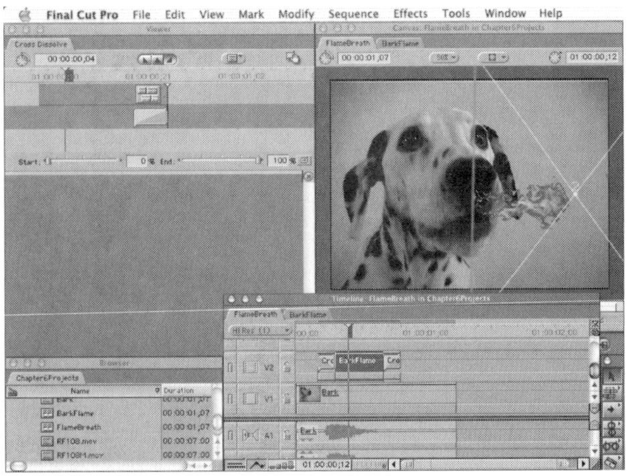

33.16

33.17

TECHNIQUE 34

INDOOR EXPLOSIONS

34.1 (CP43)

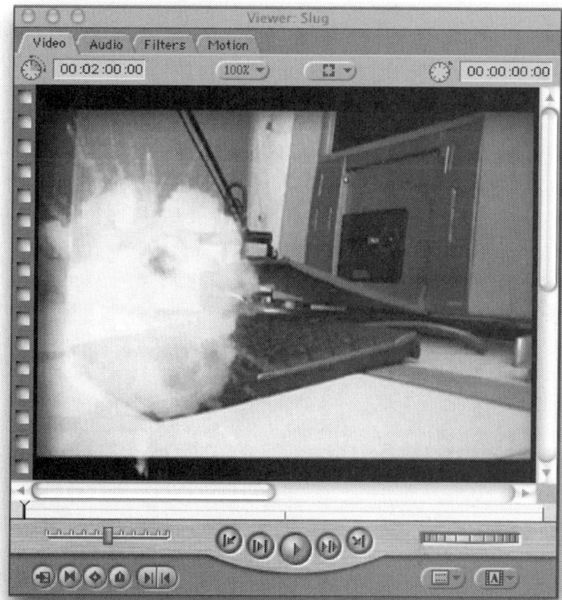

34.2 (CP44)

The secret behind any well-executed indoor explosion is the apparent destruction of your subject matter without actually destroying it in the process. Final Cut Pro 3 allows us to create the illusion by using a simple mask and a single frame of still imagery.

The steps you will create to achieve this illusion are to overlay an explosion clip on top of a video track, then gracefully and seamlessly replace the object and explosion with a still image, making it look like your subject has been destroyed.

STEP 1: OPEN THE PROJECT

- Look for the bin labeled **Indoor Explosions** in the Chapter 6 Projects folder.
- Double-click to open the **IndoorExplosion** timeline sequence.
- After you do so, you see the original robot clip already in place in the timeline, as shown in **Figure 34.3**.

34.3

STEP 2: CREATE KEYFRAMES AND MARKERS

- In the canvas window, move the play head to the 3-second position in the timeline. Alternatively you can also click the timecode field in the upper-right corner of the canvas window and type in **3** and **;** (semicolon) to force the play head to the 3-second point in the timeline.
- Place a marker here, as shown in **Figure 34.4** to help synchronize the action that you'll add later (keyboard shortcut "m").

STEP 3: ADD A STILL FRAME TO FOOL THE VIEWER

- Notice that a still frame is created from the first frame of the clip to use in your matte mask here.
- Drag the media item **stillframe.tif** onto the canvas window and choose the **Superimpose overlay** after it's presented. You now see that a second video track entitled **V2** has been added to the timeline window in **Figure 34.5**.

34.4

34.5

NOTE

Remember, pressing "n" toggles the snapping feature on and off. It will help you to easily drop it into the right position if it is toggled on.

TIP

Remember, if the clip icons in the timeline are too small to easily work with, you can enlarge your view of them by using the Command+ keyboard shortcut.

- Drag the left edge of this still frame clip in V2 to the right until it snaps to the marker location at the 3-second point as you see in **Figure 34.6**.
- With the clip highlighted in the V2 track, choose **Effects ➢ Video Filters ➢ Matte ➢ Mask Shape**. This is shown in **Figure 34.7**.
- Double-click the **V2** video clip to display a preview of the matte window in the viewer as shown in **Figure 34.8**. Note that the matte window is a default rectangular shape.

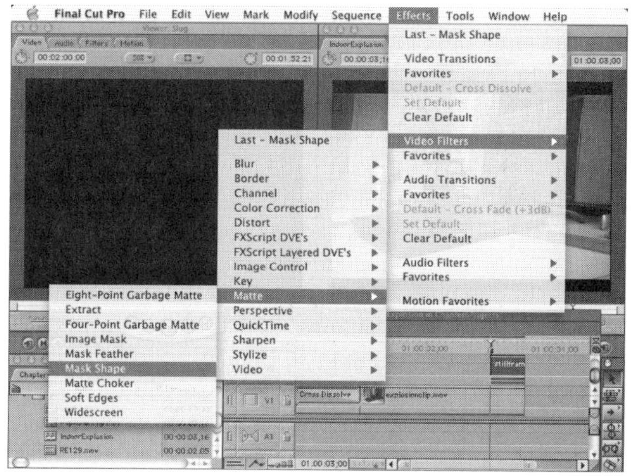

34.7

34.6

34.8

STEP 4: CHANGE THE SIZE, SHAPE, LOCATION, AND EDGES OF THE MATTE MASK

- In the viewer window, separate the Video tab from the Filters tab by dragging it to one side of your screen. After you do this, you can see the results of your operations in the viewer window as you can see in **Figure 34.9**.
- In the Filters tab window, change the Horizontal scale of the matte window to **29**, the Vertical scale to **60** and the Center location of the window to **–111, –24** as you can see in **Figure 34.10**.
- Add a blurry edge to the matte window you just created by choosing **Effects ➢ Video Filters➢ Matte ➢ Mask feather** from the menu as you see in **Figure 34.11**.

> **NOTE**
>
> **These settings create a matte overlay at a specified vertical scale size and location that allows the background video to show through around the matte overlay, effectively hiding the little robot in the scene.**

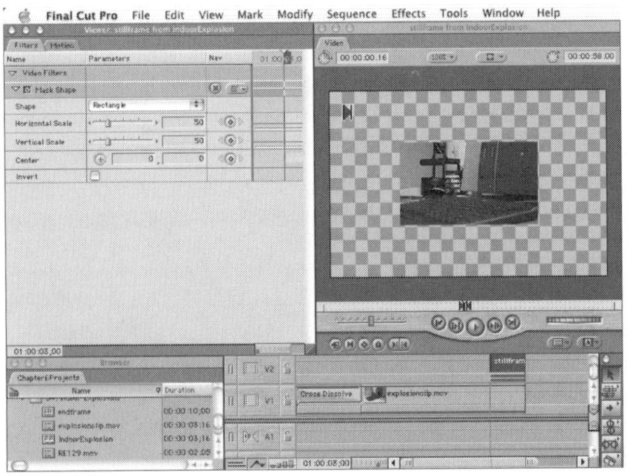

34.9

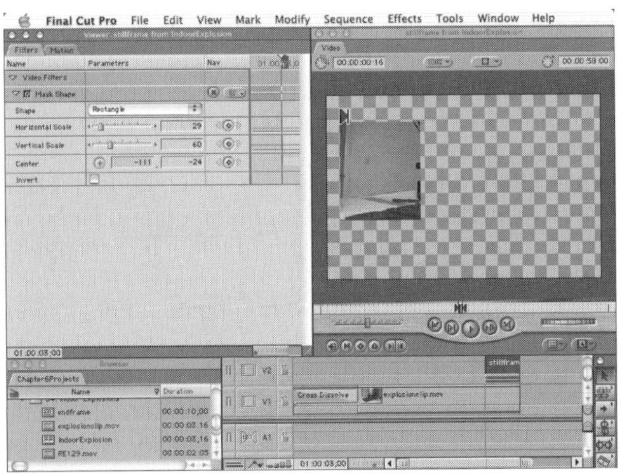

34.10

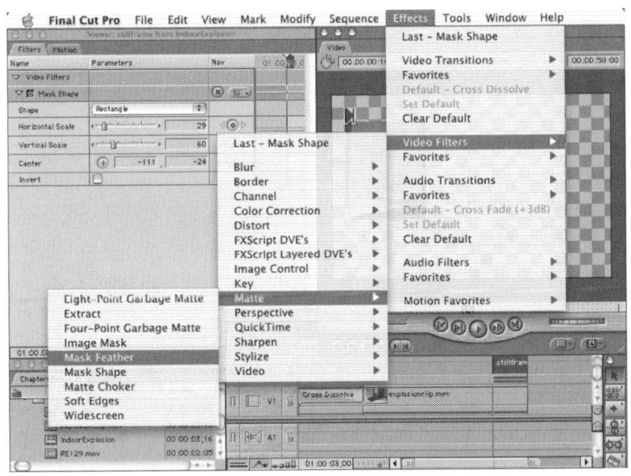

34.11

■ You see the Mask feather filter effect appear in the Filters tab window. The "Soft" value slider controls the degree of feathering the transition between the matte overlay and the background behind it.

■ Set the Softness value to **22** as shown in **Figure 34.12**.

STEP 5: QUICK PREVIEW

■ You can preview individual frames of your new composition by using the arrow keys on the keyboard to manually scrub the play head back and forth one frame at a time from the three-second marker.

■ See how the transition between one frame and the next is pretty abrupt. Add a smoother transition between these moments in time.

> **NOTE**
>
> **In the event there is some color, lighting, or tone difference between the still image and video clip, the feathered edge helps soften the transition between the matte window and the background video.**

STEP 6: ADD A DISSOLVE TRANSITION

■ From the **Window** menu, choose **Effects** to see the bin containing all the video effects and transitions.

■ Double-click to open the Video Transitions bin and then double-click to open the Dissolves bin.

■ Click and drag the cross dissolve transition from the bin onto the media clip in the V2 track and snap the beginning of the transition icon to the left edge of the stillframe clip.

■ As you can see in **Figure 34.13**, the length of the V2 clip is fairly short, so the transition icon may try to fill most of the length of the V2 clip.

■ Double-click the transition icon on the clip in the V2 video track to load it into the Viewer.

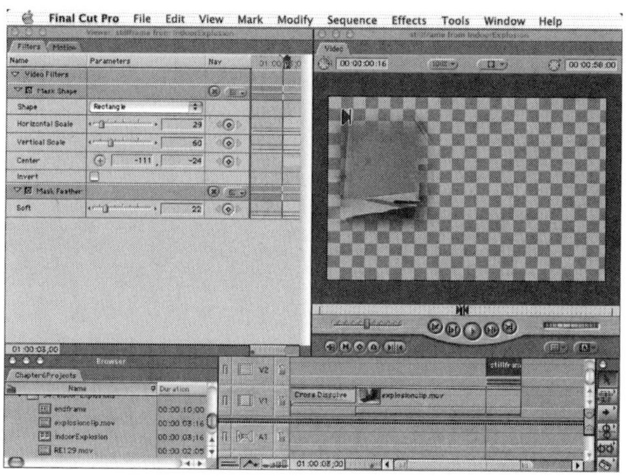

34.12

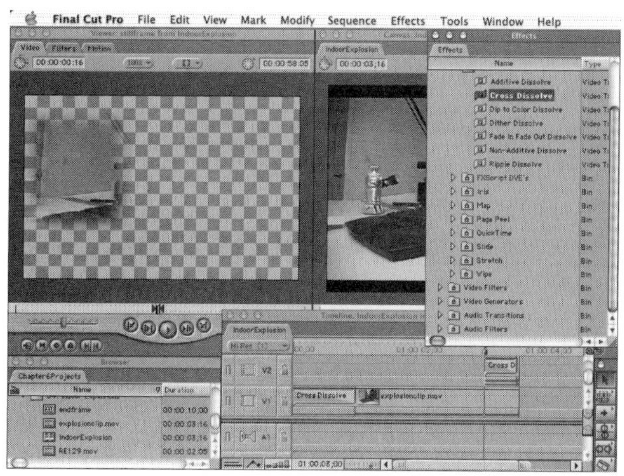

34.13

■ Adjust the duration of the transition by typing **7** and pressing return in the timecode field in the upper-right area of the viewer window to set the length of the transition to 7-frames. You can also drag the left edge of this transition icon to the left to shorten it up. When you do, you see a yellow assistance field appear that indicates how many frames the transition will occupy. **Figure 34.14** shows this feature in action.

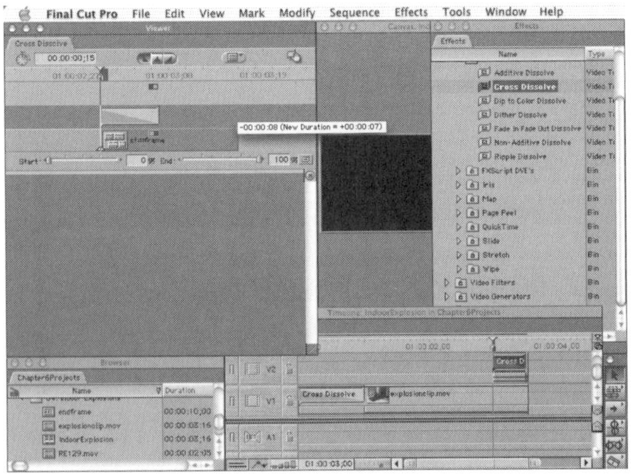

34.14

STEP 7: ADD MORE STILL DATA

■ Click and drag the clip media icon called **endframe.tif** in the browser window into the V1 video track in the timeline. Release the mouse button after the clip snaps to the end point of the **explosionclip.mov** clip. In **Figure 34.15**, you can see how this gives you a few extra seconds of still image to persist after the explosion dissipates.

NOTE

Final Cut Pro 3 provides assistance in controlling many aspects of your video compositions in the form of an automatic pop-up field that appears when adjusting the length of a clip or transition.

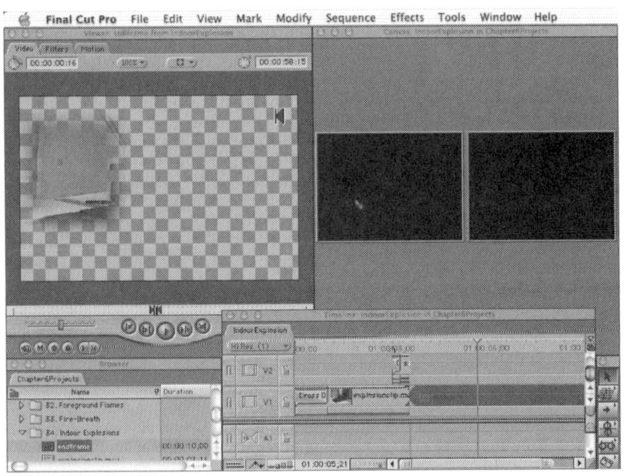

34.15

34.16

STEP 8: ADD THE EXPLOSION

■ Time for the pyrotechnics. Click and drag the icon for the clip **RE129.mov** into the timeline window and create a new video track in V3 before releasing the mouse button. Position the new video track data at the end point of the clip in the V2 video track as shown in **Figure 34.16**.

STEP 9: CHANGE THE COMPOSITION MODE AND POSITION

■ Click to select the clip in V3 of the timeline window.

■ Choose **Modify ➢ Composite Mode ➢ Screen** as shown in **Figure 34.17**. This changes the layer interaction between the new explosion track and the underlying video tracks, so you can see though it, yet allow all the lighter pixels to remain opaque.

STEP 10: REPOSITION THE EXPLOSION

■ You may notice the explosion is just a bit off target.

■ Enable the Image + Wireframe view under the View menu (or use "w").

■ Drag the location of the explosion clip directly over the robot image as shown in **Figure 34.18**.

STEP 11: YET ANOTHER PREVIEW

■ Option-drag the play head across the timeline where the transitions and interactions between all of the video clips happen to preview the effect. Remember, your computer may not require the option-key enhancement to force a preview of your render.

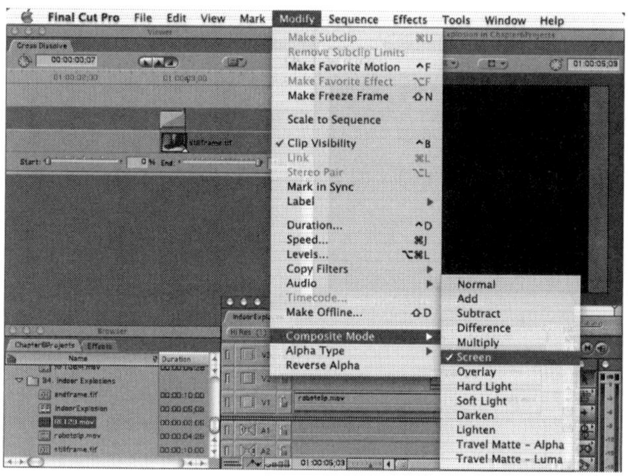

34.17

34.18

34.19

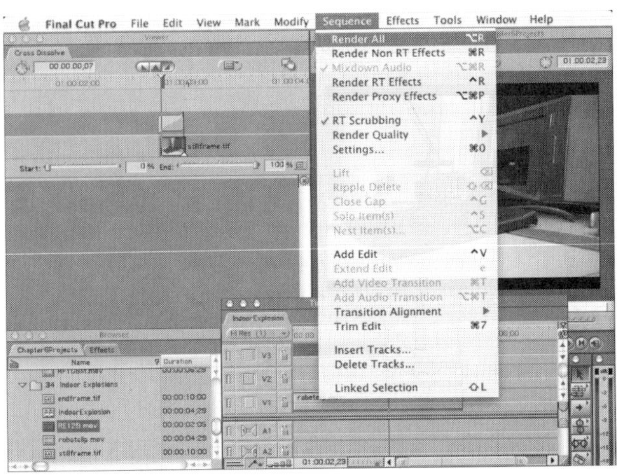

34.20

STEP 12: SYNCHRONIZE THE TIME

- You want to make sure the explosion happens at the right moment in time. Make sure the location of your V3 explosion video track begins a frame or two prior to the disappearance of the robot in the video track. You can click the video clip in V3 and drag it into a few frames earlier in the track to make this happen as shown in **Figure 34.19**.

STEP 13: RENDER THE CLIP

- Choose **Sequence** ➢ **Render All** as shown in **Figure 34.20** to save your movie with the new effect applied.

You can see how adding an explosion video track can enhance any video that you may be creating. This is a perfect opportunity to combine the effects in this chapter to others that you have read in previous chapters, such as laser beams and electric shocks, to create some incredible multiple effects in your video project.

For professional-grade explosions, (and you can never have too many explosion clips in your portfolio) consider purchasing the high-quality media clips from ArtBeats.

CHAPTER 7

MORE ADVANCED MATTE EFFECTS

In this chapter, I demonstrate matte effects involving matte windows, where in essence you cut "a window" within one track of video, so that you can see another video behind it. The purpose of these techniques is to simulate something that otherwise would not be possible within the context of the real-world environment. By using the tools provided by Final Cut Pro, you are able to make them look real.

The user has control over the attributes of these windows including size, shape, position, and definition, defined as either a hard or fuzzy transition between the matte windows in the background.

In these techniques you learn how to match up simple camera techniques and angles with the special effects inherent within Final Cut Pro. In this chapter, you enhance these techniques with a variety of composite effects, by adding one layer of video on top of another.

Swirly Text

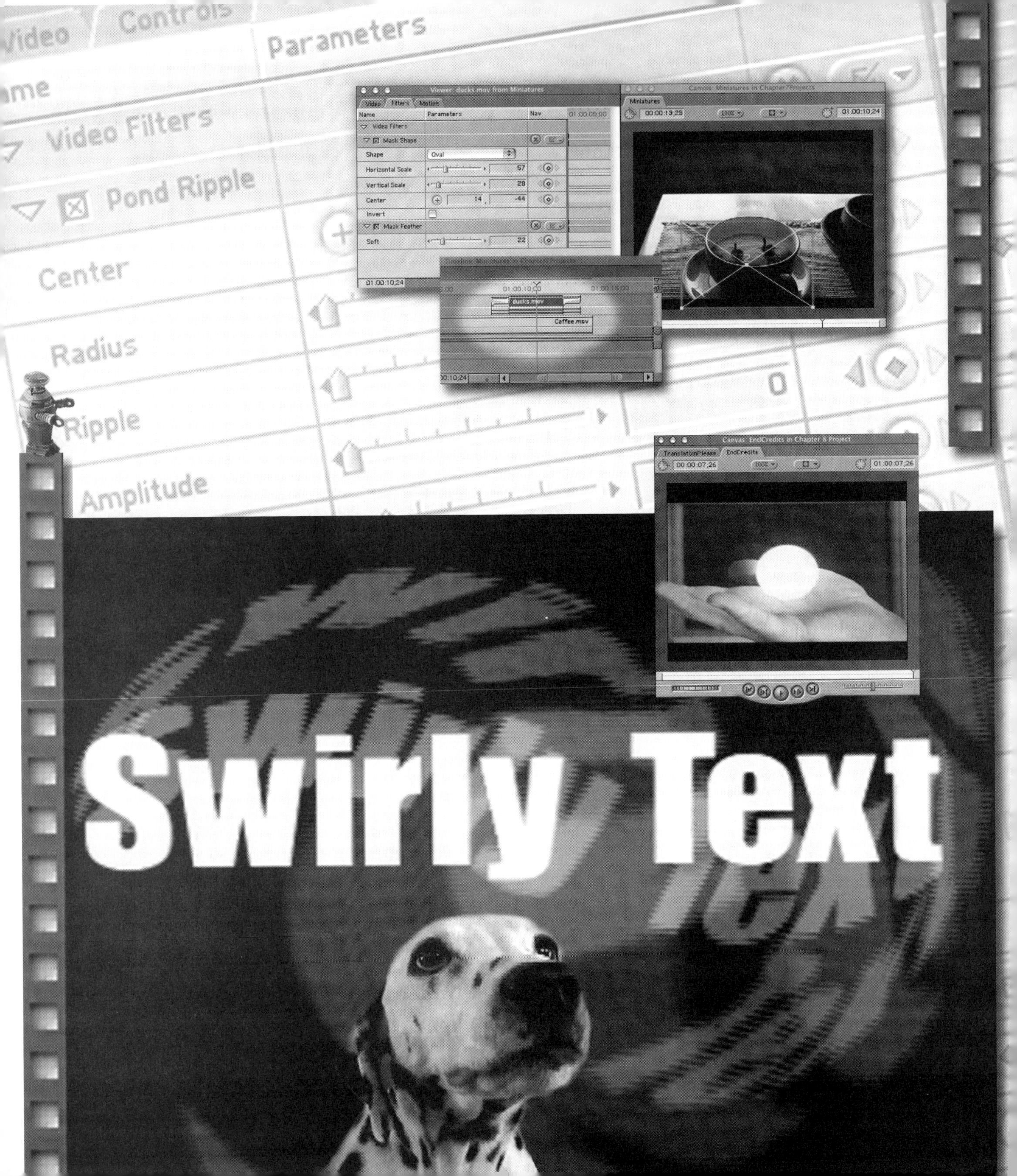
Video
Controls
Parameters
Video Filters
Pond Ripple
Center
Radius
Ripple
Amplitude

TECHNIQUE 35

MINIATURE PEOPLE AND THINGS

35.1 (CP45)

35.2 (CP46)

This technique shows another easy way to accomplish the size deception technique. The secret to accomplishing this successfully is to make sure that the camera angles for the inset video and the background video are consistent.

STEP 1: OPEN THE SEQUENCE

- Make sure that any previous project tabs that were open have been closed.
- Look for the bin in the Chapter 7 Projects folder labeled **Miniature People and Things**.
- In the file you find the sequence called **Miniatures**. Double-click to open it.
- Play through the movie once to get an idea as to where you'll be adding your inset media track. **Figure 35.3** shows the play head at a moment in the timeline where your miniature ducks should begin appearing.

STEP 2: MARK YOUR INSERTION POINT

- The coffee is poured right up until the 8-second mark.
- Move the play head to a position right at 8-seconds into the clip (identified as 8;08, or 8-seconds, 8-frames) in the video track of the timeline window. A shortcut for this is to click in the **canvas** window, and then click in the **timecode field**, where you type in **8**, ;(semicolon), **08**, and then press **Enter**. This tells Final Cut Pro to move the play head to the 8 second, 8-frame position in the timeline window as shown in **Figure 35.4**.

> **NOTE**
>
> **In case you didn't guess the spot, we don't want the ducks appearing before the coffee has been poured into the coffee cup.**

35.3

35.4

STEP 3: ADD THE OVERLAY VIDEO TRACK

- Find the video clip called **duck.mov** and drag its icon onto the timeline window at the play head insertion point.
- Watch for the cursor change when it becomes a down-facing arrow, which then allows you to snap the left edge of the clip at the insertion point marking the location of the playhead.
- After you accomplish this, you've created a new video track labeled **V2** that has the ducks video clip on top of the base video track as you can see in **Figure 35.5**.

TIP

Remember, this process can be made a little easier if the snapping feature is enabled. The keyboard shortcut "n" toggles snapping on and off.

35.5

STEP 4: ADD A DISSOLVE TRANSITION TO THE INSET TRACK

- Open the **effects** window by choosing **Window ➢ Effects**. Next, open the video transitions bin inside of this folder. You find another folder entitled **Dissolve** that contains a collection of various dissolve transitions that you can work with. This demonstration uses the dissolve transition.

35.6

35.7

■ Click and drag the **cross dissolve** icon onto your clip in the V2 video track, snapping the left edge of the icon to the left edge of the clip as seen in **Figure 35.6**

■ Repeat the previous step by adding a dissolve transition for the right edge of the clip in the V2 video track as shown in **Figure 35.7**.

STEP 5: RESIZE THE CLIP IN V2

■ Select the ducks clip in V2 and enable wire frame handles in order to resize it. You can also accomplish this step by using either the shortcut w and cycling through the various wireframe options, or by choosing **Wireframe** + **Picture** from the **View** menu as shown in **Figure 35.8**.

■ Re-size the clip by dragging one of the corner handles towards the center of the frame.

35.8

NOTE

You can also adjust selected clip items numerically in the Motion tab. If you want to adjust this frame size numerically, double-click the clip in the timeline to see it in the Viewer, and then click the Motion tab of the Viewer window and set the scale to 55. This repositions the image in the window to a smaller size at the same center point, and in this case, gives you access to other Motion tab settings at the same time.

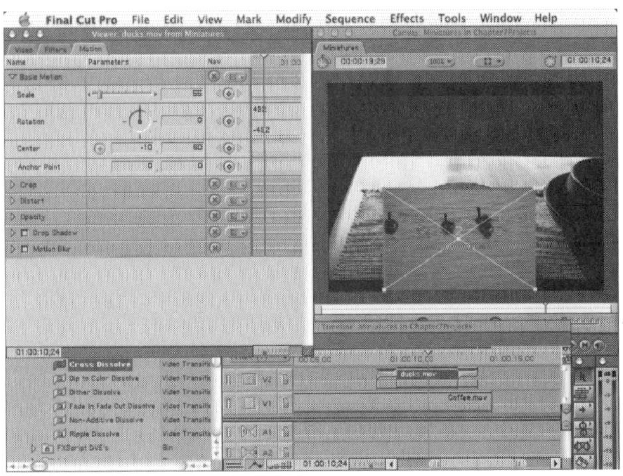

35.9

35.10

■ Set the center point of the clip to **–10, 60** respectively. This places the ducks overlay in the proper position for the next step where you will add a matte mask window. **Figure 35.9** shows the location and Motion tab settings.

STEP 6: CREATE A MATTE WINDOW

■ Double-click the clip in the V2 video track to see it in the Viewer.
■ From the **Effects** menu, choose **Video Filters ➢ Matte ➢ Mask shape**.
■ You now see the ducks clip that used to fill your entire window frame inside a small rectangular window on top of your V1 video track as shown in **Figure 35.10**.

> **NOTE**
>
> **Even though you repositioned the video clip in the V2 track, you use this control to re-position the matte window — through which you can see the video clip.**

35.11

STEP 7: CHANGE THE SHAPE OF THE MASK WINDOW

■ Click the **Filters** tab in the viewer window to see the mask shape settings.
■ Change the pop-up menu that appears from **Rectangular** to **Oval**.
■ Set the **Horizontal Scale** to **57** and the **Vertical Scale** to **29**.
■ Change the center point of the matte window to **14, –44** as shown in **Figure 35.11**.

STEP 8: FEATHER THE EDGES OF THE MATTE WINDOW

You want this window to blend in better with its background, so you need to replace the sharp edges with a feathered edge so that it blends better with the cup of coffee.

■ From the **Effects** menu, choose **Video Filters ➢ Matte ➢ Mask Feather**. This applies a default 2-pixel feathered edge to your matte mask.
■ You just softened the transition between the video source and the matte window.
■ Click to activate the **Filters** tab. Look for the **Mask Feather** settings and set the **"Soft"** value to **22** as you see in **Figure 35.12**.

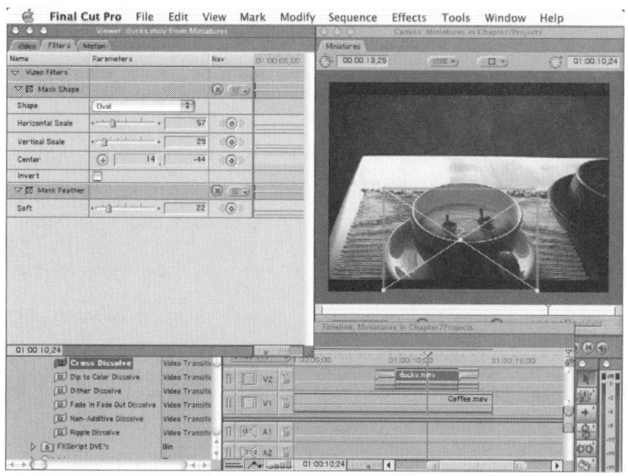

35.12

35.13

STEP 9: RENDER THE CLIP

- From the **Sequence** menu, choose **Render All** as shown in **Figure 35.13** to see results of the changes you made.
- After you finish, close this project tab by **Control-clicking** on the tab name or use the keyboard shortcut Control-W.

This technique showed you another great way to use matte windows to help create an illusion based on a simple size deception. The secret here is to remember to keep your camera angles consistent between both your inset foreground shot and your background shot.

TECHNIQUE 36

GIGANTIC HOUSE PETS

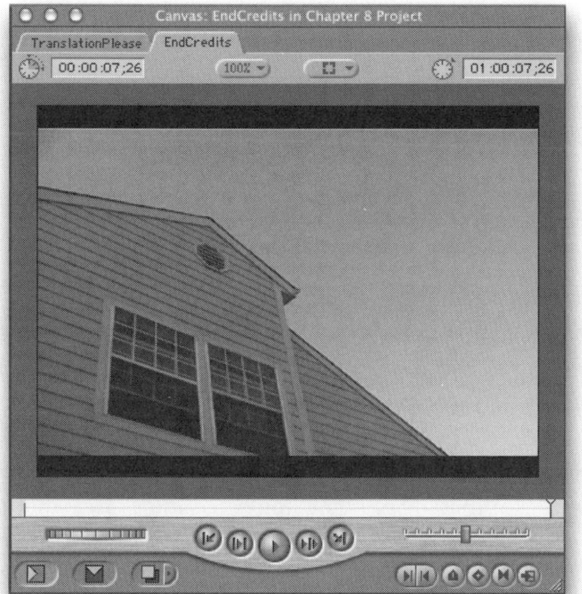

36.1 (CP47)

36.2 (CP48)

Gigantic house pets is another size deception that uses a matte window to composite two different video tracks together giving the illusion of one giant-sized pet looking over the top of one residential home. The secret to this effect, like the previous one, is making sure that your camera angles are consistent for both subjects. For example, if you are looking up at the home from a low eye level, you want to make sure that the shot you take of your pet, in this case, is also taken from that same low angle upwards as well.

STEP 1: OPEN THE FILE

If you still have other sequences open in the timeline, make sure to close them now so you aren't distracted in the upcoming techniques.

- Find the bin in your browser window called **Gigantic Housepets**.
- Open the bin and double-click the sequence titled **Giants**.

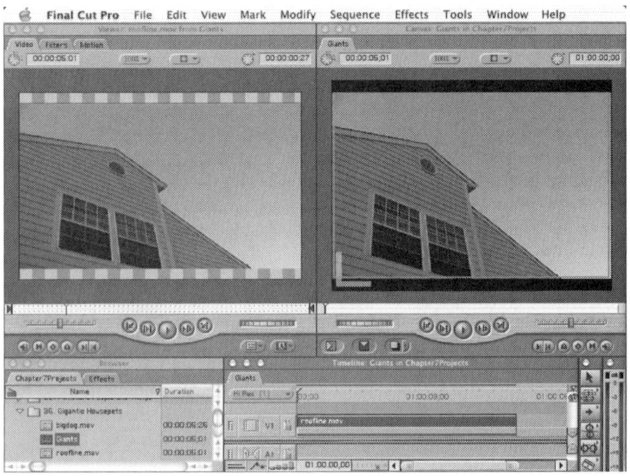

36.3

36.4

- You see in **Figure 36.3** that a base video track already exists in this timeline.
- Your task here is to add a matte window so that you can see a giant pet in the sky.

STEP 2: ADD THE GIANT PET

- Drag the video clip titled **bigdog.mov** onto the canvas window and choose the **superimpose overlay**, when it is presented as shown in **Figure 36.4**.

STEP 3: CREATE THE MATTE WINDOW

Previously with matte windows, you used color keying or a generated symmetrical shape from within the program. In this example, you use an imported piece of artwork as your window.

Creating a mask window that is not square, rounded, oval, or rectangular only requires a few additional steps compared to choosing the automatic matte

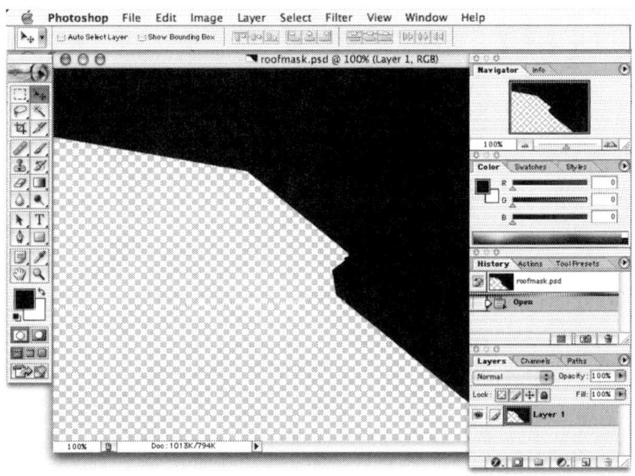

36.5

frames in the generator filters. Creating this effect is possible by using a simple color key filter. For this technique you add your own travel matte made from a still frame of the video clip.

In this case, the matte was easy to create by using your favorite painting program because the roofline is a simple polygon with straight edges. The shape of the house was easy to paint out, creating a simple window through which the video in the V2 track is shown.

- Click and drag the mask matte entitled **roofmask.psd** onto the **canvas** window and choose the **superimpose** overlay when it is presented.

Figure 36.5 shows the roofmask.psd document being created in the Adobe Photoshop environment. You can see how it is a simple one-color matte window in the shape of a house.

- The till image fills the entire length of the clip automatically.
- Because the V1 video track is the current target as indicated by the yellow film clip icon, the matte is installed into a new V2 video track directly above the V1 video track, forcing the gigantic dog into a brand new V3 video track above them all.

NOTE

The two worlds of computer graphics and digital video define the shape of their pixels differently; depending on how you've set up your version of Final Cut Pro, the proportions of the mask artwork may not exactly match the dimensions and proportions of the video window.

You can compensate for this difference in the canvas window by selecting the V2 video track, enabling wire frame handles, and then holding down the shift key while you click and drag on one of the corner handles to resize the clip in order to fit the frame. You know if you succeeded when the mask edges match up with the roofline without showing any gap in the video image. Be prepared for a little experimentation to make this fit perfectly.

STEP 4: MAKE THE MATTE A WINDOW

- Click the **bigdog.mov** video clip in V3 to select it.
- From the **Modify** menu, choose **Composite mode ➢ Travel Matte-Alpha** as shown in **Figure 36.6**.

36.6

- This forces the matte object you just placed in the V2 video track to become a window in the shape of all of the black pixels.

Figure 36.7 shows a well-matched and proportioned mask in place.

STEP 5: RENDER THE CLIP

- From the **Sequence** menu, choose **Render All,** as shown in **Figure 36.8**, to see results of the changes that you made.
- After you finish, close this project tab by Control-clicking on the tab name or use the keyboard shortcut Control-W.
- Now you have a huge dog's nose towering over the roofline of your home.

This technique is another favorite that can help you create the illusion of an 80-foot tall pet. The secret is in creating an easy to define window edge and keeping your camera angles consistent between the foreground and background shots.

> **NOTE**
>
> **The matte window for this demonstration was created by exporting a single frame of the video clip as a photoshop file, then manipulating it in Photoshop to create the mask.**

36.7

36.8

TECHNIQUE 37

MATTE WINDOWS IN OBJECTS

37.1 (CP49)

37.2 (CP50)

This technique is similar to the previous one, but in this technique you reshape a rectangular video frame in order to fit a distorted rectangular shape in the background of your video clip.

For example, you could have a video playing within a flat-looking, but irregularly shaped surface of another object, such as an oven, a microwave, a television set, or any flat surface object where you can paste in a video picture. The secret to this technique is that the object onto which you will display this video frame must have straight edges. These straight edges makes it very easy to create a rectangular shape and distort it in order to display the video in perspective within the object because it has four corners and straight edges between them.

STEP 1: OPEN THE FILE

- Make sure that any other project tabs previously opened are closed.
- Open the **Chapter 7 Projects** folder.
- Locate the bin called **Matte Windows in Objects.**
- Double-click to open the **Matte Surfaces** sequence and load it into your timeline window as you see in **Figure 37.3.**

37.3

STEP 2: ADD THE SECOND VIDEO TRACK

- A video clip has already been inserted in the V1 video track.
- Drag the second video clip called **batwing.mov** into the timeline window, creating a new video track in V2, snapping the **right edge** of the clip to the end of the video clip in the V1 video track as shown in **Figure 37.4.**
- Watch for the cursor to become a down-facing arrow before you release the mouse button.

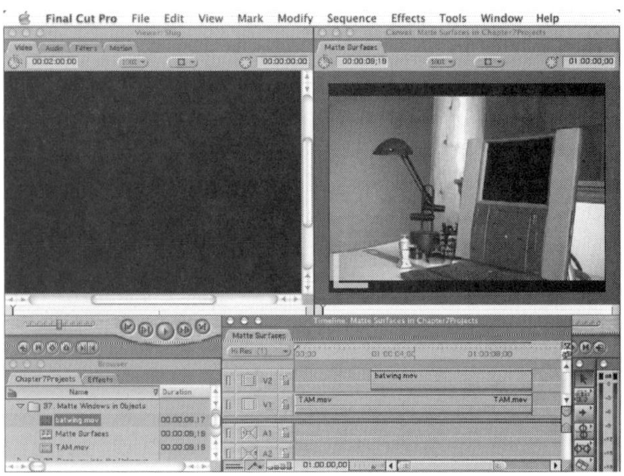

37.4

NOTE

As you view this 9-second sequence, you notice a nice four-sided shape in the middle of the object. In this case, it is the display screen of the 20th Anniversary Macintosh. This space is where the video sequence will be placed.

NOTE

This video clip is in the correct position when the right edge snaps to the right edge of the base video track in V1 and the two right edges line up.

STEP 3: ADD A TRANSITION TO EITHER END OF THE V2 CLIP

■ If the **Effects** tab is visible in your **browser** window, open it by clicking its tab as shown in **Figure 37.5**.

■ Open the video **Transitions** folder and find the **Dissolve** folder.

■ Open the **Dissolve** folder and choose the **Cross Dissolve** icon.

■ Drag the **Cross Dissolve** icon onto the V2 video clip and snap its left edge to the left edge of the V2 video clip.

■ You see a Dissolve Transition Effect icon added to the clip.

■ Do the same thing for the right edge of the V2 video clip as shown in **Figure 37.6**, which eases the video clip in and out of the sequence smoothly.

STEP 4: RESIZE AND REPOSITION THE CLIP IN V2

■ Click to select the video clip in V2.

■ Enable the Wire frame view (use the keyboard shortcut W or choose **View ➢ Image + Wireframe**).

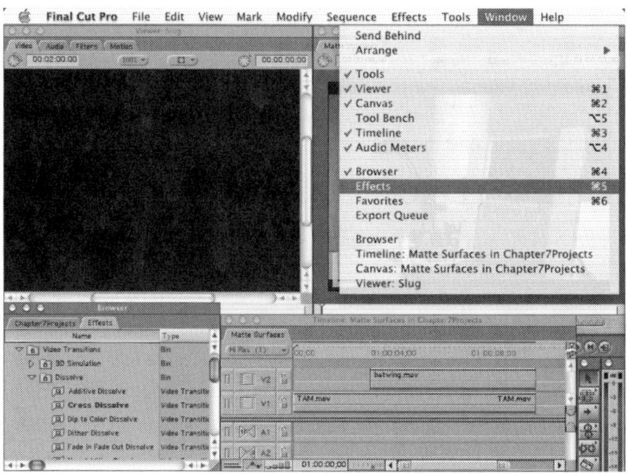

37.5

■ Click and drag one of the corner handles toward the center of the frame to resize the image.

■ Move the wire frame V2 video clip in the canvas window towards the video screen in the computer in the V1 video clip. Position it with the lower-right corner of the V2 clip over the lower-right corner of the computer's screen area.

■ If you want to match this example numerically, double-click the video clip in V2 and choose the **Motion** tab in the **viewer** window. Set the scale to **33**, and the center to **41, –19** as shown in **Figure 37.7**.

37.6

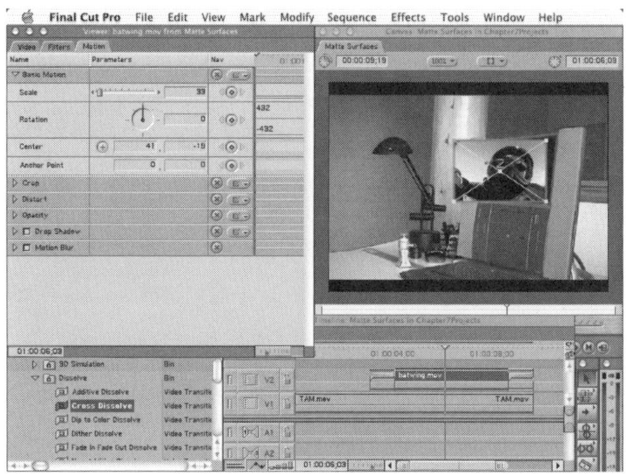

37.7

STEP 5: DISTORT THE INSET VIDEO IMAGE

The overlaid video track has regular rectangular borders and would look correct if your base video track was a straight-on picture with perfect proportions. Dropping that into a regular rectangular shape would be too easy. Don't let your effects change the way you tell your story, in essence letting the "tail wag the dog."

- Use the keyboard shortcut D or choose the **Distort** tool in the Tool palette.
- Select the clip in V2, with the wire frame controls still enabled.
- Click and drag the corner handles of the wire frame to match the corners of your rectangular flat surface of the computer's screen.
- If you want to more precisely define the shape of the distorted rectangle, you can enter numeric values into the specified areas within the Motion tab of the viewer window. First, open the **Distort** option in the **Motion** tab and then enter these numbers (as shown in **Figure 37.8**):

  Upper Left: –32, –105
  Upper Right: 216, –129
  Lower Right: 189, 123
  Lower Left: –53, 105
  Aspect Ratio: –12.5

> **TIP**
>
> **As you might guess, this task may be made easier if you magnify your view of the subject by increasing the view percentage. You can easily zoom in to an image using the simple keyboard shortcut: Command +.**
>
> **Throughout this book, you're provided with a method for defining your effects using numeric values in the Motion or Filter tabs. This is a convenient feature that will allow you to match these values in future clips, exactly duplicating an effect or position.**

STEP 6: CHANGE THE OPACITY

The clip in the V2 video track is too bright for the setting and looks unnatural. Reducing the opacity helps both to darken the inset image and blend it better with its surroundings.

- Click to select the clip in V2.
- Click to select the **Motion** tab in the **viewer** window.
- Change the opacity setting in this window to **66%** as you see in **Figure 37.9**.

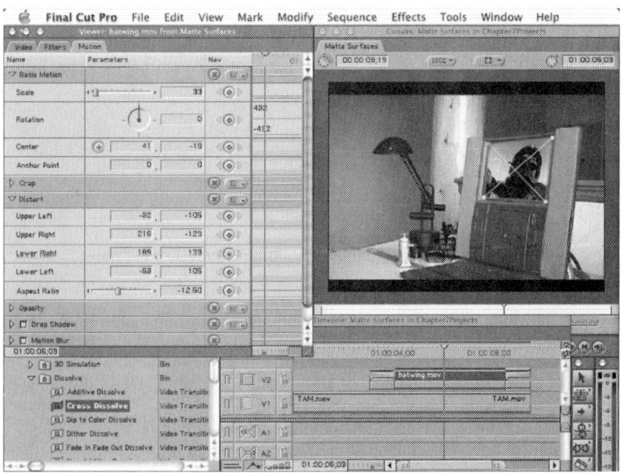

37.8

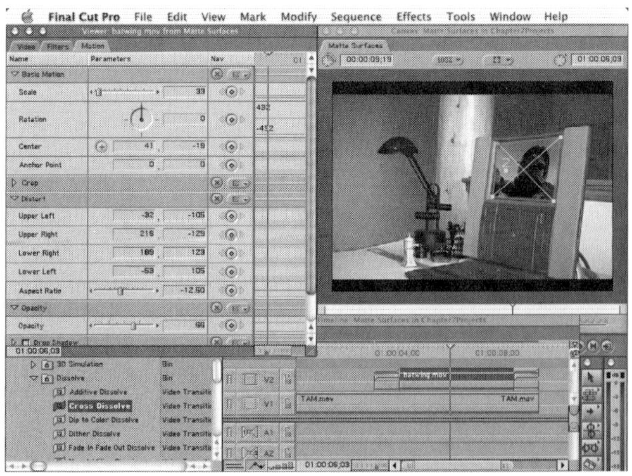

37.9

STEP 7: RENDER THE CLIP

- From the **Sequence** menu, choose **Render All** as you see in **Figure 37.10** to see results of the changes that you made.
- You now added a secondary video clip to any ordinary appliance.

Now that you know this technique, you can add this effect to other rectangular flat objects, such as picture frames, oven doors, and television screens.

In this technique you learned how to inset a distorted video clip onto any flat surface. The secret, of course, is in distorting the video frame and adjusting the Composite mode of the overlaid video track.

With this technique you can place any video image into any other video image.

37.10

DOORWAY INTO THE UNKNOWN

38.1 (CP51)

38.2 (CP52)

This basic technique is the same as before, but with this technique we are animating a matte window so that it becomes visible over the course of time.

When we see a door open, what we are essentially seeing are two parallel lines moving apart, one stationary and the other one in motion. For this example you use a CD-ROM door, where the lines moving apart are horizontal.

This technique has two secrets. The first secret is the control of the size and shape of the matte window as well as the speed at which the CD-ROM drawer is opening. Because we are using a stationary camera, it allows you to easily integrate one scene into the other. The use of the matte window allows you to create in imperceptible change between the two scenes.

The second secret lies in the fact that you use a regular rectangular shape with straight hard edges, through which we can create our matte window.

STEP 1: OPEN THE PROJECT

- Make sure you close any previously opened project tabs.
- Look for the bin titled **Doorway into the unknown** in the **Chapter 7 Projects** folder.
- Double-click the sequence entitled **Doorway**.
- In **Figure 38.3** you see that a base video track called **opening.mov** is already placed to help you along.

STEP 2: ADD THE INSET VIDEO TRACK

- Play this clip once to see how and where the door opens.
- Move the play head to the 6-second point in the timeline.
- Look for the timecode field in the canvas window, click in it, and type **6: (Return)** (that's 6, a colon, and Return). This is your insertion point for the inset clip that appears in the doorway.
- Click and drag the movie clip **what.mov** from the **browser** window into the **timeline** window, dropping the clip at the insertion point where you left off at the play head. Watch to see that the cursor becomes a down-facing arrow before you release the mouse button.
- Notice that a new V2 video track has been added to your timeline window as you see in **Figure 38.4**.

STEP 3: RESIZE THE CLIP

- Notice that the newly placed V2 video track is a little longer than the V1 video track. Shortening that is easy.
- Click to select the newly added clip in the V2 video track.

38.3

38.4

■ Reduce the length by dragging the right edge over to the left edge until it snaps to the end point of the clip already in place.
■ While that video clip is selected, enable the Wire frame view by using either the keyboard shortcut W, or by choosing **View ➢ Image + Wireframe**. The Wire frame view is shown in **Figure 38.5**.
■ In the canvas window, click the corner handle and drag it inward until the inset video clip frame is about half of its original size.
■ If you want to position and size the inset clip in the V2 track, select the **Motion** tab in the **viewer** window and enter the following values:

Change the Scale setting to 50%
Change the center point to –11, –8

■ Click and drag the wire framed clip down and to the left a bit to more closely center the image in the square area where the hatch will open.

STEP 4: CREATE THE VIDEO MATTE WINDOW

■ Double-click the clip in V2 to show it in the Viewer.
■ Choose **Effects ➢ Video Filters ➢ Matte ➢ Mask Shape**.
■ You see that the video image now appears in a clipped and smaller window than before. You want to position the matte window to fit precisely within the rectangular shape of the open door.
■ You can play with this positioning for hours, but a shortcut method is to enter the following values in the **Filters** tab of the **viewer** window (as shown in **Figure 38.6**):

Horizontal Scale: 53
Vertical Scale: 55
Center: 34, –39

TIP

It might help to get a closer look at your work by using the keyboard shortcut Command+ to zoom into the image. A close-up look can help with your positioning efforts.

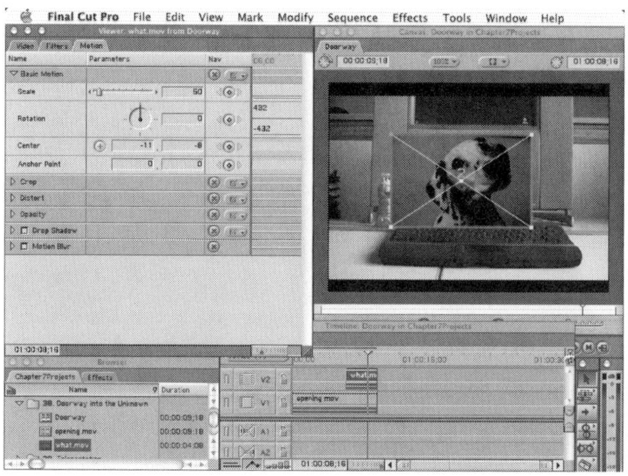

38.5

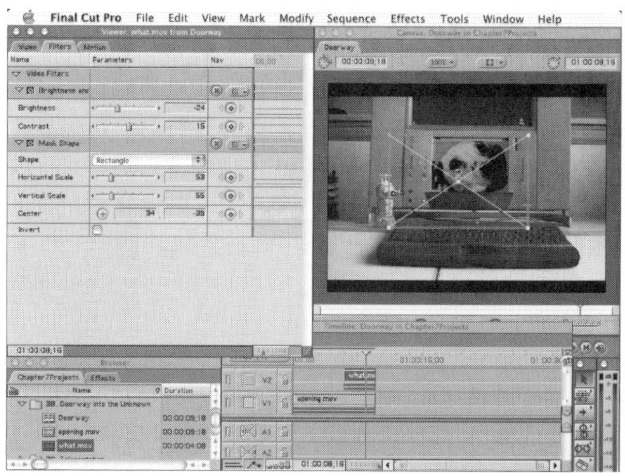

38.6

STEP 5: SOFTEN THE EDGES OF THE MATTED WINDOW

■ From the menu, choose **Effects ➢ Video Filters ➢ Matte ➢ Mask Feather** as you see in **Figure 38.7**.

STEP 6: ADD THE WIPE EFFECT

■ Move the playhead to the beginning of the clip in V2. (You can use the up-arrow shortcut key to accomplish this.)
■ If you preview the clip right now, you'll see that the inset video clip just appears as the doorway behind it opens. You need to simulate the opening of the door by creating a wipe transition for the appearance of the inset video clip.
■ Display the **Effects** bin by choosing **Windows ➢ Effects** or the **Command-5** shortcut key.
■ Open the **Video Transitions** bin. Next, open the **QuickTime** bin inside of it and look for the **Wipe** icon.
■ Click and drag the **Wipe** icon onto the timeline onto the clip in the V1track, so that the left edge of the Wipe Transition icon matches up with the left edge of your clip in V2 as shown in **Figure 38.8**.
■ Double-click the **Wipe Transition** icon in the V2 video track to see it in the **viewer** window.
■ The default values for this Wipe effect won't work. You need to change the direction and duration of the wipe to make this look natural.
■ Change the Wipe Type to **Slide Vertical** in the pop-up menu of the **Wipe** tab.
■ Now the only element left is to synchronize the wipe transition with the door opening. You can do this easily by changing the duration of the transition.
■ In this demonstration, the duration is only 1-second and 4 frames. Click in the **Duration** field of the **Wipe** tab and type in **1;** (semicolon) **4** and press **Enter**.

NOTE

You can leave the feathering values set at 2 for the purposes of this demonstration, because our project is in low-resolution. In high-resolution projects, you may want to adjust this value either up or down to better fit the needs of your project.

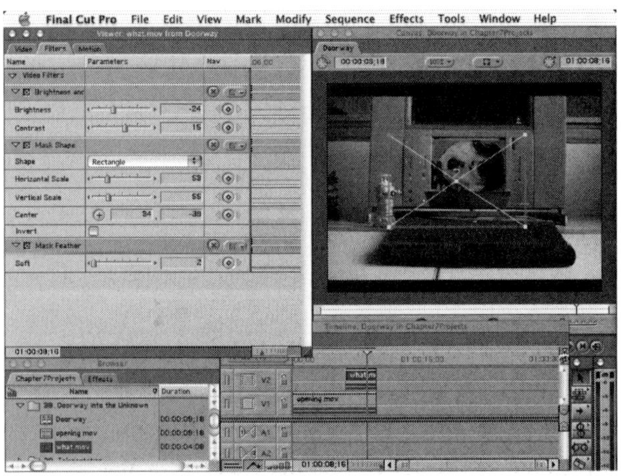

38.7

38.8

■ This field sets the duration of the effect to a precise frame length that appears to follow the opening door of the V1 video clip as shown in **Figure 38.9**.

STEP 7: RENDER THE CLIP

■ From the **Sequence** menu, choose **Render All** to save your movie with the new effect applied as shown in **Figure 38.10**.

This technique is especially fun because it allows you to create a video surprise in just about any scene. Because the edges of the inset window are straight and vertical, it's easy to insert additional video data as well as keyframe the motion of the creation of the matte window.

NOTE

A good way to test this effect is to use the arrow keys on your keyboard and manually scrub the play head one frame back and forth.

NOTE

Your mileage may vary. Not all doors open at the same speed, not all video clips are playing at the frame-rate that this one is. Be prepared to spend some time experimenting with the duration of the transition in your projects.

Look around and notice how many other objects or openings in your home have straight edges to them and can easily be modified with a good wipe transition.

38.9

38.10

TECHNIQUE 39

TELEPORTATION

39.1

39.2

This technique takes advantage of layers of video and still image to create the illusion of having something in the foreground disappear magically into thin air. This technique is similar to the ones that use multiple travel mattes, but in this case you use only one mask and a Wipe Transition effect to cause the object to disappear.

With the Teleportation effect, you add different filter effects that give the appearance of the object changing its molecular structure as it disappears.

NOTE

One of the secrets to the success of this effect is making sure that your original camera shot is made from a tripod or stationary camera mount. Your still image has to occur from the same angle or position as the action sequence in the foreground.

39.3

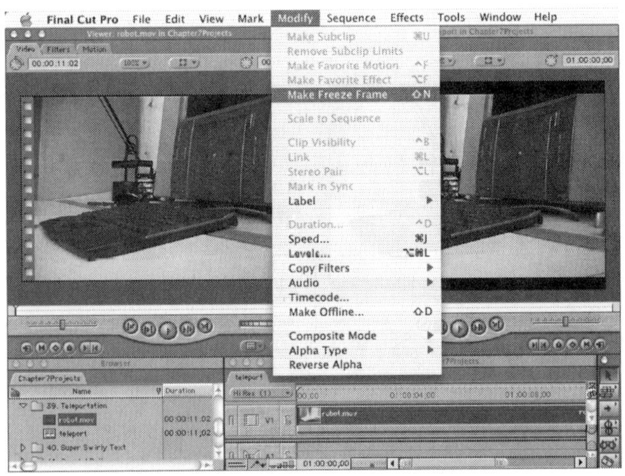

39.4

STEP 1: OPEN THE PROJECT FILE

- In the **Chapter 7 Projects** folder, look for the project bin called **Teleportation** to get **Figure 39.3**.
- Double-click on the Sequence icon in the bin to see in the timeline window and to open it.
- Play it through once to get an idea as to where the transitions need to occur.

STEP 2: CAPTURE A STILL FRAME FROM THE BEGINNING OF THE CLIP

- Double-click the **robot.mov** clip in the bin to see it in the Viewer. Use the up-arrow to move the play head to the beginning of the clip in the viewer window.
- From the menu, choose **Modify ➢ Make Freeze Frame** (or use the keyboard shortcut Shift-N) as shown in **Figure 39.4**.

STEP 3: ADD THE STILL CLIP TO THE BIN

- Click and drag the image from the Viewer into the bin so that it highlights the bin folder, which adds this project as a clip media item.

39.5

■ Click to select the name of the still image and name it **BeamOut**.

■ You captured this clip now, so that you can use it later in the main clip. This is an unmodified image of our scene without our subject in it. When you create the Transportation effect, this background will remain after the subject disappears by teleporting away. **Figure 39.5** shows the clip as it appears in your project bin.

STEP 4: NEW TRACK, NEW CLIP

■ Click to select the clip in the V1 track so that it is highlighted.

■ Hold down the **Option** and **Shift** keys and then click and drag up until you see the down-facing arrow.

■ This sequence creates a duplicate video track named **V2** as shown in **Figure 39.6**.

STEP 5: PROGRESSIVELY "DE-REZ" THE SUBJECT

■ Move the play head to the 9-second mark in the timeline window by clicking in the canvas window in the timecode field, type **9** and **;** (semicolon), and then press **Enter**. This moves your playhead to the 9-second mark of the clip.

■ Double-click the clip in the **V2** video track to view it in the viewer window and then click to expose the Filters tab.

■ Choose **Window ➢ Effects** or use the keyboard shortcut Command-5 to make the Effects bin visible.

■ Open the **video filters** folder and choose **Blur**. Drag the icon for **Wind Blur** into the **Filters** tab of the **viewer** window.

■ Keyframe this moment in time by clicking the **Keyframe** button for each of the following attributes and setting the following values: **Direction: 0**, **Radius: 0**, **Steps: 1** as you see in **Figure 39.7**.

■ Move the playhead to the 10-second mark by entering **10** and then **;** and return in the timecode field. This is one second beyond where we originally started in our step.

■ As you see in **Figure 39.8**, keyframe the **Radius**, **Steps**, the **Horizontal Scale**, and the **Vertical Scale**. Change those values to the following:

Radius: 33

Steps: 10

You've just created a transition for your video image inside of the matte window that changes over the course of a one second period.

39.6

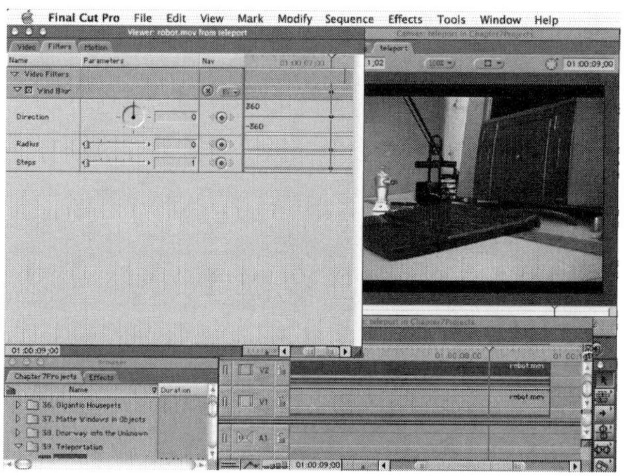

39.7

STEP 6: MAKE A WINDOW FOR THE TRANSITION

To contain the actual effect to a small area in the video frame, you'll create a mask matte window through which the effect can be seen.

- Go back to the **effects** window and choose **Video Filters**. Open up the **Matte** folder and choose **Mask Shape**. Drag this icon into the **Filters** tab of the **viewer** window.

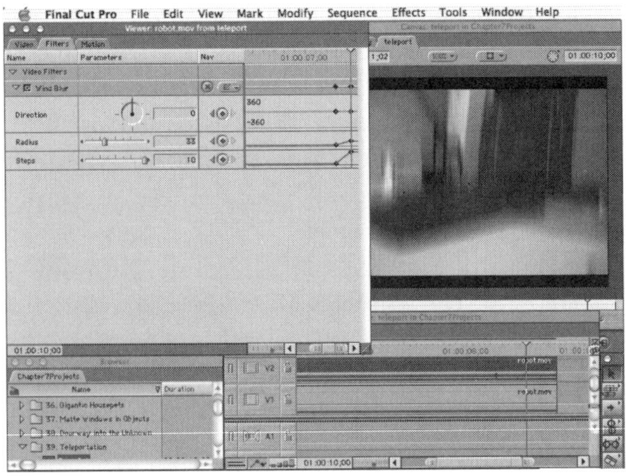

39.8

- Go back once again to the **effects** window and choose **Video Filters**. Open up the **Matte** folder and choose **Mask Feather**. Drag this icon into the **Filters** tab of the **viewer** window, giving the matte window a softer edge.

Figure 39.9 shows the results of this action in progress.

- Set the geometry of the mask shape values to those shown in **Figure 39.10**.
  Horizontal Scale: 11
  Vertical Scale: 50
  Center: –106, 3
- Set the Soft value to **11**.

This creates a soft-edged mask window through which your teleporting robot appears as seen in **Figure 39.10**.

TIP

You may want to separate the Filters tab from the viewer window so you can see the effects of the next steps.

39.9

39.10

STEP 7: BEAM ME UP!

- In the bin for this project, double-click on the still image you just labeled **BeamOut** to load it into the **viewer** window.
- Change the duration of this clip to one second. In the Duration field, which you'll find in the upper-left corner of your viewer window, enter **1** and the **;** as shown in **Figure 39.11** and then press **Enter**. This clip is now only one second in duration.
- Click and drag the **BeamOut** still image clip into the timeline window as shown in **Figure 39.12**. This creates a V3 video track. The objective is to snap this clip to the end of the timeline in the V3 video track. Watch for the cursor to change to a down-facing arrow as the right edge of the clip snaps to the right edge of the movie clip in V2.
- Move the play head to the beginning of the BeamOut clip.
- Double-click the clip in **V3** to see it in the **viewer** window.
- Click the **Motion** tab and set the opacity to **0**. Click the **Keyframe** button to keyframe the opacity as shown in **Figure 39.13**.
- Use the down-arrow keyboard shortcut to move the play head to the end of this video clip.

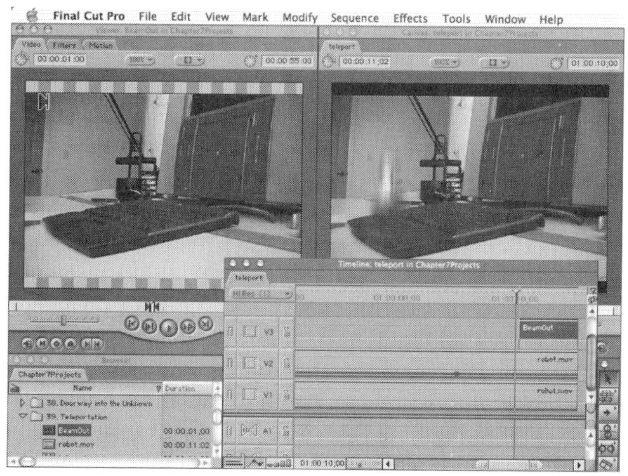

39.12

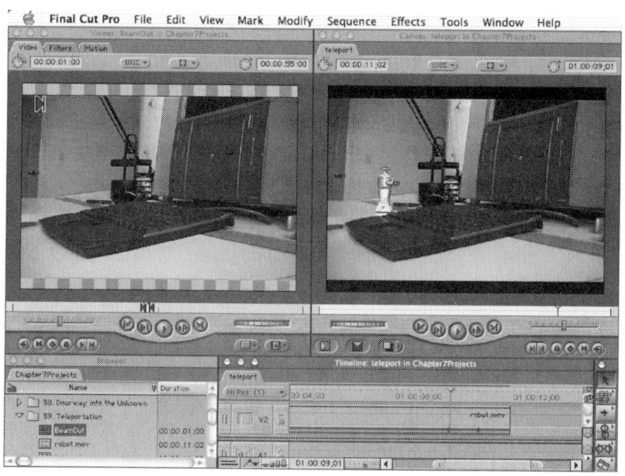

39.11

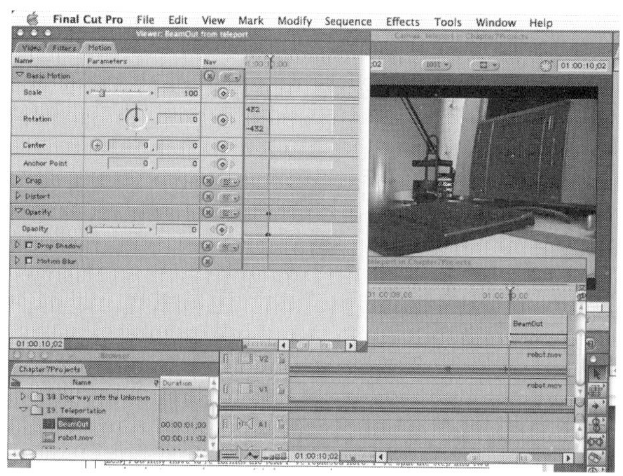

39.13

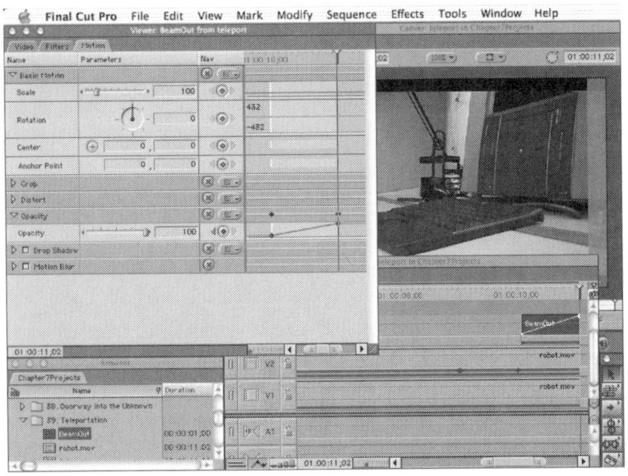

39.14

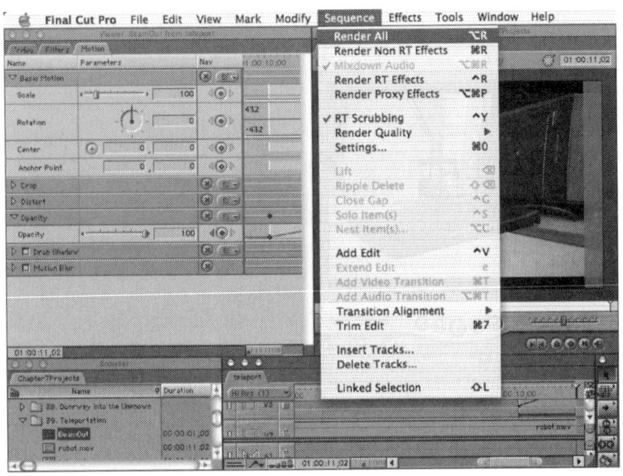

39.15

- **Keyframe** the opacity by clicking the keyframe button and set the opacity to **100** as shown in **Figure 39.14**.
- This opacity produces an effect of the still image gradually becoming opaque in the course of a one second time duration.

STEP 8: RENDER THE CLIP

- From the **Sequence** menu, choose **Render All** (as shown in **Figure 39.15**) to save your movie with the new effect applied.

This technique is especially useful when you need to have selected family members or employers disappear suddenly. Your favorite science fiction television show for (almost) the past 40 years used this technique to transport cast members onto strange new worlds and new civilizations, boldly going where no one in television had gone before.

The difference here is that Final Cut Pro 3 and your home camcorder make the technique less expensive and far more convenient to accomplish than was possible in the Hollywood back lots of the 1960s.

TECHNIQUE 40

SUPER SWIRLY TEXT

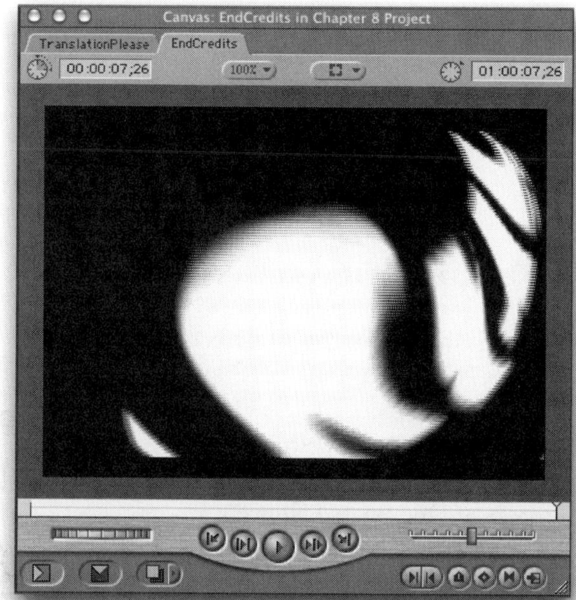

40.1

40.2

One of Final Cut Pro's strong points is its wide variety of advanced filter effects that you can use in almost any combination to enhance a video you create. One of the best features of using a combination of these filter effects is to set up a sequence so that each filter will make a transition over the course of a particular period of time. In this particular technique, you essentially move backwards in time and create a series of effects that cause a portion of text to transition from a state of unreadable distortion to a state where the text is highly readable.

STEP 1: OPEN THE PROJECT FILE

- Open the **Chapter 7 Projects** folder.
- Open the bin entitled **Super Swirly Text.**
- Double-click on the icon labeled **Super Swirly Text** and load it into your timeline window as shown in **Figure 40.3.**

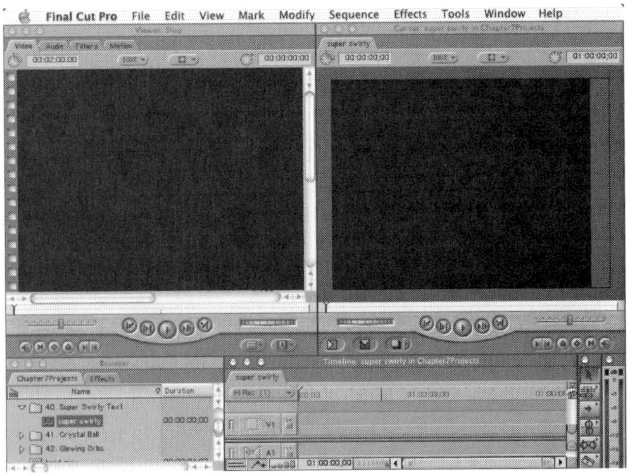

40.3

STEP 2: CREATE A TEXT OBJECT

- Select the **Video** tab in the **viewer** window, then click the **Generator** button and choose **Text ➢ Text.**
- Select the **Controls** tab in the **viewer** window, and change the font to **Impact** (or any fat style sans serif font).
- Change the font size to **122 points** and the color to **white.**
- Click the **Video** tab and in the **Duration** field enter **3, ;** (semicolon), and **return** for a 3-second duration as you see in **Figure 40.4.**

STEP 3: ADD MULTIPLE FILTERS

- From the menu, choose **Effects ➢ Video Filters ➢ Distort ➢ Pond Ripple.**
- From the menu, choose **Effects ➢ Video Filters ➢ Distort ➢ Whirlpool.**
- From the menu, choose **Effects ➢ Video Filters ➢ Distort ➢ Fisheye.**

As you see in **Figure 40.5**, you just applied three radically different video filters to a single object in the video channel of this clip.

40.4

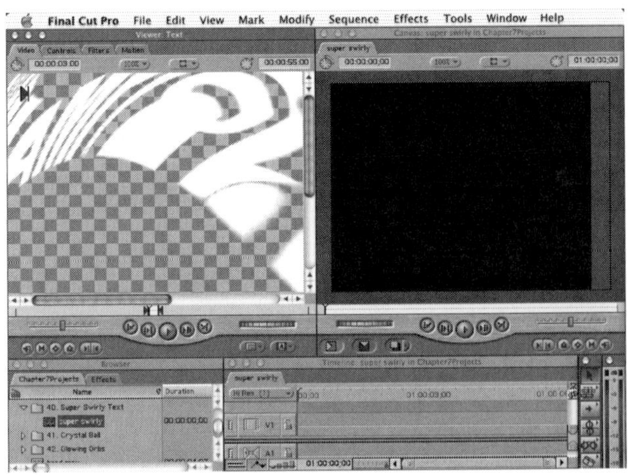

40.5

STEP 4: KEYFRAME AND ADJUST

■ Move the play head to the beginning of the clip in the **video** window.

■ Click the **Filters** tab and set a **keyframe** for all of the **Pond Ripple**, **Whirlpool**, and **Fisheye** settings in this particular moment of time by clicking the keyframe button for each of the following values. Set the following values as shown in **Figure 40.6**:

Pond Ripple:

Keyframe the Radius value at 100.
Keyframe the Ripple field value at 12.
Keyframe the Amplitude value at 22.

Whirlpool:

Keyframe the Whirlpool Amount value at 360.

Fisheye:

Keyframe the Fisheye Radius value at 200 and the Amount at 100.

STEP 5: KEYFRAME AND CORRECT

■ Go to the **video** window and use the down-arrow key to move the play head to the end of the 3-second clip.

■ Click to select the **Filters** tab and keyframe this moment in time by settting keyframes for all of the settings with a value of zero (as shown in **Figure 40.7**):

Pond Ripple:

Keyframe the Radius value at 0.
Keyframe the Ripple field value at 1.
Keyframe the Amplitude value at 0.

Whirlpool:

Keyframe the Whirlpool Amount value at 0.

Fisheye:

Keyframe the Fisheye Radius value at 0 and the Amount at 0.

The result here is that over the course of three seconds, this text clip morphs itself from something totally unrecognizable back to a readable piece of text.

STEP 6: ADD THE TYPE TO THE SEQUENCE

■ Click the **Video** tab again to show your video clip in its original form.

■ Click and drag this clip into the **canvas** window and choose the **Insert** overlay.

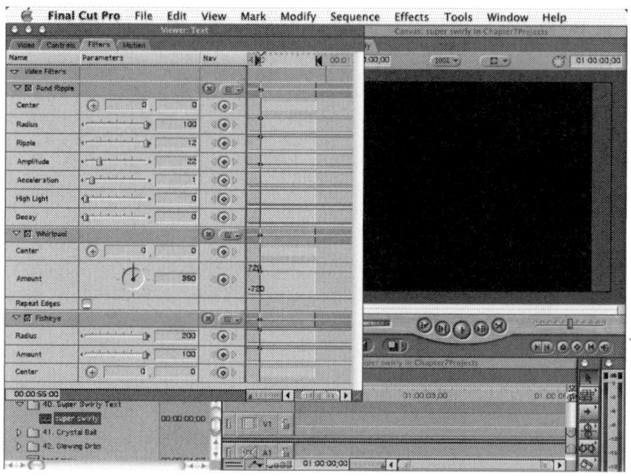

40.6

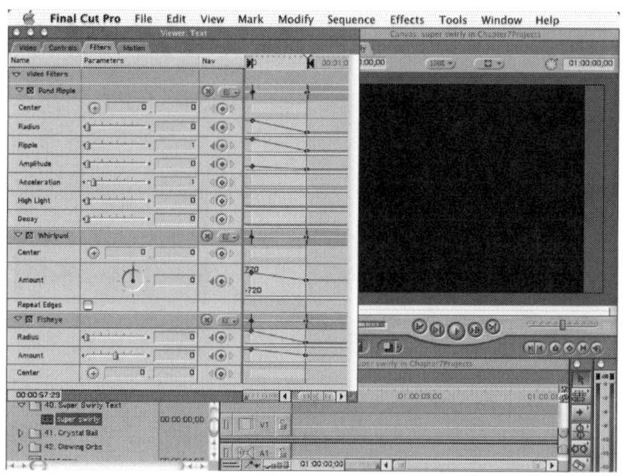

40.7

- Preview this clip by dragging the play head back and forth in the **canvas** window. (If your machine has a less robust processor and memory configuration, you may have to force the preview render by using the **Option** key while you drag the play head to force Final Cut Pro to render this clip a frame at a time.)
- **Figure 40.8** shows how this text clip transforms from something unrecognizable to a clean and readable portion of text.

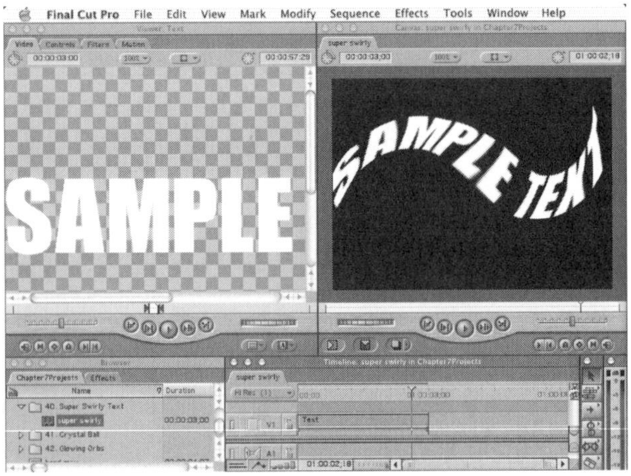

40.8

STEP 7: DRAG THE CLIP INTO THE PROJECT BIN

- Click in the center of the **Video** tab of the **viewer** window and drag the frame down into the project bin. Release the mouse button when the Super Swirly Text folder icon highlights.
- You will see an icon appear in your bin that says **Text**. Rename that icon to **Swirly Text**.

Figure 40.9 shows the results of this step.

TIP

One of the benefits of this technique is that the text remains live with all of the transition and filter effects applied to it as it is saved in your bin. To reproduce it, all you do is drag the icon into the timeline as often as is needed. When you need to save it, just drag the frame preview from the video window, down into your bin.

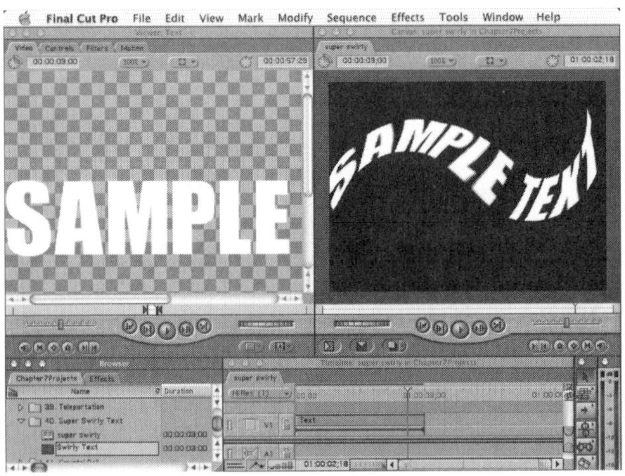

40.9

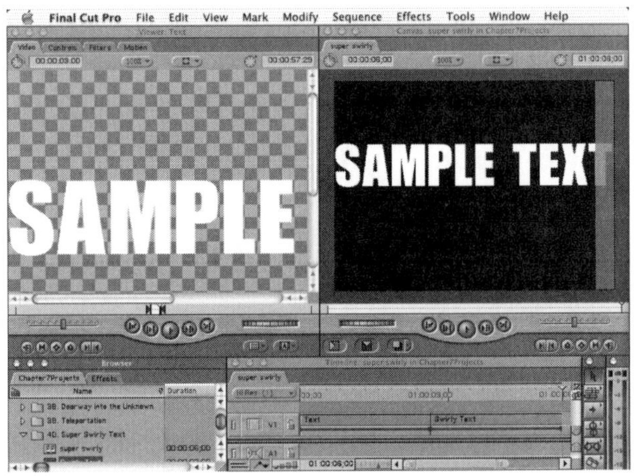

40.10

STEP 8: ADD YOUR NEW ICON TO THE TIMELINE

- Click the **Swirly Text** icon that you have just created and drag it onto the timeline window as shown in **Figure 49.10**.
- Place it at the end of the original clip that was already there by allowing it to snap to that location. You should now have two identical clips occurring in sequence.

STEP 9: EDIT THE TEXT OF THE SECOND CLIP

- In your timeline, double-click on the second clip. You can see it in the viewer window.
- Click the **Controls** tab. Replace the text that reads **Sample Text** with the words **Swirly Text**. You see that change instantly made in your canvas window as shown in **Figure 40.11**.
- If you scrub your play head back and forth by using the Option and arrow keys, you will see that the same video effect is applied to the text that now reads Swirly Text.

STEP 10: RENDER THE CLIP

- From the **Sequence** menu, choose **Render All** (shown in **Figure 40.12**) to save your movie with the new effect applied.

This technique takes an interesting twist on the application of special effects. Instead of applying a filter and transition that occurs over time, the filter and transition happens in reverse.

The real advantage of this technique is that you can save this clip and re-apply it to any video track maintaining all of the filter applications. So for example, you could change the text to a group of new words or make changes to the typeface or size of the text. The filters remain intact and are applied to the text changes that have taken place.

40.11

40.12

TECHNIQUE **41**

LOOK INTO THE CRYSTAL BALL

41.1 (CP53)

41.2 (CP54)

This technique is another matte window overlay, except the difference with this one is that you use a distortion filter in addition to the matte window that allows the video inset window to appear spherical. Applying it is easy and generally fun to accomplish.

How often do you need to consult the wisdom of a mystical crystal ball in your video projects? Here's a technique that shows you how to create your own mystical crystal ball effect by using a common snow-globe souvenir. The technique is easily customizable. You can place anyone's head, any special effect, and any mystical response emanating from any common mystical crystal ball.

For this demonstration, I consult the very wise and sage Dalmatian for advice from a mystical snow-globe, which as we all know, is almost a like a real crystal ball.

STEP 1: OPEN THE PROJECT FILE

- Make sure that any previous project tabs are closed.
- In your **Chapter 7 Projects** folder, find the **Crystal Ball** sequence.
- Double-click on the **Crystal Ball** sequence icon to open the sequence.
- You see in **Figure 41.3** the base video clip is already inserted into the timeline for you.

41.3

41.4

STEP 2: ADD THE MYSTICAL HEAD

- Move the play head in the timeline window to the 4-second point in the timeline.
- You can do this quickly and efficiently by double-clicking in the **Timecode** field in the lower-left corner of the **timeline** window and typing in the number **4**, then a **;** (semicolon), and either **Enter** or **Return**.
- Click and drag the clip media item **thesage.mov** into the timeline placing its left edge at the location of the play head in the V2 video track. When you do, it should snap into place.
- Release the mouse button when the cursor changes to a down-facing arrow.

Your workspace should look like the one shown in **Figure 41.4**.

STEP 3: CREATE THE MATTE WINDOW

- Double-click the **video clip** in the **V2** video track to see it in the **viewer** window.
- From the menu, choose **Effects ➢ Video Filters ➢ Matte ➢ Mask Shape.**
- Change the settings for that filter by clicking the **Filters** tab in the **viewer** window and change the shape to **oval.**
- Change the **Horizontal Scale** to **55** and the **Vertical Scale** to **88** as you see in **Figure 41.5.**

STEP 4: FEATHER THE MATTE WINDOW

- Double-click the **video clip** in the **V2** video track to see it in the **viewer** window.
- From the menu, choose **Effects ➢ Video Filters ➢ Matte ➢ Mask Feather.**
- Click on the **Filters** tab of the **viewer** window, and set the **Soft** value to **33** as you see in **Figure 41.6.**

STEP 5: SPHERIZE

Now to warp the face of the sage a little bit.

- Double-click the **video clip** in the **V2** video track to see it in the **viewer** window.
- Make the image look as if it is wrapped around the inside of the sphere.
- From the menu, choose **Effects ➢ Video Filters ➢ Distort ➢ Fisheye.**
- Make the settings for this effect in the **Filter** tab as follows**: Radius: 33**, **Amount: 22** as shown in **Figure 41.7**.

STEP 6: RESIZE THE SAGE

- Click to select the clip in the V2 video track.
- Enable the wire frame handles, by using either the keyboard shortcut **W**, or choose **View ➢ Image + Wireframe**.
- Click and drag any corner handle towards the center of the frame.
- Click the **Motion** tab in the **viewer** window and enter the following values (as shown in **Figure 41.8**): **Scale**: **52**, **Center**: **–3**, **31**.

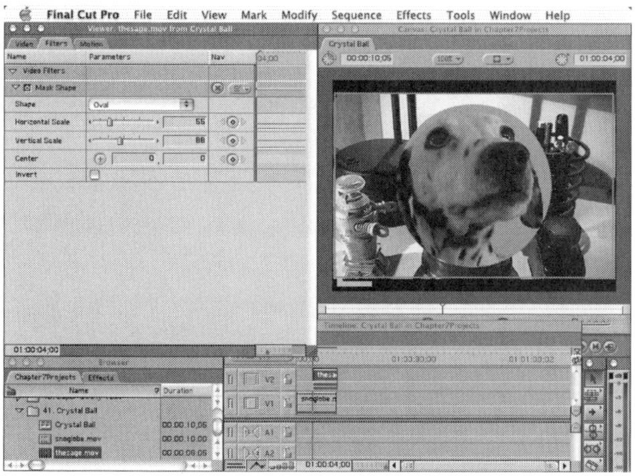

41.5

41.6

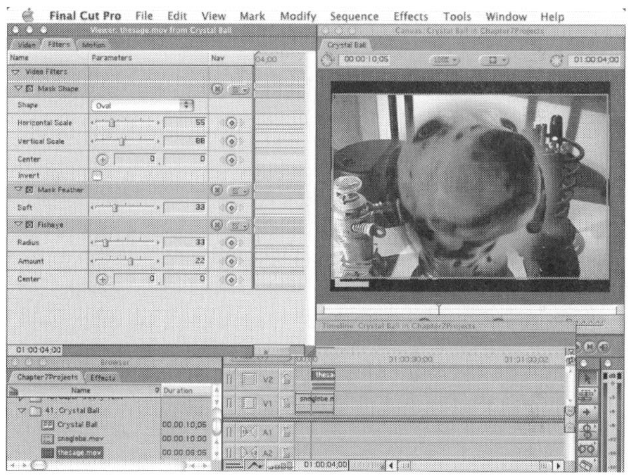

41.7

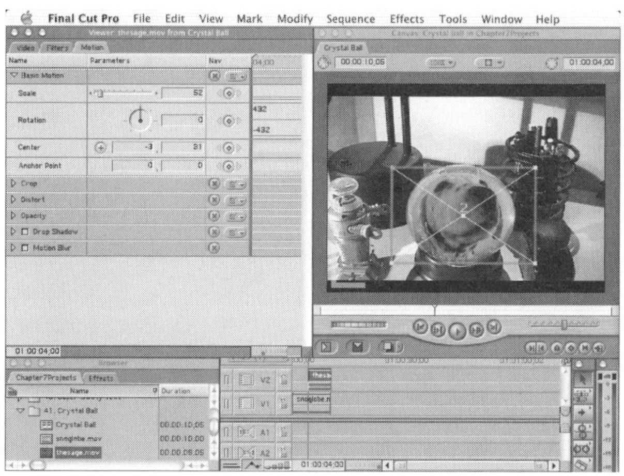

41.8

41.9

NOTE

Your work space layout may be a little different from the one shown here. You may want to separate the Effects tab from the browser window to easily drag filter effects onto your clips.

41.10

STEP 7: FADE IN, FADE OUT

- Of course your mystical sage head should appear gradually. The Final Cut Pro 3 dissolve transition effect is easily applied here.
- Display the **effects** window. From the menu, choose **Window ➢ Effects** (or use the keyboard shortcut Command-5).
- Open the **Video transitions** bin and then open the **Dissolve** bin.
- Drag the **Cross Dissolve** icon onto the left edge of the clip in the V2 video track.
- Drag the **Cross Dissolve** icon onto the right edge of the clip in the V2 video track as you see in **Figure 41.9**.

Final Cut Pro dissolves the appearance and disappearance of the matte window video data.

STEP 8: RENDER THE CLIP

- From the **Sequence** menu, choose **Render All** as shown in **Figure 41.10** to see results of the changes that you made.
- After finished, close this project tab by Control-clicking on the tab name or use the keyboard shortcut **Control-W**.

In this technique you learned to combine a filter and a matte mask to create a unique special effect that fits in well with any video presentation. Best of all, the tools to create the effect exist entirely within Final Cut Pro 3. You can wrap an image around any spherical round object and make it believable!

TECHNIQUE 42

GLOWING ORBS

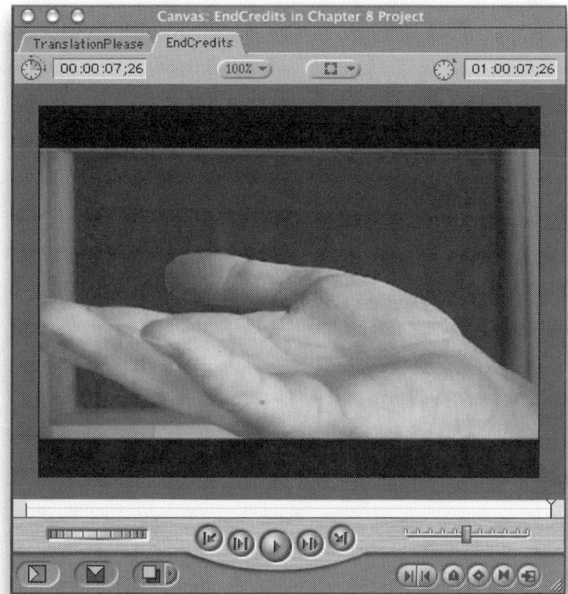

42.1 (CP55)

42.2 (CP56)

Making glowing orbs that float across any video scene is another great technique. Glowing orbs are easy and dramatic, and best of all, Final Cut Pro contains all the tools you need to accomplish this.

STEP 1: OPEN THE PROJECT FOLDER

■ Open the **Chapter 7 Projects** folder. If you have any previous project tabs open in the timeline, close them now to avoid any confusion as you progress through this technique.

■ Locate and open the bin called **Glowing Orbs**.

■ Double-click the bin to open the sequence **Glowing Orbs**. As shown in **Figure 42.3**, you now see this clip in your timeline window.

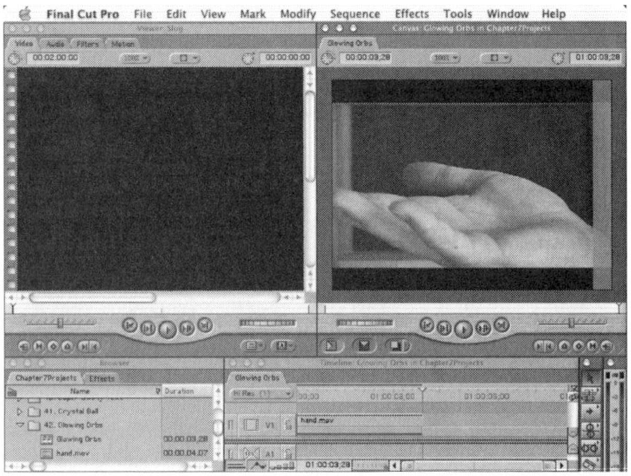

42.3

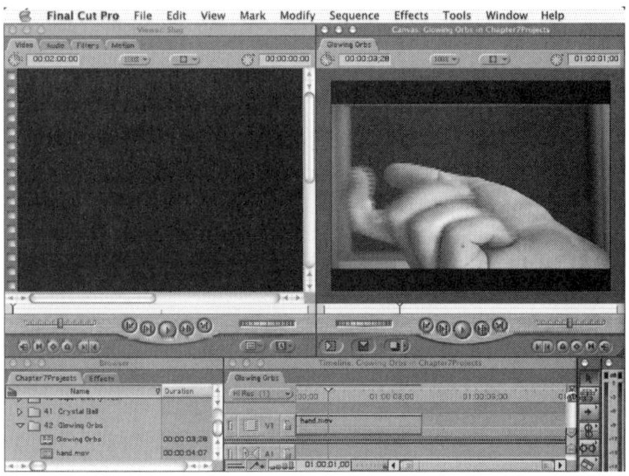

42.4

STEP 2: PLAY THROUGH THE CLIP

■ Move the play head to the 1-second mark on your timeline as shown in **Figure 42.4**. This section is where your glowing orb will appear.

STEP 3: DUPLICATE THE CLIP

■ Click to select the clip in the V1 video track.

■ Hold down the **Option** and **Shift** keys while you drag the clip up to create an additional video track, a copy of the selected track, into V2 as shown in **Figure 42.5**.

STEP 4: ADD A FAKE LIGHT SOURCE

■ Double-click to view the **V2** video track in the **viewer** window.

■ From the menu, choose **Effects ➢ Video Filters ➢ Matte ➢ Mask Shape**.

■ From the menu again, choose **Effects ➢ Video Filters ➢ Matte ➢ Mask Feather**.

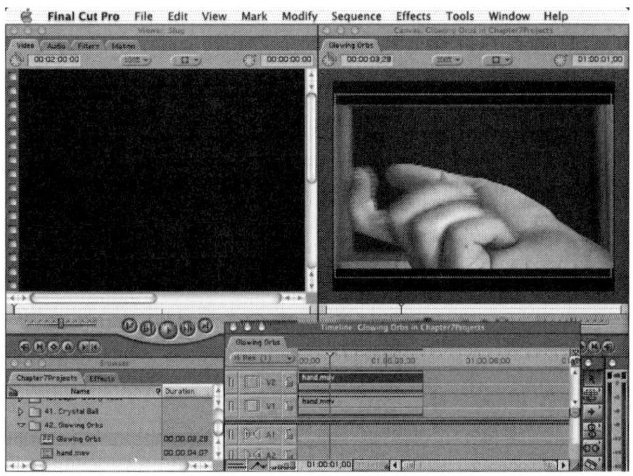

42.5

- Click the **Filters** tab to set keyframes for the following attributes:
  Horizontal Scale: 34
  Vertical Scale: 39
  Shape: Oval
  Softness: 55
- From the menu, choose **Effects ➢ Video Filters ➢ Image Control ➢ Brightness and Contrast**.
- In the **Filters** menu of the **viewer** window, change the Brightness to **33**, and the Contrast to **33** as well.

As you see in **Figure 42.6**, these settings give the illusion of a small, feathered area that has been more brightly lit than its surroundings.

STEP 5: TRANSITION VISIBILITY

- Click the **Motions** tab in the **viewer** window.
- In the **Opacity** setting, keyframe and set the value to **0**.
- Move the play head to the **1-second, 11-frames** position of the clip by using the **timecode** field in the **canvas** window.
- Create another keyframe and set the value to **100** as shown in **Figure 42.7**. This setting causes the Lighting effect to transition and gradually brighten over time.

STEP 6: MAKE THE ORB

- Move the play head back to the original entry point at **1-second** in the timeline.
- In the **Video** tab, click the **Video Generator** button in the **viewer** window and choose **Shape ➢ Circle**.
- Click the **Controls** tab,and set the following:
  Size: 33%
  Softness: 2%
  Color: Hue 66, Saturation 22, V 100
  Duration: 3-seconds

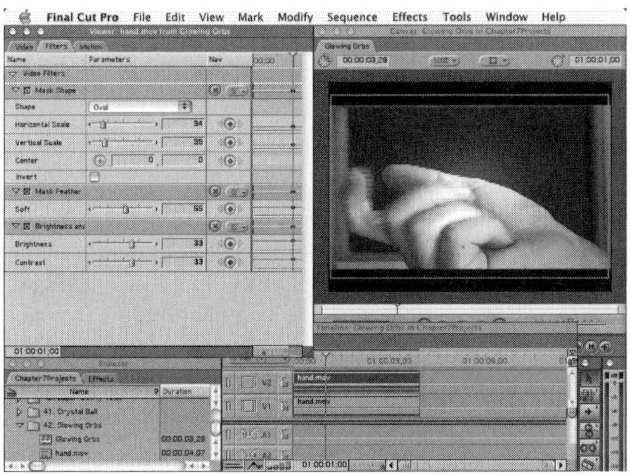

42.6

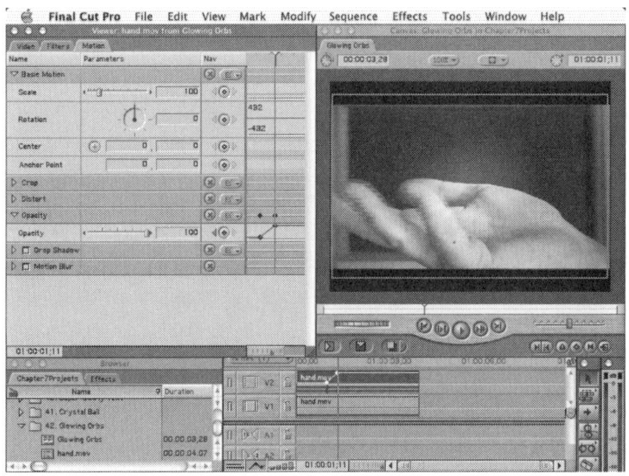

42.7

- Click the **Video** tab in the **viewer** window and drag the thumbnail down into the bin, which creates a new clip in the **Glowing Orbs** bin that is automatically titled **Circle**.
- Double-click on the thumbnail currently named **Circle** and change its name to **Orb**.

Figure 42.8 shows the results of these instructions.

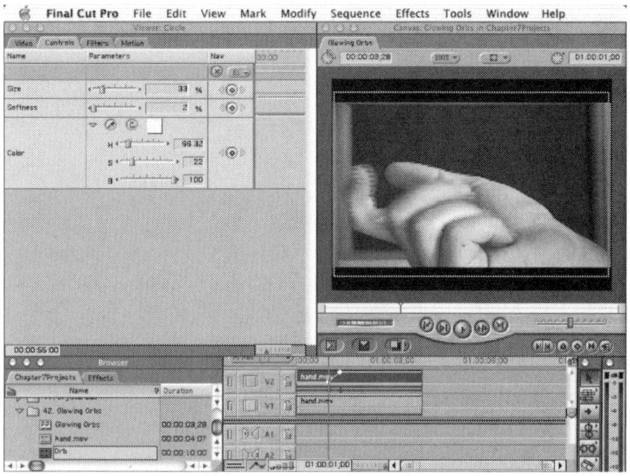

42.8

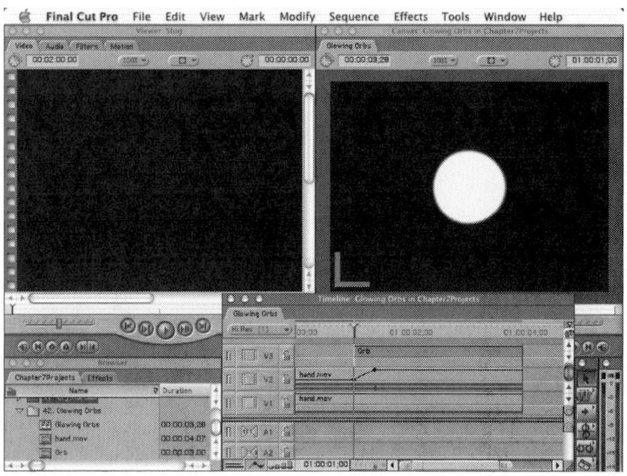

42.9

STEP 7: ADD THE ORB TO THE TIMELINE

- Click and drag the orb onto the timeline. Watch for the cursor to change to a down-facing arrow and release the mouse button when the left edge of the clip snaps at the play head location at 1-second in the timeline. You also create a new video track, V3, as shown in **Figure 42.9**.

STEP 8: TRANSITION THE APPEARANCE OF THE ORB

- Move the play head to the start of the orb clip.
- Click the **Motion** tab and choose the **Scale** setting.
- Click the **Keyframe** button and set the scale to **0**.
- Move the play head to the end of the clip by using the down-arrow key shortcut on your keyboard.
- Click the **Keyframe** button and set the size to **100** as shown in **Figure 42.10**.

Now the orb appears to magically grow out of thin air.

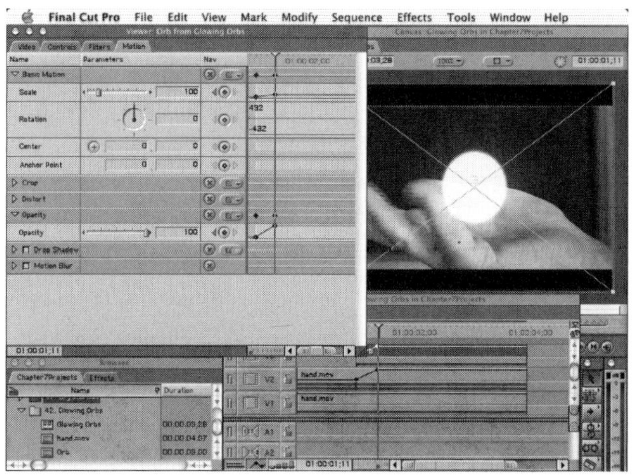

42.10

STEP 9: RENDER THE CLIP

- From the **Sequence** menu, choose **Render All** as shown in **Figure 42.11** to see results of the changes that you made.
- After finished, close this project tab by Control-clicking on the tab name or use the keyboard shortcut **Control-W**.

As in any additive illusory technique, manipulating your base video track aids in completing a believable simulation. In this case, you added a matte window with a contrast and brightness change that simulated an additional light source or a glow around the artificial orb that you added. Enhancing this technique is easy by moving the orb and the lighting effect across time with a Motion tab.

42.11

CHAPTER **8**

ADVANCED TEXT AND TILTING TECHNIQUES

Stylish application of simple text treatments in your video project can add a professional flair. This chapter introduces some easy-to-accomplish special effects using the Final Cut Pro built-in text tools combined with some techniques and effects you already know.

Textual information in a video presentation can enhance your video presentation as a supplemental caption to the video information, as a complete informational presentation, or as a completely stylized video matte window.

Follow along with the steps and see how these simple enhancements can change the overall look and feel of your video projects.

Advanced Text
Jitter!
Scrolling text
Subtitles...
Fuzzy Drop Shadows
Three Dimensional Text
Crawling Text
a long time ago, in a galaxy far, far away,
The exciting view from above...

TEXT CRAWLS

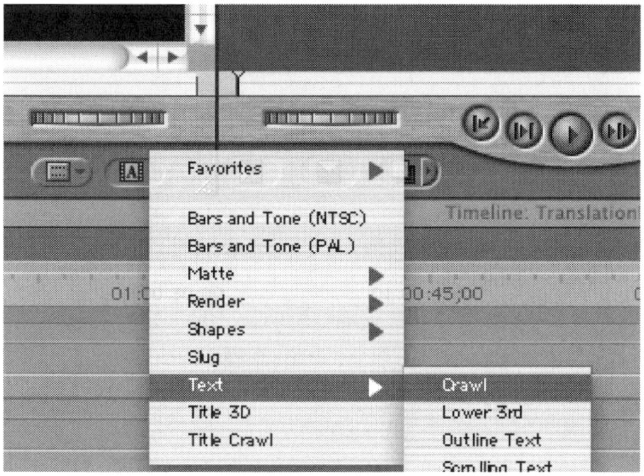

43.1

43.2

Text crawls are a useful style-technique that adds a kind of news-feed look to your video clip. Text crawls can contain and present informational data to your clips and give a feeling of urgency or data transmission.

The technique shown here shows you how to introduce a simple line of text that crawls horizontally across the screen as your main video message plays.

Text crawls are useful to present supplemental textual information without creating an overt distraction from the video information.

NOTE

Don't confuse crawling text with scrolling text. A text "crawl" displays text as a single line of text moving horizontally across the video frame. "Scrolling" text moves a column of text vertically up or down the video frame.

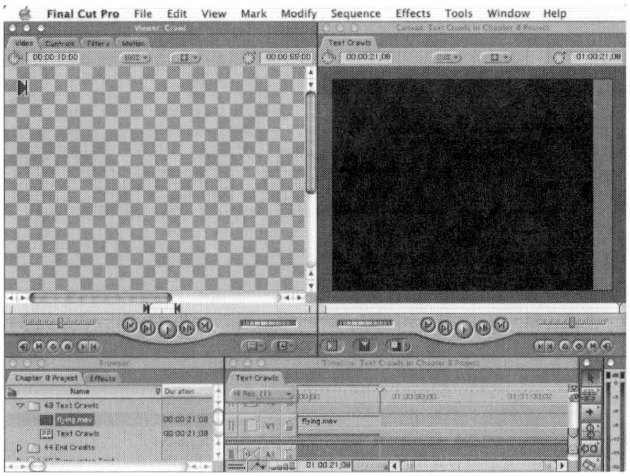

43.3

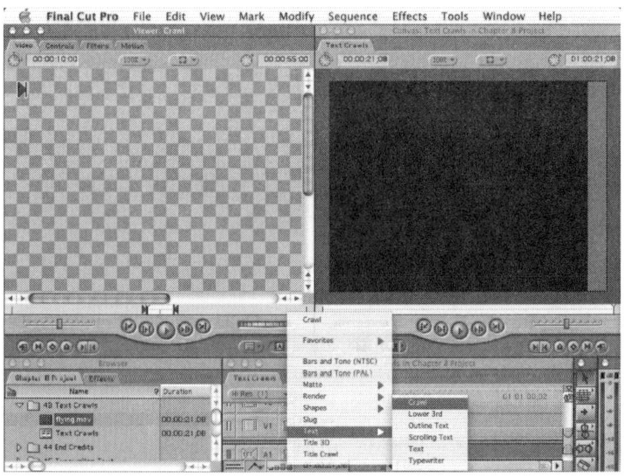

43.4

STEP 1: OPEN THE FILE

- Make sure you close any previously opened project tabs.
- Look for the bin called **Text Crawls** in the Chapter 8 Projects folder.
- In the bin, you find the Text crawl Timeline sequence in **Figure 43.4** in which you build your crawling text information.
- Double-click the **Text Crawls** sequence icon to display it in the timeline window. You see that there is a clip already there called **flying.mov**.

STEP 2: CREATE THE CRAWLING TEXT

- Click the **Video Generator** icon in the **viewer** window and use the pop-up menu to choose **Text ➢ Crawl** to create the text as you see in **Figure 43.4**.
- Final Cut Pro then creates an automated text crawl effect that waits for you to insert your text message

TIP

Add spacing if your font is compressed and hard to read at the size you specified. This demonstration has it set to 5. Remember for most people, moving text is a little harder to read than static text.

STEP 3: DEFINE THE TEXT OBJECT ATTRIBUTES

- Click the **Controls** tab to expose the text attributes and their controls.
- Type the following words of wisdom into the text field: **It is far better to be down here wishing you were up there, than up there wishing you were down here . . . Launches are optional, landings are mandatory . . .**
- Set the Font type to **Arial**.
- Set the size of the type to **36**.
- Set the style to **plain**. (You can change the color easily, but for this demonstration, leave it white.)
- Set the location to **95**.
- Leave the direction on Left.

Figure 43.5 shows all of these settings in place.

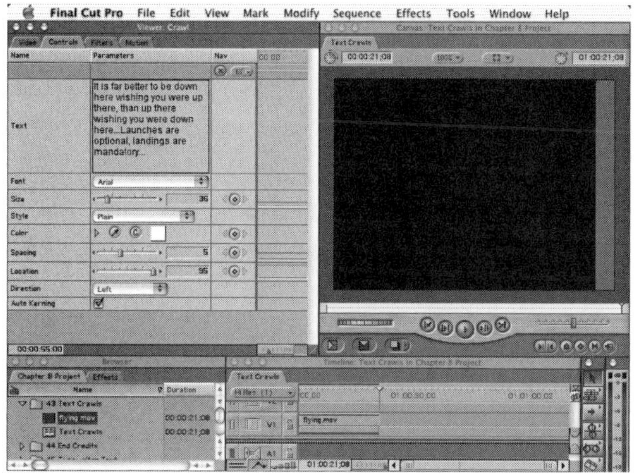

43.5

STEP 4: ADD THE CRAWLING TEXT TO THE BIN AS AN OBJECT

- Click the **Video** tab to display the video preview of the effect. (You won't see anything in this window because the text begins and ends off-screen.)
- Click and drag from the center of this window down into the **Text Crawls** project bin. Release the mouse button after the bin icon highlights.
- You now see a new icon in the bin labeled **crawl.** Click the name of the icon to select and change its name to something more intuitive and relevant to your project. For this demonstration, change it to **flight rules text** as shown in **Figure 43.6**.

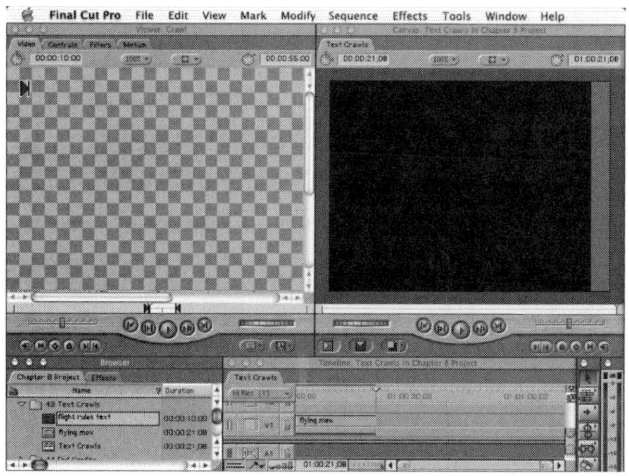

43.6

> **NOTE**
>
> **You can change the direction of the crawl as well. In western cultures, text is read as it crawls to the left, in eastern cultures on the other hand, text crawls to the right.**

> **NOTE**
>
> **If you've left the wireframe view on from previous projects, you should turn it off for this step.**

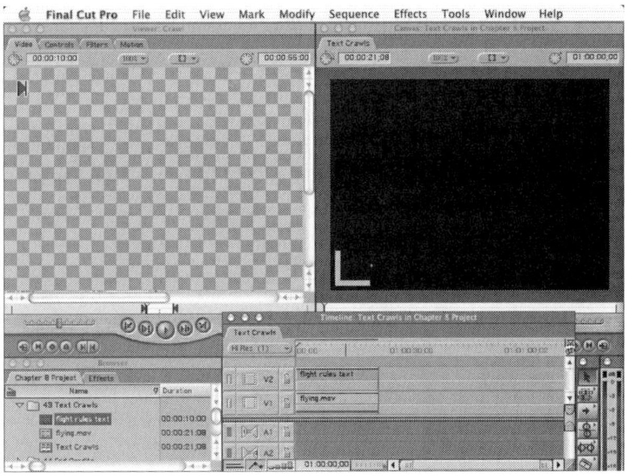

43.7

43.8

STEP 5: ADD THE CRAWL TO THE TIMELINE

- Set the play head to the beginning of the clip in the timeline.
- Click and drag the **Flight Rules** text clip icon from the browser window onto the canvas window and choose the **Superimpose** overlay after it's presented.
- You see a new video track added to the timeline labeled **V2** containing the crawling text as shown in **Figure 43.7**.

STEP 6: PREVIEW THE EFFECT

- You can see a rough preview of the effect by using the left and right arrow keys to scrub the play head back and forth across the timeline one frame at a time. You can also drag the play head in the timeline back and forth.
- Final Cut Pro renders and displays each frame of the video in sequence. **Figure 43.8** shows how this point in your progress might look.

NOTE

Like any other clip media item, you can set the duration for the clip. Final Cut Pro treats the item as a static media type, even though the contents of the media has motion. In this example, the flying.mopv clip is 20+ seconds long, and the default still media duration is 10-seconds, so there won't be any issues when importing this clip item into the sequence's timeline. If you're ever faced with an error message saying "Insufficient content for edit," the secret is to adjust the duration of the imported clip to be the same as or shorter in duration than the media already in the timeline.

STEP 7: FINE-TUNE THE TEXT ATTRIBUTES

After you add crawling text to your timeline, you can still easily edit it.

- Double-click the text item in the **V2** video track in the timeline window.
- Click to display the **Controls** tab in the **viewer** window, as shown in **Figure 43.9**.
- Make your incremental changes to any of the text attributes and see them instantly applied in the preview of the canvas window.

43.9

STEP 8: PREVIEW AGAIN AND RENDER THE CLIP

- Using the arrow key shortcut, preview your changes as you make them to see that they are working with your video project.
- Choose **Sequence ➢ Render All,** as shown in **Figure 43.10** to finish the project.

Adding a text crawl can add a feeling of urgency or simple data transmission to any video clip. This demonstration shows you how to add a line of text that crawls across the screen horizontally as your video plays through.

You can use this technique to present information as a data stream, a closed captioned text description service, or to supplement the information presented in the video without creating overt distraction to the video information.

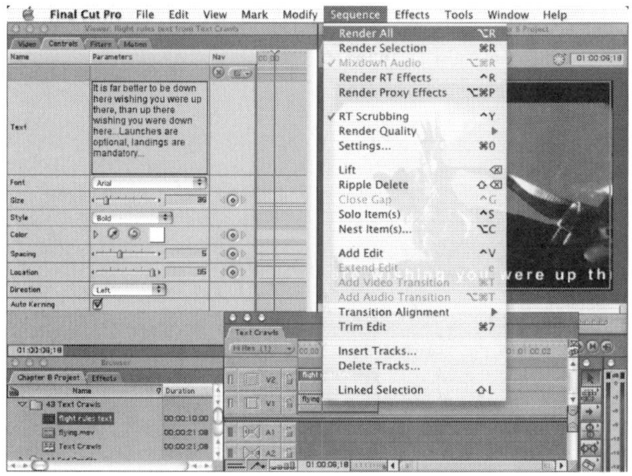

43.10

NOTE

Final Cut Pro calculates the speed of the crawl based on the length of the text crawl clip. You can control this by keyframing the beginning and ending points of the crawling text in the timeline.

TECHNIQUE 44

SCROLLING TEXT

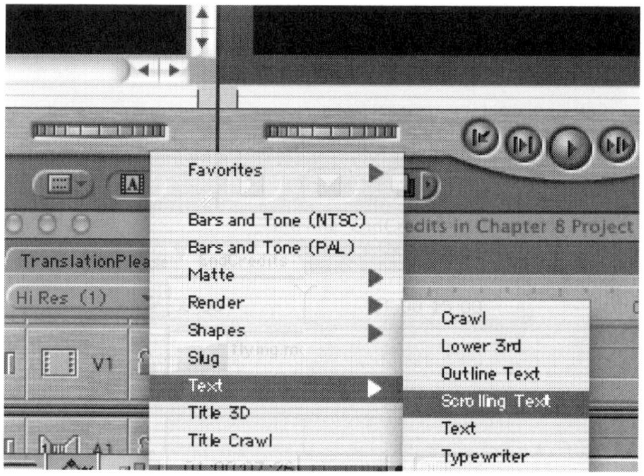

44.1

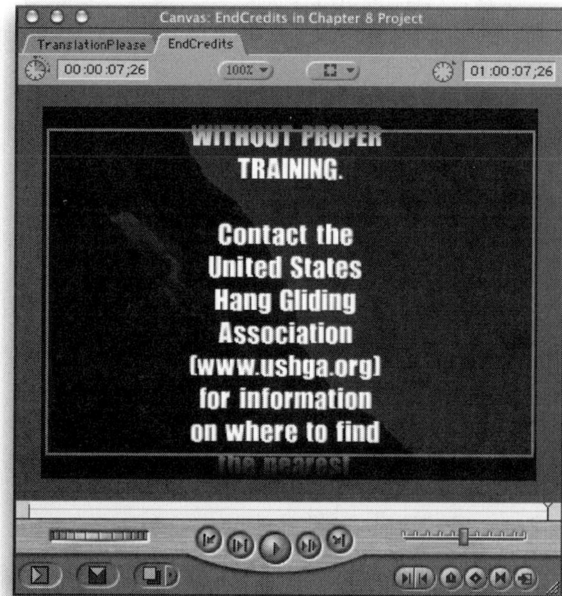

44.2

Scrolling text is an effect where a column of text "scrolls" vertically up your video frame area. Scrolling text is commonly seen at the end of a movie where the credits for the production are displayed.

Final Cut Pro affords you precision and control in the placement and execution of scrolling text in your video projects. This demonstration shows you how to easily apply the effect over any video clip and control the effect.

44.3

44.4

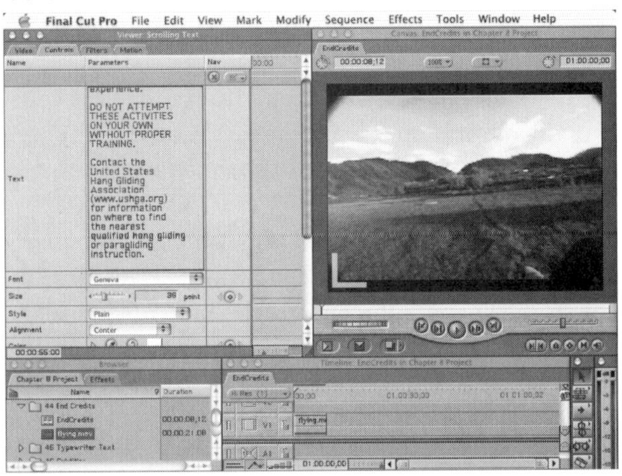

44.5

STEP 1: OPEN THE SAMPLE PROJECT

- Make sure you close any previously opened project tabs.
- Look for the bin labeled **End Credits** in the Chapter 8 Project folder.
- Open the file and double-click the **End Credits** timeline icon to view it in the timeline window as seen in **Figure 44.3**.

STEP 2: CREATE SCROLLING TEXT FOR THE CLIP

- Create a scrolling text effect by using the auto-generator pop-up menu in the viewer window.
- From the menu, choose **Text ➢ Scrolling Text** as shown in **Figure 44.4**.

STEP 3: ADD YOUR TEXT CONTENT

- In the **viewer** window, click the **Controls** tab.
- Because your end credits can be somewhat lengthy due to the amount of information being displayed, you may want to cut and paste text into the text field in the controls tab window.
- From your Desktop or Finder, find the text file in your sample files folder called **ScrollingText.txt**.
- Open the file using any text-editing program. If you're using OSX, then it will automatically open with TextEdit. If you using OS9, then the file will open with SimpleText. Any other text-editing application, such as AppleWorks or Microsoft Word, will work as well.
- Select all of the text by either choosing **Edit ➢ Select All** or Command-A, and then choose **Edit ➢ Copy**. The text is now on the clipboard and ready to paste into the Final Cut Pro viewer window's Control tab.
- Click in the **text field** of the **Controls** tab and choose **Edit ➢ Paste**. You see the text automatically flow into the text field as in **Figure 44.5**.

STEP 4: ADJUST THE SCROLLING TEXT ATTRIBUTES

- Set the text attributes to the following, as shown in **Figure 44.6**:

  Font: Impact (it's bold and impactful)
  Size: 36 points
  Style: plain
  Alignment: Center
  Color: Use white for this demonstration to stand out against all the colors present in the video clip.
  Spacing: 1
  Leading: 0%
  Indent: 10%
  Gap Width: 5%
  Fade size: 11%
  Direction: Up

STEP 5: ADD THE SCROLLING TEXT OBJECT TO YOUR BIN

Click the **Video** tab of the **viewer** window and drag the video frame from the viewer window down into the **End Credits** bin, releasing the mouse button when the **End Credits** bin icon is highlighted.

- You see a new icon, called **Scrolling Text**, created in the End Credits bin. Click to highlight the name of the icon and change it to **scrolling disclaimer** as shone in **Figure 44.7**.

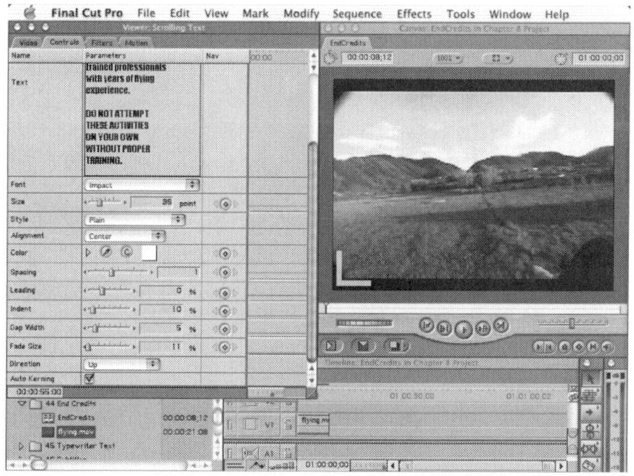

44.6

44.7

TIP

A note of caution about sans-serif versus serif type faces. Serifed type faces are the fonts you see with little "feet" that rest on the baseline of a line of text and at the end of the vertical stroke in text characters. Given the resolution of today's television and video monitors, serif fonts will likely be hard to read at smaller sizes. It's a good practice to use sans serif fonts for video. It's easier to read, especially when it's moving.

44.8

44.9

STEP 6: ADD THE TEXT OBJECT TO THE TIMELINE

- Click and drag the Scrolling Disclaimer icon into the canvas window and choose the superimpose overlay when presented.

You see that the clip is added to the timeline in a new video track labeled **V2**, and the clip automatically fills the timeline for the length of the base clip as shown in **Figure 44.8**.

STEP 7: PREVIEW THE EFFECT

- Click to select the canvas window.
- Use the left- and right-facing arrow keys to move the play head back and forth. This forces the play head to scrub over your video clips, which causes Final Cut Pro to render each frame of the clip as shown in **Figure 44.9**. You can also use your mouse to drag the play head back and forth.

STEP 8: ADJUST THE LENGTH OF THE SCROLLING CLIP

- To emphasize the information in the scrolling text, you can extend the scrolling text beyond the end of the base video track in V1 until it changes to the split-arrow cursor, indicating that you can now select the edge of the clip.
- Click and drag the right edge of the scrolling text clip to the right, extending the length of the clip beyond the end of the video clip in V1 of the timeline track.
- Extending the clip length allows the scrolling text to play against a black background beyond the end of the video clip that it is superimposed over. When there is no video image present, Final Cut Pro renders text effects on a black background by default. **Figure 44.10** shows this effect.

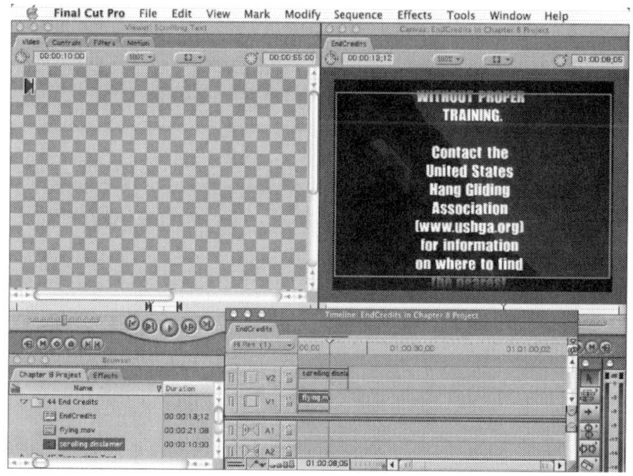

44.10

STEP 9: PREVIEW AND RENDER THE FINAL EFFECT

- Choose **Sequence ➢ Render All** as shown in **Figure 44.11** to preview and render the final effect again and to render the entire clip with the effect in place.

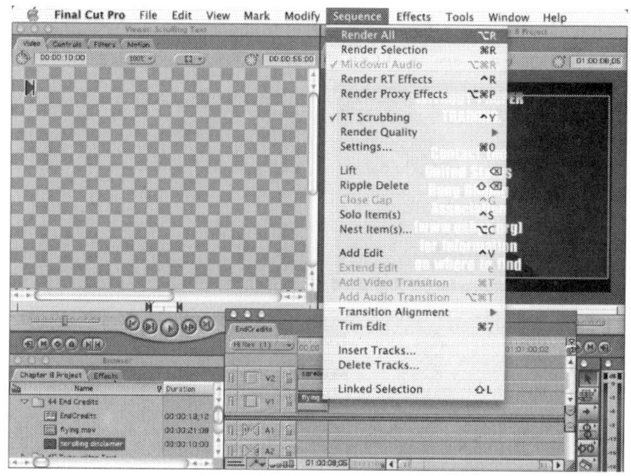

44.11

Scrolling text is an easy-to-accomplish and easy-to-control effect that lends a movie-like feeling to your video project. You can use scrolling text to convey large volumes of information as it can be displayed in a columnar format, filling the video frame while you can control the speed of the scroll.

TECHNIQUE 45

TYPEWRITER TEXT

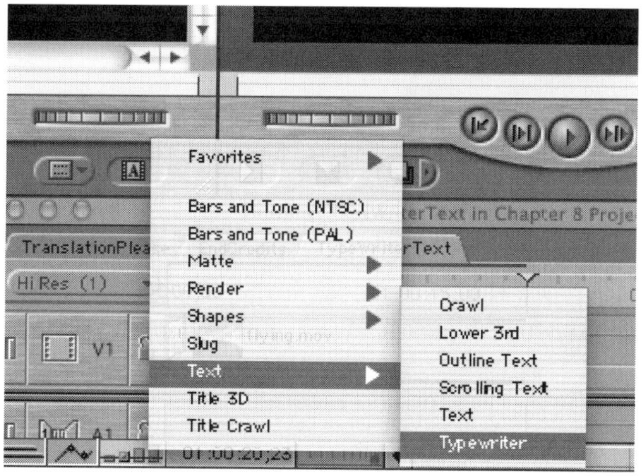

45.1

45.2

This technique demonstrates a rather stylized presentation of text. In this example, the typewriter text video filter automates a simple text-animation technique and adds a level of character to your video presentation.

Final Cut Pro allows you to create this typewriter effect in a few short and simple steps. In this demonstration, I show you how to insert several typewriter text clips and control the pacing of the typed characters.

45.3

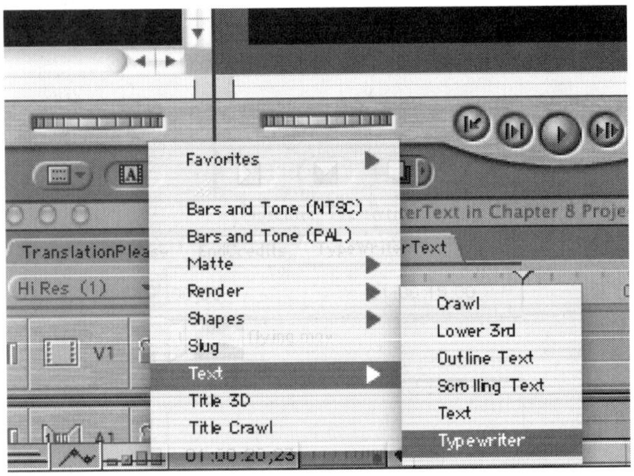

45.4

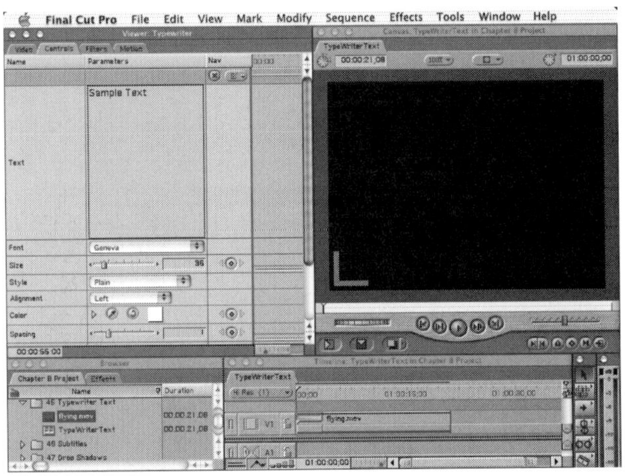

45.5

STEP 1: OPEN THE FILE

- Make sure you close any other previously opened project tabs.
- In the Chapter 8 Project folder, look for the bin titled **Typewriter Text**.
- In the **browser** window, double-click on **Typewriter Text** sequence icon to load it into your timeline window as shown in **Figure 45.3**.

STEP 2: CREATE A TYPEWRITER TEXT EFFECT

- Click the **Video Generator** button in the **viewer** window. Choose **Text ➢ Typewriter**, as shown in **Figure 45.4**.
- Click to display the **Controls** tab in the **viewer** window as shown in **Figure 45.5**.

STEP 3: SET YOUR FIRST TEXT CLIP ATTRIBUTES

- Click to display the **Controls** tab in the **viewer** window.
- In the text field, type the words **The Sky**.
- Set the font to **Courier** (looks like a typewriter) and apply the following attributes:

  Size: 66
  Style: Bold
  Color: White
  Spacing: 1
  Location: 50
  Indent: 10
  Pause: 20

■ Click to expose the **Video** tab in the **viewer** window.
■ Click and drag the thumbnail preview of the typewriter clip into the Typewriter Text bin on your browser window.
■ Rename the new text icon in the browser window to **thesky** as shown in **Figure 45.6**.

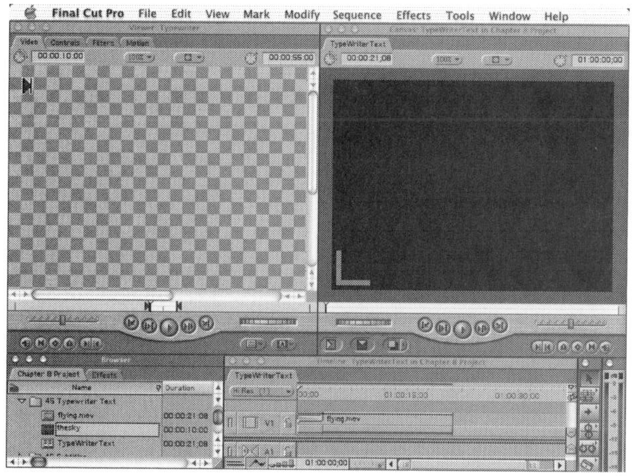

45.6

STEP 4: ADD THE CLIP TO THE TIMELINE

■ Click and drag the new text clip onto the timeline window in **Figure 45.7**.
■ You see the new video track named **V2** appear in the timeline with the typewriter text clip filling the entire duration of the sequence.

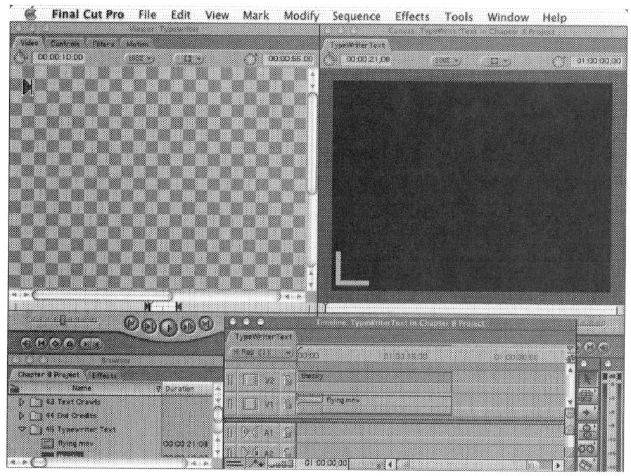

45.7

STEP 5: SET THE DURATION OF THE CLIP

■ Double-click the **typewriter text clip** in the V2 video track of the timeline window.
■ Click the **Video** tab in the **viewer** window.
■ Set the duration of the text effect to **2-seconds** by typing **2** and **;** (semicolon) in the duration field followed by the **Return** key.
■ Now you see that the typewriter clip in **Figure 45.8** is only a short part of the total sequence length.

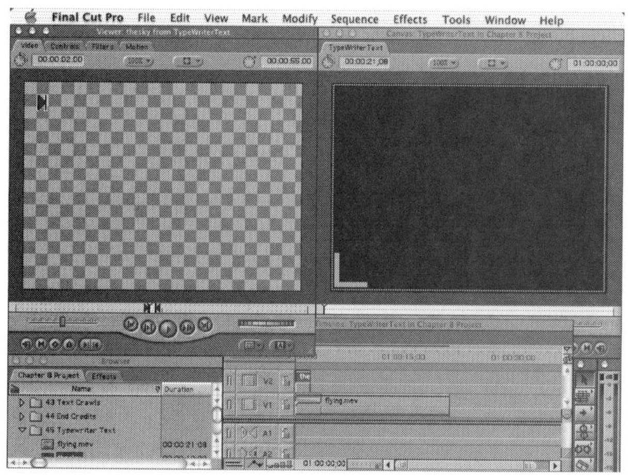

45.8

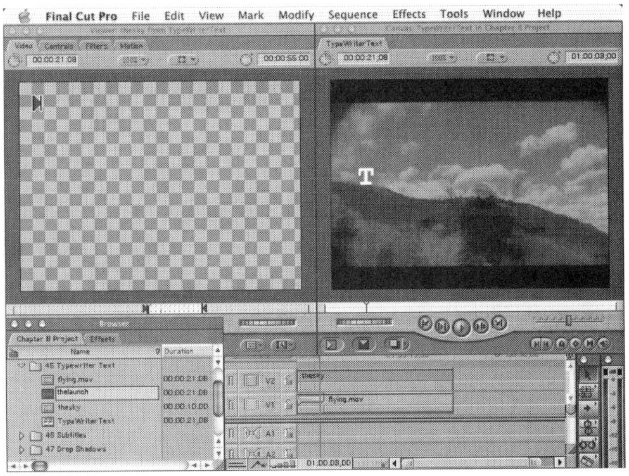

45.9

45.10

45.11

STEP 6: CREATE ANOTHER TEXT CLIP

- In the **viewer** window, click the **Controls** tab.
- Change the text in the text field to **The Launch**.
- Leave all the other text attributes the same.
- Click to expose the Video tab.
- Drag the thumbnail preview of the clip down into the typewriter text bin icon.
- Rename the new text clip item in the bin **thelaunch** as shown in **Figure 45.9.**

STEP 7: ADD THIS CLIP TO THE TIMELINE

- In the canvas window, set the location of the play head to the 3-second point by typing in **3** and **;** (semicolon) into the timecode field and then press the Return key.
- Click and drag the new clip in the bin onto the timeline at the 3-second location of the play head. Release the mouse button when the cursor changes to a down-facing arrow.

STEP 8: CREATE ANOTHER NEW TYPEWRITER TEXT CLIP

- Click in the **Controls** tab again in the viewer window.
- Change the text in the text field to **The Flight**.
- Click the **Video** tab and drag the thumbnail preview down into the Typewriter Text bin.
- Click the name of the new clip item in the bin and change its name to **theflight** as shown in **Figure 45.10.**

TIP

If you have the snapping feature-enabled (keyboard shortcut "n" toggles this feature), then you will have more control over exactly where this clip snaps into place.

STEP 9: ADD THE NEW TYPEWRITER TEXT CLIP TO THE TIMELINE

- In the timeline window in **Figure 45.11**, set the play head location to the **7-second** point by clicking in the timecode field at the lower-left corner of the window and typing in **7** and **;** (semicolon) and then press the **Return** key.
- Click and drag the new clip item **theflight** into the timeline as you did in the previous step. Make sure that the insertion arrow is a down-facing arrow and place the clip onto the V2 video track at the location of the play head, as shown in **Figure 45.12**.

45.12

STEP 10: ANOTHER NEW TYPEWRITER TEXT CLIP

This step repeats the previous step, changing the content of a new text item.

- Click in the **Controls** tab again in the **viewer** window.
- Change the text in the text field to **The Dream**.
- Click the **Video** tab and drag the thumbnail preview down into the Typewriter Text bin.
- Click the name of the new clip item in the bin and change its name to **thedream** as you can see in **Figure 45.13**.

45.13

STEP 11: ADD THE NEW TYPEWRITER TEXT CLIP TO THE TIMELINE

As completed previously, this step duplicates previous steps, adding new content to the text item.

- In the canvas window, set the play head location to the **7-second** point by clicking in the timecode field and typing in **10** and **;** (semicolon), then press the Return key.
- Click and drag the new clip item **thedream** into the timeline as you did in the previous step. Make sure that the insertion arrow is a down-facing arrow and place the clip onto the V2 video track at the location of the play head as **Figure 45.14** shows.

45.14

45.15

45.16

45.17

STEP 12: ONE MORE NEW TYPEWRITER TEXT CLIP

One more clip. Just like the previous steps.

- Click in the **Controls** tab again in the **viewer** window.
- Change the text in the text field to **The Landing**.
- Click the **Video** tab and drag the thumbnail preview down into the Typewriter Text bin.
- Click the name of the new clip item in the bin and change its name to **thelanding** as **Figure 45.15** shows.

STEP 13: ADD THE LAST TYPEWRITER TEXT CLIP TO THE TIMELINE

- In the canvas window, set the play head location to the **7-second** point by clicking in the timecode field and typing in **13** and **;** (semicolon), and then press the **Return** key.
- Click and drag the new clip item **thelanding** into the timeline as you did in the previous step. Make sure the insertion arrow is a down-facing arrow and place the clip onto the V2 video track at the location of the play head as shown in **Figure 45.16**.

STEP 14: PREVIEW AND RENDER THE SEQUENCE

- As **Figure 45.17** shows, choose **Sequence ➢ Render All** to complete this project demonstration.

This technique automates a simple text animation technique, which adds a bit of character to any video presentation. As you see, the technique is easy to produce and execute and provides an informal, artistic enhancement to any text application in Final Cut Pro.

TECHNIQUE 46

SUBTITLES

46.1

46.2

Subtitles are a common recognizable method to help clarify spoken content or add a new lingual dimension to your video presentation. Creating subtitles in Final Cut Pro is an easy process and allows you to add textual data support to your video image.

Because Final Cut Pro supports multiple (nearly limitless) video tracks in a project, adding multiple subtitles on multiple tracks is easy, thereby enabling you to create a single video with as many language subtitles as you need.

STEP 1: OPEN THE FILE

- Make sure you close any previously opened project tabs.
- Double-click the sequence titled **TranslationPlease** to open it.
- You see a base video track appear in your timeline window as seen in **Figure 46.3**.

STEP 2: CREATE THE FIRST SUBTITLE

Click the **Effects** generator icon in the viewer window.

- From the menu, choose **Text ➢ Lower Third**.

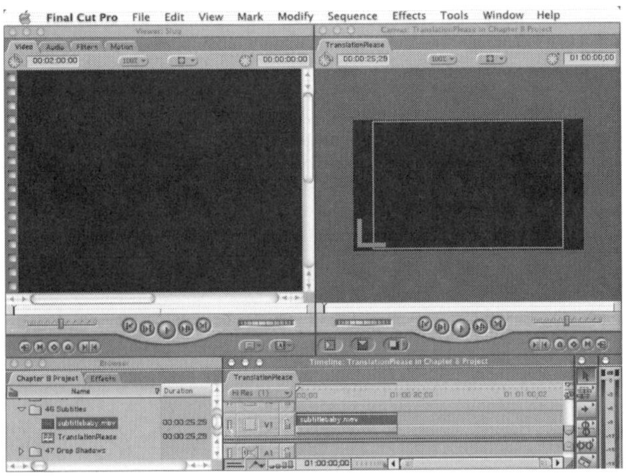

46.3

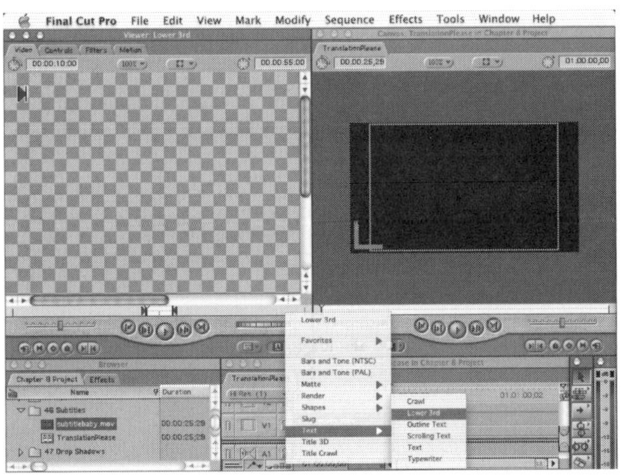

46.4

- This effect creates a two-line text object that automatically occupies the lower third of the video frame as shown in **Figure 46.4.**

STEP 3: SET THE ATTRIBUTES FOR THE TEXT

- Click the **Controls** tab in the **viewer** window to expose all the attribute settings.
- Change the text in the Text 1 field to **Translation**.
- Set the Font to **Times.**
- Set the Style to **Bold/Italic.**
- Set the Size to **36.**
- Set the color to a lighter shade of **gray** or **silver**. To change a font color, click the color swatch in the Font Color Parameters area. A color selection dialog box appears where you can select different color models. Click the **Crayon** icon near the upper-right corner. Click on the Silver crayon.
- Set the text in the Text 2 field to **What? Strained peas again?**
- Set the Font to **Helvetica.**
- Set the Style to **plain.**
- Set the Size to **33.**
- Set the Tracking to **2.**
- Leave the Font color **white.**
- Set the Background to **solid.**
- Set the Opacity to **33.**
- Leave the Color **black.**

Figure 46.5 shows these settings in place.

STEP 4: ADD THE TEXT CLIP TO THE BIN

- Click the **Video** tab to see the text preview of the text clip.

> **TIP**
>
> **A good rule of thumb is to use a half-second per word of spoken text.**

- Click and drag the thumbnail preview of the clip to the bin.
- Change the name of the new text clip in the bin to **subtitle 1** as seen in **Figure 46.6**.

STEP 5: CHANGE THE DURATION OF THE TEXT CLIP

- Double-click on the **subtitle 1** text clip in the bin to display it in the viewer window.
- Change the duration of the clip in the Duration field to **2-seconds.** Click in the Duration field in the upper-left corner of the Video tab and type **2;** (semicolon) and press Return.
- In the timeline window, place the play head at the 2-second point of the video clip in V1 by clicking in the timecode field in the lower-left corner of the timline window and typing **2;** (semicolon) and press Return as **Figure 46.7** shows.
- Click and drag the **subtitle1** text clip into the timeline. Insert the clip in the V2 video track at the 2-second point where the play head is resting.
- Double-click the text clip in V2 of the timeline to display it in the viewer window.
- Click the **Motion** tab in the viewer window.
- Click the delta next to the word Opacity to expose the opacity settings. Set a keyframe at this point by clicking the keyframe button for the opacity setting. Make sure that the opacity is set at **100%.**

NOTE

Your view of the content in the viewer window may or may not include a full view of the content you're creating. The best solution for this, and to make sure that you're seeing everything that is in the window, is to set the viewer and canvas windows to the magnification "Fit Window" so both the entire video clip frame and the entire generator clip frame are visible in the screen shot.

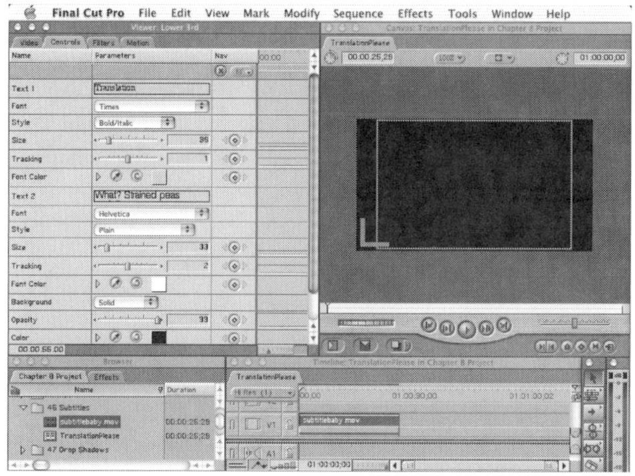

46.5

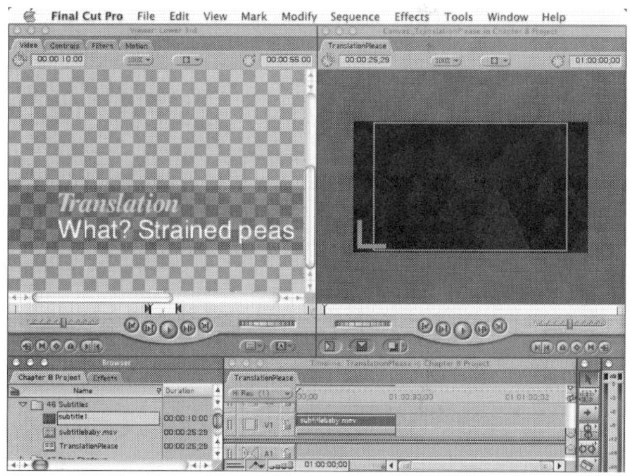

46.6

46.7

■ Move the play head to a new position approximately 1-second further into the Motion tab's timeline or about halfway through the text clip's duration.

■ Keyframe this location by clicking the keyframe button as seen in **Figure 46.8**.

■ Use the down-arrow shortcut to move the play head to the text clip's out point.

■ Create another keyframe in the opacity setting for this moment.

■ Change the opacity for this keyframe to **0**. This setting causes your sub-head to gradually disappear over the course of one second in your video clip.

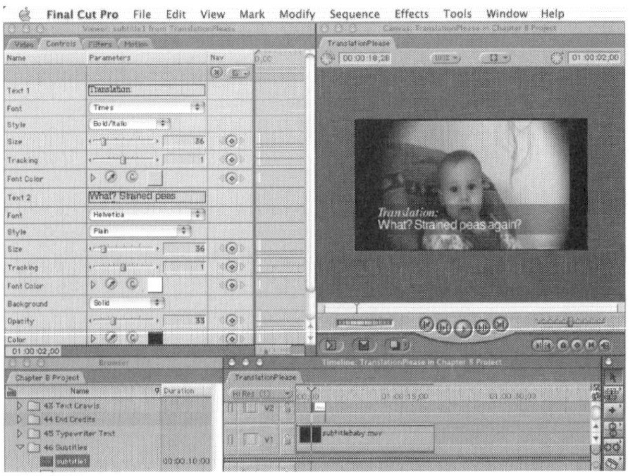

46.8

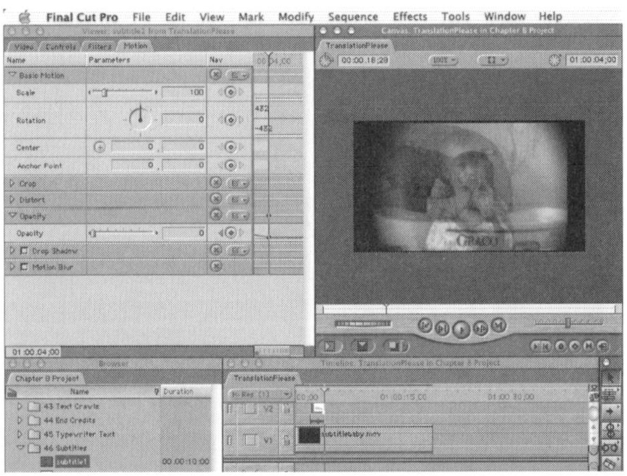

46.9

■ You just created a clip that appears at a specific moment in time, and then fades from view as time passes.

Figure 46.9 shows the opacity keyframed at this moment at 0%, while the canvas window shows the video track transitioning between two scenes in the base video track. Because the text clip is invisible, or 0% opaque, it isn't seen.

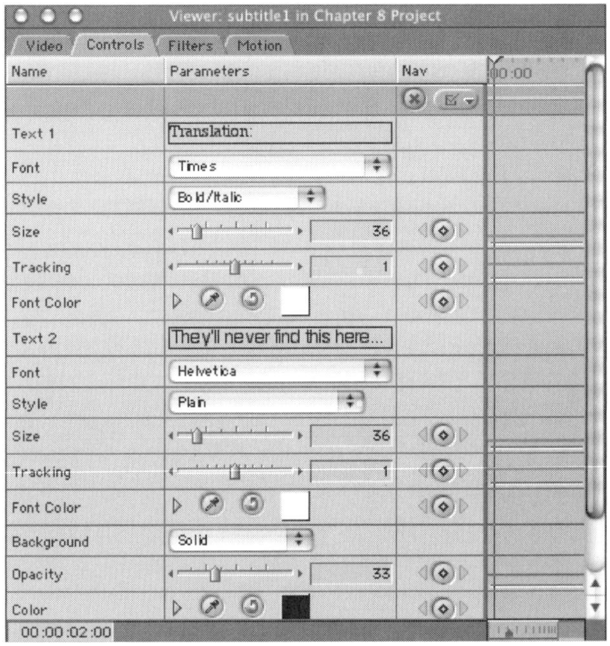

46.10

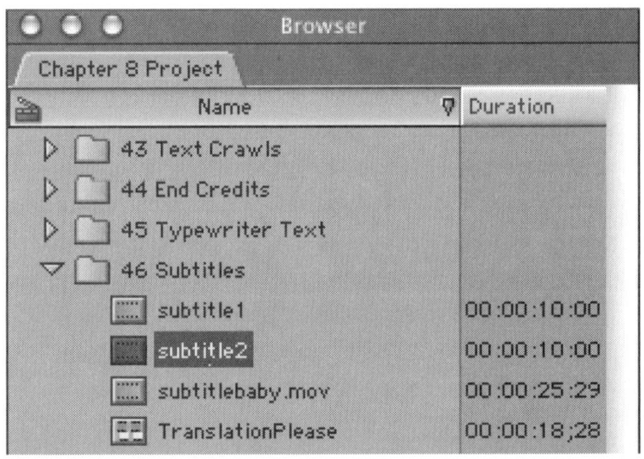

46.11

STEP 6: CREATE THE NEXT SUBTITLE

- Double-click the **subtitle 1** clip item in the bin to see it in the viewer window.
- Click the **Controls** tab and change the text 2 field contents to **They'll never find this here** as **Figure 46.10** shows.
- Click the **Video** tab in the **viewer** window.
- Set the duration of the new text clip to **2-seconds** by typing in **2:** (colon) into the duration field and press **Return**.
- Click in the center of the **Video** tab in the **viewer** window and drag from the viewer window down into the browser window and place the clip into the Subtitles bin. Release the mouse button when the **Subtitles** Project bin is highlighted.
- Rename the clip **subtitle 2** as **Figure 46.11** shows.

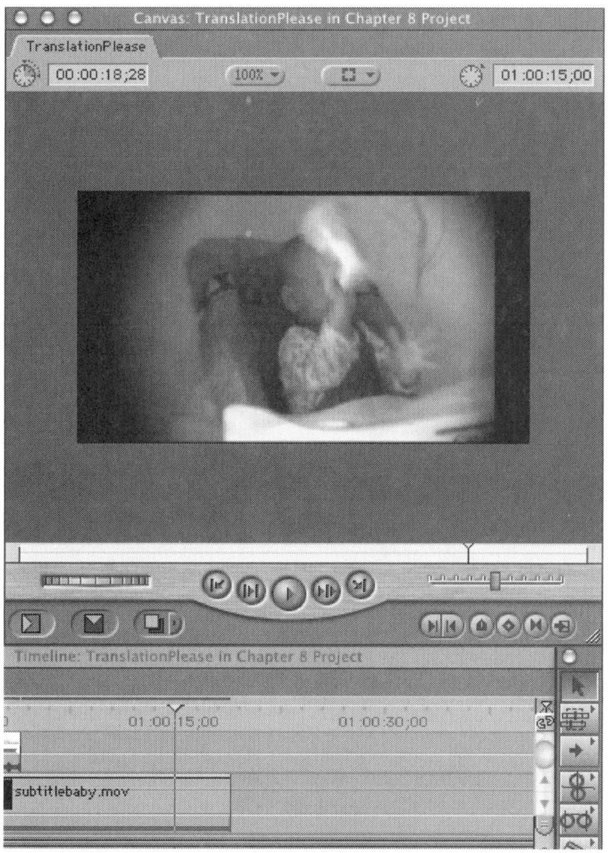

46.12

STEP 7: ADD THE SECOND SUBTITLE TO THE TIMELINE

- Click the **canvas** window to activate it.
- Set the timecode value in the timecode field to **15-seconds** into the sequence by typing **15;** (semi-colon) in the timecode field and press **Return**. **Figure 46.12** shows your results.
- Click and drag the **subtitle 2 text** clip into the timeline at the location of the play head and release the mouse button when the cursor becomes a down-facing arrow as **Figure 46.13** shows.
- You just added a second distinct text clip to the timeline that contains different text contents, while carrying all the attributes and transitions of the original text clip.

46.13

46.14

STEP 8: RENDER THE CLIP

- Choose **Sequence ➢ Render All** from the menu as shown in **Figure 46.14** to render the entire clip with the effect in place.

This technique shows you how easy it is to create subtitles as an overlaid video track in your Final Cut Pro projects. As simple a technique as this is, Final Cut Pro enables you to manipulate as many attributes of the subtitle text as you can imagine, from types style, color, composition mode, and includes special effects.

TEXT WITH DROP SHADOWS

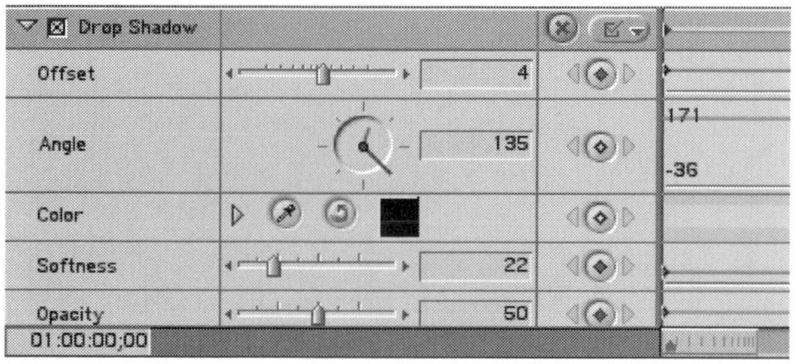

47.1

47.2 (CP58)

One more special effect for the application of text into a video project, drop shadows on any imported track adds the illusion of depth and dimension.

47.3

47.4

47.5

STEP 1: OPEN THE PROJECT

- Make sure you close any other previously opened project tabs.
- In the bin entitled **Drop Shadow**, find the timeline called **dropshadow**.
- Double-click on the timeline to open it and load it into the timeline window as you see in **Figure 47.3**.

STEP 2: CREATE A TEXT OBJECT

- Create a text object using the **Video Generators** button pop-up menu in the viewer window. Choose **Text ➢ Text**.
- Set the attributes of the text to:
  Font: Sand
  Size: 66
  Content: In the text field, type in the words **The Dream of Flight** with a line break between "Dream" and "of" as you see in **Figure 47.4**.

STEP 3: ADD THE DROP SHADOW

Adding a drop shadow to type is a convenient one-step process in Final Cut Pro.

- Choose the **Motion** tab in the **viewer** window.
- Click the check box next to the drop shadow setting as shown in **Figure 47.5**.

STEP 4: DEFINE THE DROP SHADOW ATTRIBUTES

Drop shadow settings are precisely controllable.

- Click the delta immediately to the left of the drop shadow setting.
- For this example, the offset value should be a little lower than the default 10. Set it to **4**.
- Make the softness a little higher by setting it to **22**.
- Set the opacity of the drop shadow to **50%**.
- Now keyframe each of these attributes by selecting the keyframe button on the right of each of those settings as you see in **Figure 47.6**.

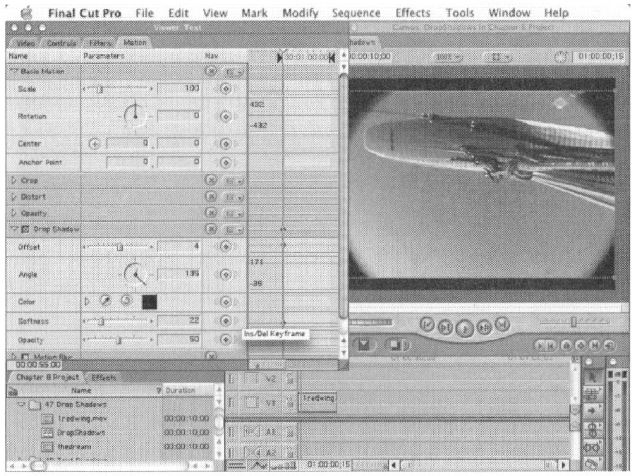

47.6

STEP 5: ADD THE TEXT TO THE TIMELINE

- Make the video window visible by clicking the **Video** tab in the **viewer** window.
- In the timeline window, set the play head to the beginning of the clip by using the up arrow keyboard shortcut as you see in **Figure 47.7**.
- Toggle the wire frame view to disable it. You see your clip object without the wire frame.
- Drag the video thumbnail into the canvas window and choose the superimpose overlay option when it is presented.

47.7

NOTE

Figure 47.7 shows just a portion of the text clip with the shadow effect applied to it in the viewer window. You can easily force your view of your content to appear completely in the window by choosing the "Fit to Window" option from the View Scale pop-up menu at the top of the viewer window as Figure 47.8 shows.

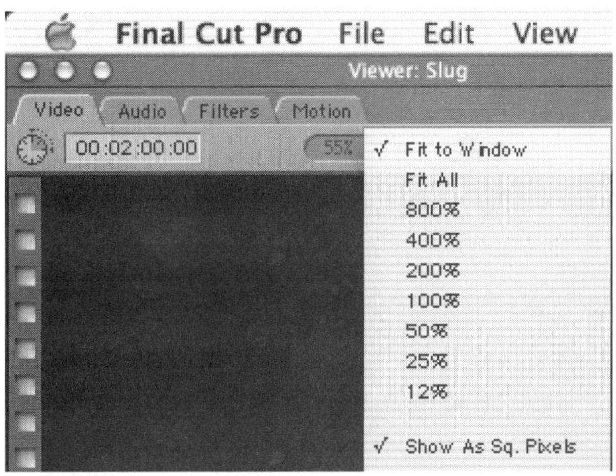

47.8

47.9

47.10

STEP 6: POSITION THE TYPE

- Select the V2 video track containing the text object you just imported.
- Enable the image + wireframe view with the "w" shortcut on your keyboard.
- Drag the type object in the canvas window into the lower third of the image area to making it float in the open area below the video subject as shown in **Figure 47.9**.
- If you want to position the type object numerically, double-click on it in the canvas window and choose the Motion tab. Set the center location to –22 and 33 respectively.

STEP 7: PREVIEW

- In the timeline window, use the arrow keys to manually scrub a frame at a time, back and forth in the timeline to get a rough preview of the work in progress, as shown in **Figure 47.10**.
- The technique is pretty striking and easy to accomplish, but you can make it better.

NOTE

You may have noticed that the procedure used here to create and edit your text object varied slightly from methods used in previous chapters. To paraphrase, Final Cut Pro provides several ways to skin almost any cat in the video production flow. The method shown here has advantages in speed, flexibility, and dynamic previews. While the concept remains the same, Final Cut Pro affords a flexibility in the method that changes to meet your preferred workflow.

STEP 8: ANIMATE THE SHADOW EFFECT

- Move the play head in the timeline to the very beginning of the clip.
- In the motion tab window, keyframe the drop shadow settings.
- Click each of the keyframe buttons next to offset, angle, color, softness, and opacity.
- Move the play head to the end of the clip (use the down arrow keyboard shortcut).
- Create a new keyframe for each of the settings at this point in the timeline.
- Now change the settings to the following:
  Offset: 22
  Softness: 99
  Opacity: 22
- Setting keyframes for each of these attributes causes Final Cut Pro to "tween" or average the effect across time between the keyframes, as **Figure 47.11** shows.

47.11

STEP 9: RENDER THE CLIP

- Choose **Sequence ➢ Render All** as shown in **Figure 47.12** to see the new effect applied.

47.12

In this technique, you discover how easy it is to define and control the application of a drop shadow to text objects. The process is simple and convenient to accomplish. Your creativity and a few simple tricks can make this simple technique as striking as your imagination will allow.

TECHNIQUE 48

TEXT OVERLAYS

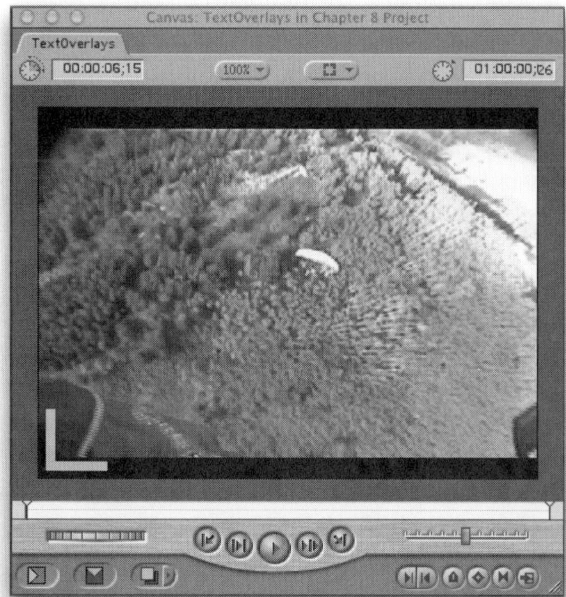

48.1

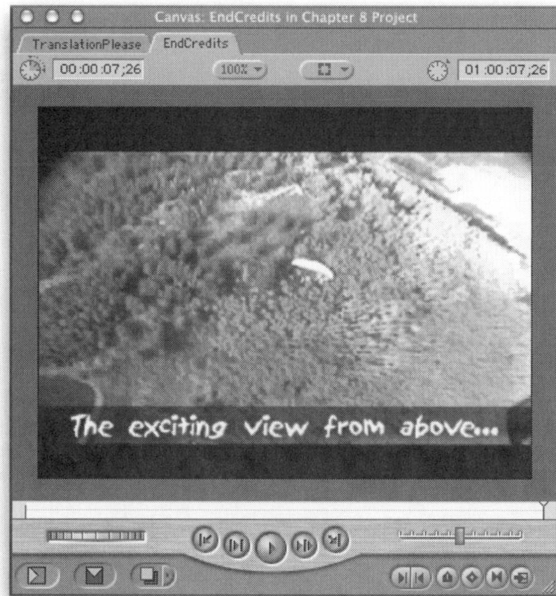

48.2 (CP60)

Watch any news show on television and you see text overlays displaying the name and brief pertinent information about any video subject presented. This technique shows you how to apply this text overlay in your own video presentation, quickly and easily.

You can easily customize this technique, which can be enhanced to include color overlay effects to the text that adds more impact to the text, while keeping it easily distinguishable against any video background.

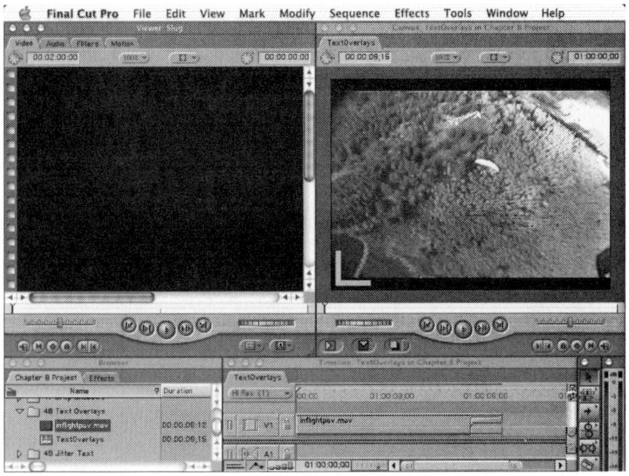

48.3

48.4

> **NOTE**
>
> A reminder here that Figure 48.4 shows just the top-right corner of your text as it is bieng composed in your viewer window. You can always force the contents of a window to fit in the window by using the pop-up view scale command at the top center of the window.

STEP 1: OPEN THE FILE

- Make sure you close any previously opened project tabs.
- In the Chapter 8 Projects folder, find the bin titled **Text Overlays.** Double-click the timeline **TextOverlays** to open it.
- After you open the timeline, you see a video track already in place in the timeline as shown in **Figure 48.3.**

STEP 2: ADD THE TEXT TRACK

- In the **viewer** window, choose the **Text Generator** pop-up menu to create a text object. Click the button and then choose **Text ➢ Text.**
- You now see the text in the video window as in **Figure 48.4.**

STEP 3: ASSIGN TEXT ATTRIBUTES

- In the **video viewer** window, choose the **Controls** tab.
- Type the words: **The exciting view from above…**
- Set the Font to **Sand.**
- Set the Size to **36** and position to the bottom of the frame by setting the origin to **0, 200** as **Figure 48.5** shows.

> **NOTE**
>
> **Set the text size to something proportionate to your video image. In this example, because the text is imported over a low-resolution QuickTime clip, the settings are smaller than you're likely to use in a full-resolution video clip.**

STEP 4: ADD THE TEXT TO THE TIMELINE

- Add the text to the timeline by clicking in the **Video tab preview** window of the **viewer** window and dragging the text preview into the canvas window. Choose the Superimpose overlay after it appears.
- Adding the text creates a second video track and fills the entire clip length with the text clip as you can see in **Figure 48.6.**

STEP 5: CHANGE THE COMPOSITE MODE

- Select the text clip in the V2 video track.
- From the menu, choose **Modify ➢ Composite Mode ➢ Screen** as shown in **Figure 48.7**.

STEP 6: CREATE A HIGHLIGHTING FIELD

- Click the **Video Generator** pop-up menu to create a custom gradient.
- From the pop-up menu, choose **Render ➢ Custom Gradient.**
- In the **video** window, click the **Controls** tab to customize the gradient.

48.5 (CP59)

NOTE

Here is a good place to try a few different composite modes and opacity settings. To change the opacity of a selection, click in the Controls tab of the viewer window and change the opacity settings you find there. Try this: Set the Opacity to 66 and change the composite mode to Overlay.

48.6

48.7

48.8

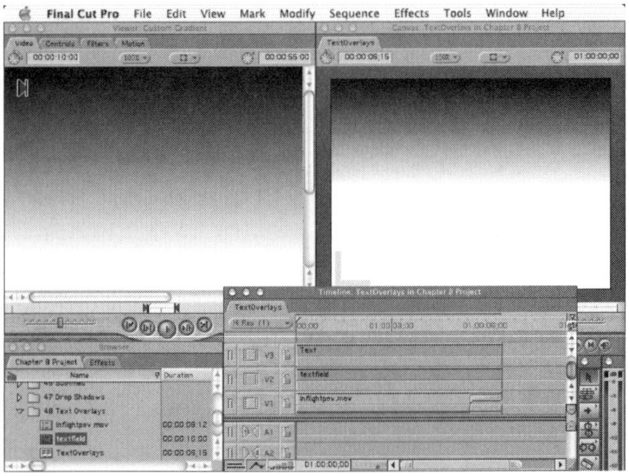

48.9

48.10

- Set the gradient direction to **0**, which makes it graduate from top to bottom.
- Click the **Video** tab and drag the gradient down into the browser window. Release the mouse button after it highlights the Text Overlays bin.
- Click to rename the custom gradient and change its name to **textfield** as shown in **Figure 48.8.**

STEP 7: ADD THE GRADIENT TO THE TIMELINE

- Drag the icon for the text field gradient from the Browser into the canvas window and choose the **Superimpose** overlay after is appears.

Note that the V1 video track is the target track so that the new gradient field inserts itself into a new track directly above the V1 video track, but below the text track that you already placed as you see in **Figure 48.9.**

STEP 8: CHANGE THE COMPOSITE MODE

- Click the **V2** video track to select it.
- From the menu, choose **Modify ➢ Composite Mode ➢ Multiply** as shown in **Figure 48.10.**

STEP 9: RESIZE THE GRADIENT FIELD

- With the gradient track selected, enable the **image + wireframe view** in the **View** menu.
- Hold down the Shift key and drag one of the corner handles toward the center of the frame to resize the overlay.
- You want the field to be just large enough to cover the height of the text and then move it to the bottom of the frame into position surrounding the text as **Figure 48.11** shows.

STEP 10: CHANGE THE COLOR OF THE OVERLAID TEXT

- With the textfield gradient still selected, click the **Controls** tab in the **viewer** window.
- Set the gradient width to **50**.
- Change the end color by clicking the end color swatch and choosing another color in the crayon color picker, as shown in **Figure 48.12**.

STEP 11: RENDER THE CLIP

- Choose **Sequence ➢ Render All** as you see in **Figure 48.13** to save your video with the new effects applied.

In this technique, you learned how to apply text as an overlaid video track or layer onto your video content. You also read how easy it is to customize the technique to fit nearly any application or presentation style.

This technique enables you to add a little more character to the background field over which your text will lay, by creating a gradient, instead of a solid field.

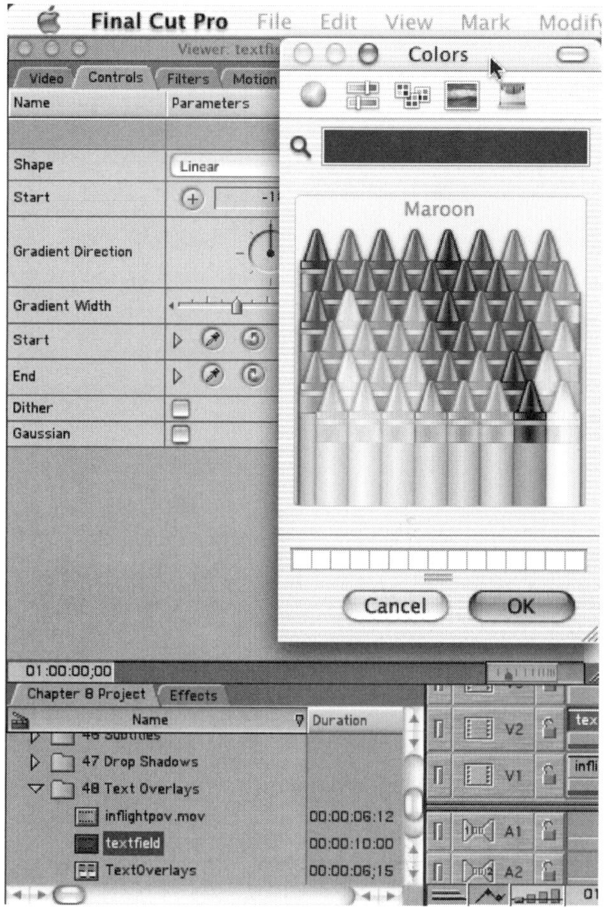

48.12

48.11

48.13

TECHNIQUE 49

JITTER TEXT

49.1 (CP61)

49.2 (CP62)

This technique is great for animating text in Final Cut Pro to introduce the text as a character of its own. While you have hundreds of ways to animate text in Final Cut Pro, this technique shows you a simple but attractive and stylish way to present the text.

This jitter-text technique is useful to create a feeling of artistic stylized motion to your text. Applying the technique is easy and it enhances an active feeling in your video presentation.

While you read the basic application and technique, you'll realize that the potential variations of the technique are nearly limitless.

STEP 1: OPEN THE PROJECT FILE

- Open the bin titled **49 Jitter Text** in the Chapter 8 Projects folder.
- **Figure 49.3** shows you that a video track is already in place.

> **TIP**
>
> **Because the type jumps around a bit, making the font and style as easy to read as possible is a good idea. A sans serif, boldface font, such as Impact or Arial Black works well for this technique.**

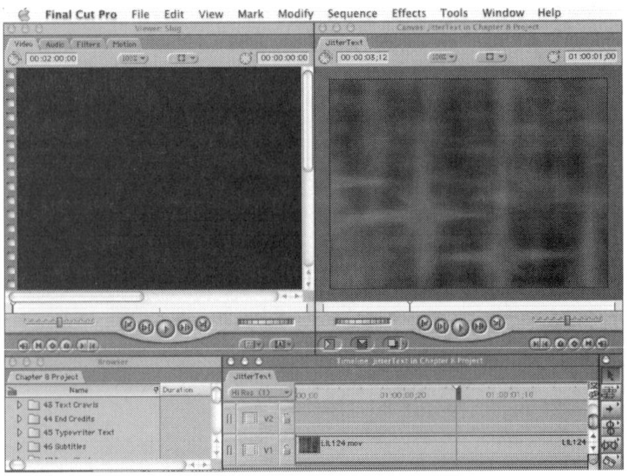

49.3

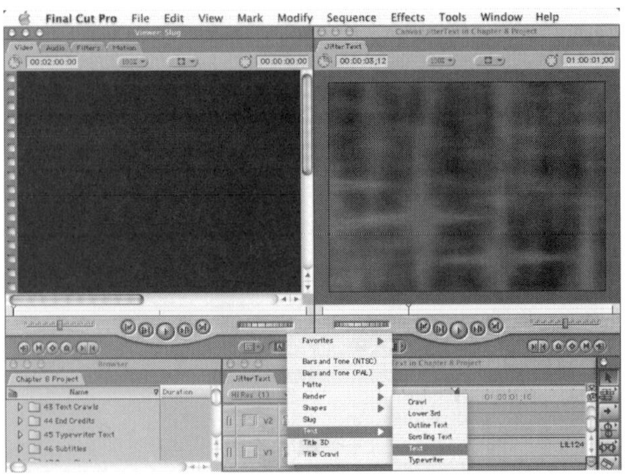

49.4

STEP 2: CREATE THE TEXT

- In the **viewer** window, use the video Object Generator pop-up menu to create a text object by choosing **Text ➢ Text** as shown in **Figure 49.4**.
- In the viewer window, click the **Controls** tab.
- In the text field, type the word **Jitter**.
- Set the Font to **Arial Black**, which is a bold, sans serif typeface.

  Set the Size to **122 points** and leave all the other settings in their default values:

  Set the Style **plain**,

  Set the Alignment **center**,

  Set the Color **white**, and the Origin **0, 0** as you see in **Figure 49.5**.
- Click to expose the Video tab in the viewer window.
- Click in the center of the viewer window and drag the text thumbnail down into the Jitter Text project bin.
- You see a new icon in the bin labeled **Text** as shown in **Figure 49.6**.

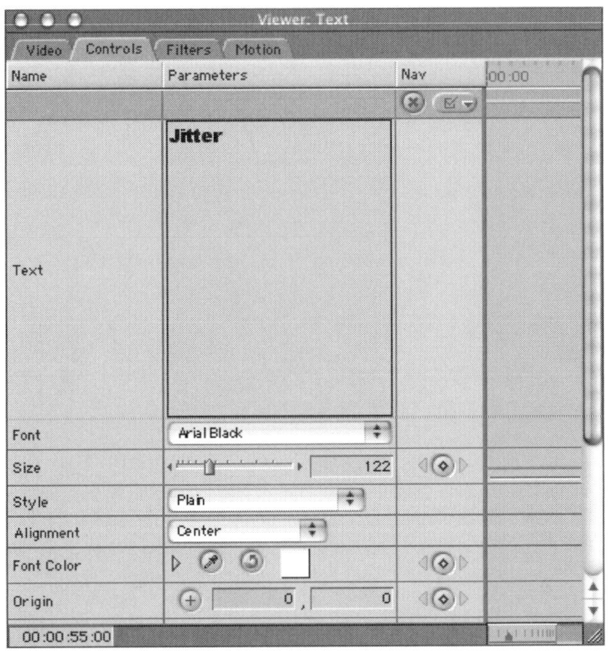

49.5

STEP 3: ADD YOUR TEXT SNIPPET

- Click and drag the type object from the Browser into the canvas window and choose the **Superimpose** overlay. You see the new type object inserted in the V2 video track, which fills the entire clip length.
- Set the duration of this type object clip in V2 to only **1-second**.
- The simplest way to accomplish this is to double-click on the clip in the V2 video track. Click in the duration field in the viewer window and type in **1;** (semicolon) and press **Return**. You see the text clip in the timeline immediately shorten to one-second in length as seen in **Figure 49.7**.
- In the timeline window, move the play head to the end of the text clip to make your next insertion point a little easier to accomplish. A good shortcut is to use the down arrow on your keyboard.

STEP 4: CREATE 2-FRAME CLIP SNIPPETS

- Double-click on the icon in the bin labeled **Text** to see it in the viewer window.
- Set the duration of the type clip in the viewer window to 2-frames by clicking in the duration field and typing in a **2** and pressing **Return**. **Figure 49.8** shows this.
- This step sets the clip up to allow you to continuously add two-frame snippets to the timeline over and over as you change subtle attributes to the type. You'll be surprised just how easy it is.

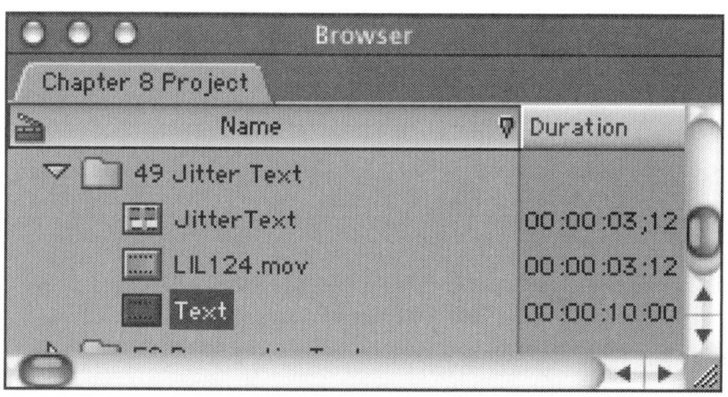

49.6

49.7

TIP

If the clips in the timeline are so small that they're inconvenient or difficult to manipulate, you can always use the keyboard shortcut Command+ to enlarge your view in the timeline window.

49.8

STEP 5: CHANGE THE ATTRIBUTES OF THE CLIP

- Click the **Controls** tab in the **viewer** window and set the Size of the type to a few points larger than the current size as shown in **Figure 49.9**.
- Click the **Video** tab again to see the type.

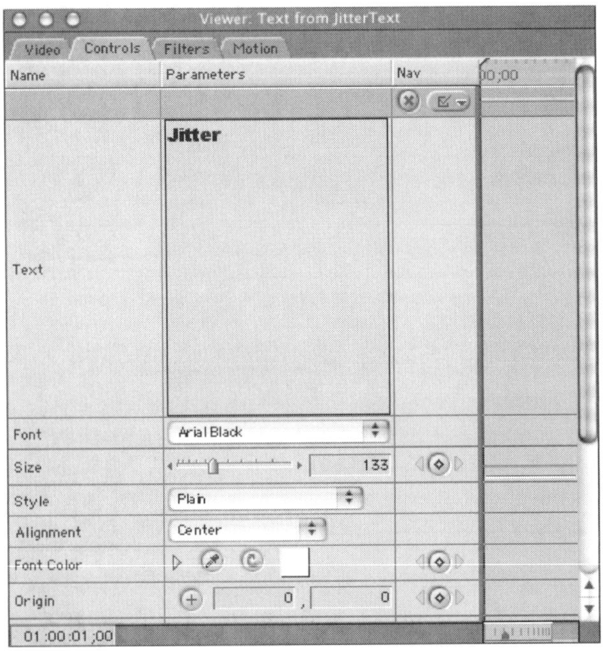

49.9

- Drag the type snippet from the viewer window to the timeline and insert the two-frame snippet at the play head location, adjacent to the 1-second clip already placed in the timeline in V2.
- You just added 2-frames of (slightly different) video to your V2 video track as you can see in **Figure 49.10**.

STEP 6: ADD TWO FRAMES OF BLURRY TEXT

- Double-click the **text clip** icon in the **browser** window to see it in the viewer window.
- Choose the **Controls** tab.
- Set Font size back to **122**.
- Click on the **Filters** tab.
- From the menu, choose **Effects ➢ Video Filters ➢ Blur ➢ Gaussian Blur** as shown in **Figure 49.11** and **Figure 49.12**.
- Set the blur value to **22**.
- Click on the **Video** tab to preview the blur effect.
- Click in the **viewer** window and drag it down into into the timeline. Let the insertion point snap to the end of the text clip in V2 as shown in **Figure 49.13**.

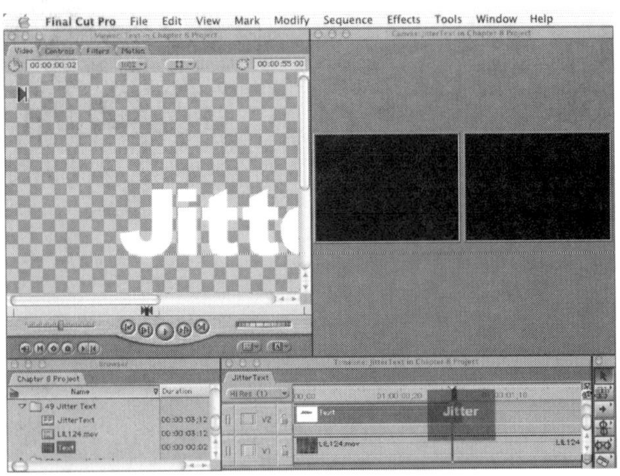

49.10

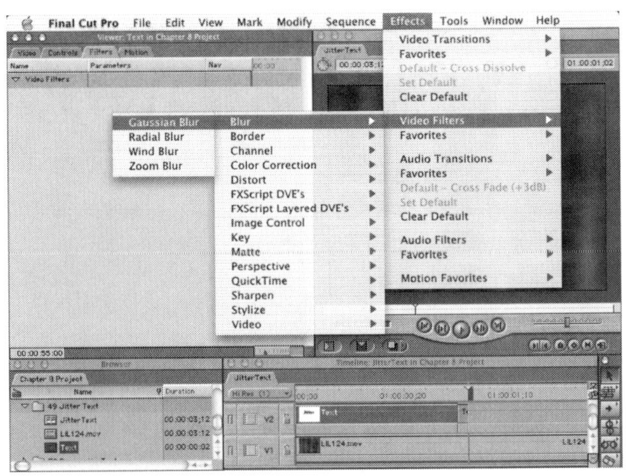

49.11

STEP 7: ADD TWO MORE FRAMES OF SHARP CLEAR TYPE

- Click back in the **Filters** tab of the **viewer** window and disable the Gaussian blur by unchecking the check box for that setting as shown in **Figure 49.14**.
- Expose the **Video** tab in the **viewer** window and add these two more unblurred type frames into the timeline at the end of the newest text clip, the same way you added the last clip, as shown in **Figure 49.15**.

STEP 8: ONE MORE BLURRED CLIP

- Double-click the **Text Clip** icon in the **browser** window.
- Click in the **viewer** window and choose the **Filters** tab.

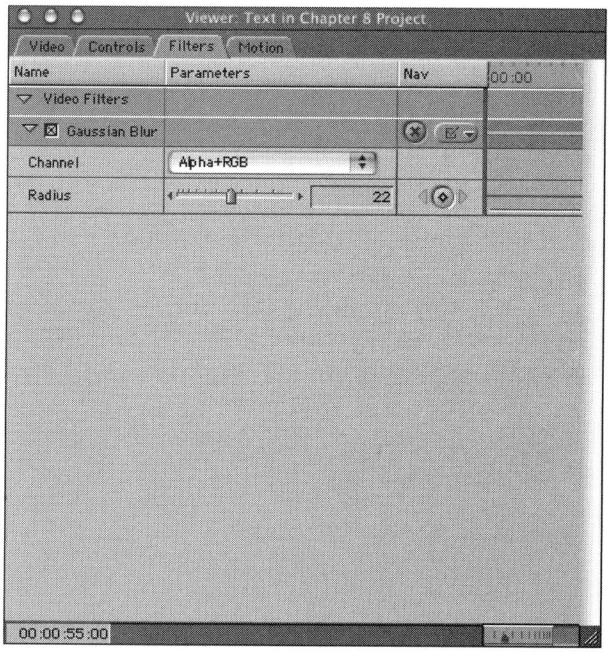

49.12

49.13

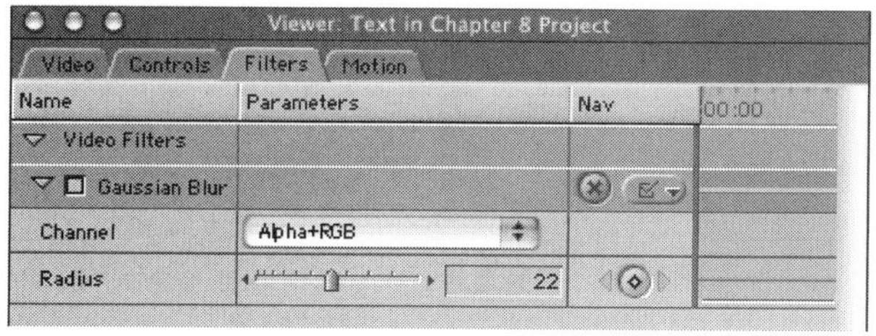

49.14

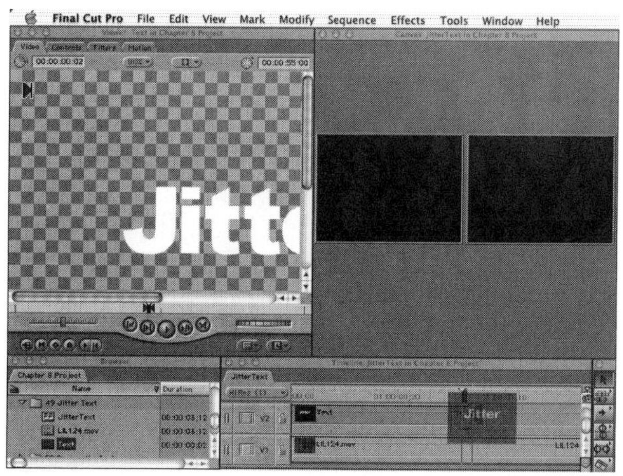

49.15

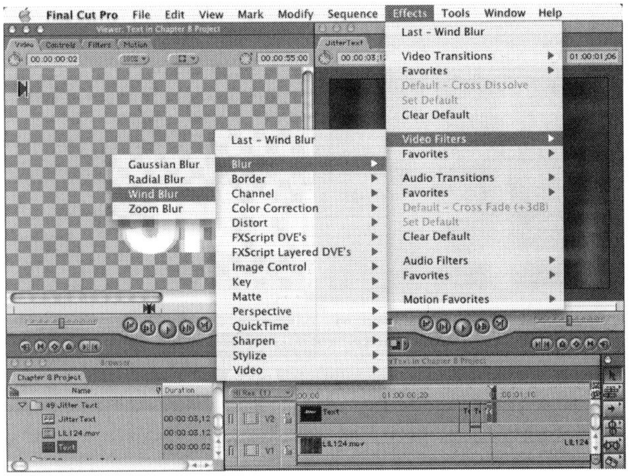

49.16

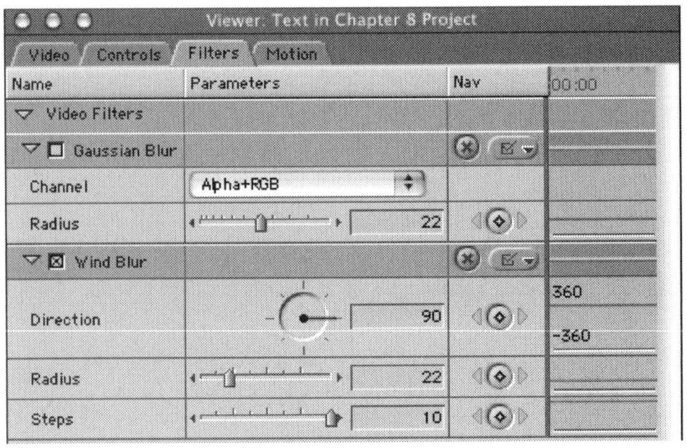

49.17

■ From the menu, choose **Effects ➢ Video Filters ➢ Blur ➢ Wind Blur** as shown in **Figure 49.16.**

Set the wind blur values to the ones shown in **Figure 49.17.**

■ Click in the **Filters** tab of the **viewer** window.
■ Set the Direction to **90.**
■ Set the Radius to **22.**
■ Set the Steps to **10.**
■ These settings give your text clip a nice horizontal blur effect.
■ Click the **Video** tab in the **viewer** window.
■ Click in the center of the video window and drag the thumbnail clip down into the timeline. Add the new text clip into the timeline at the end of the previous clip as shown in **Figure 49.18.**

STEP 9: NEST THE CLIPS

While initially tedious, the process can be made a bit easier if you nest the clips and save them for future use in other projects.

■ Select all the 2-frame mini-clips in V2 by dragging the arrow cursor around them in the V2 timeline.
■ From the menu, choose **Sequence ➢ Nest Items** as shown in **Figure 49.19.**

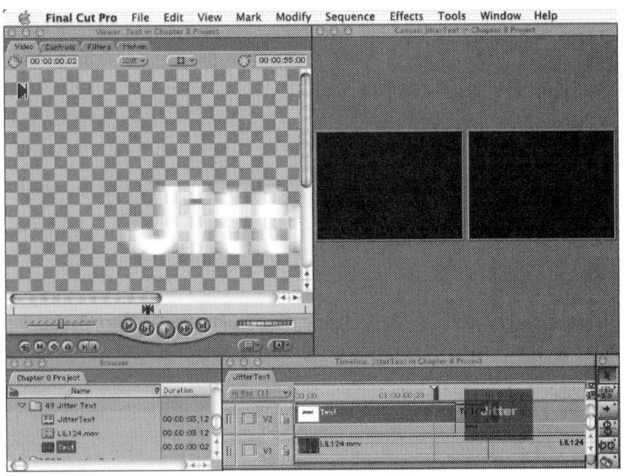

49.18

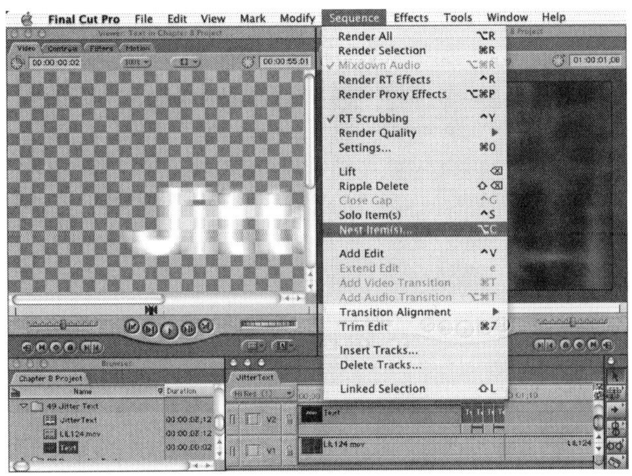

49.19

- A dialog box prompts you to name the newly nested clip as shown in **Figure 49.20**. Name this nested clip **jitterytext**.

STEP 10: CLONE THE NESTED CLIP

- Now that you nested the collection of 2-frame clips into a single clip, you can easily duplicate the nested clip over and over to fill the remaining length of the video.
- Click to select the nested **jitterytext** clip. Hold down the Option and Shift keys and drag the nested clip up into the space directly above its location. This creates a new V3 video track and an exact copy of the original nested clip directly above the clip as shown in **Figure 49.21**.
- Click and drag the newly copied clip into the V2 video track adjacent to the first nested clip. The result should look like **Figure 49.22.**

> **TIP**
>
> **You can mix things up a bit by selecting one of the nested clips and reversing the order of the frames in the clip by choosing Modify ➢ Speed and clicking the Reverse frames option in the Speed dialog box.**

49.20

49.21

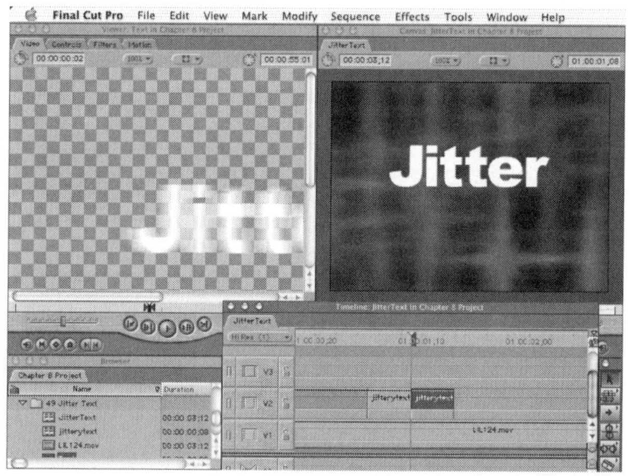

49.22

> **NOTE**
>
> **Nesting a clip has advantages in manipulating the group of sub-clips if needed later.**

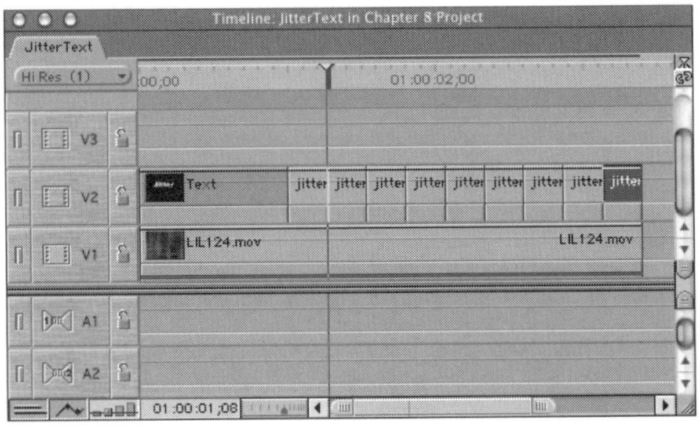

49.23

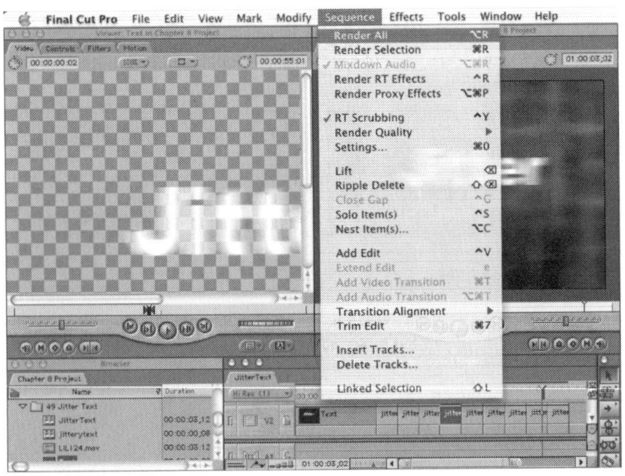

49.24

STEP 11: LATHER, RINSE, REPEAT

- Repeat the last step, duplicating the nested clip over and over until you fill the rest of the length of the timeline as shown in **Figure 49.23**.

STEP 12: RENDER THE CLIP

- Choose **Sequence ➢ Render All** as you see in **Figure 49.24** to see results of the changes that you made.
- After you finish, close this Project tab by Control-clicking on the tab name or use the keyboard shortcut Control-W.

In this technique, you read how to apply animated text as a simple, yet effective design element to your video presentation. Because the steps are simple and easy to apply, you can see how easily you can create nearly limitless variations of the technique.

Though tedious, the technique is easily extensible allowing you to build on the technique and make it as long and as variable as you can imagine.

TECHNIQUE **50**

TEXT IN PERSPECTIVE

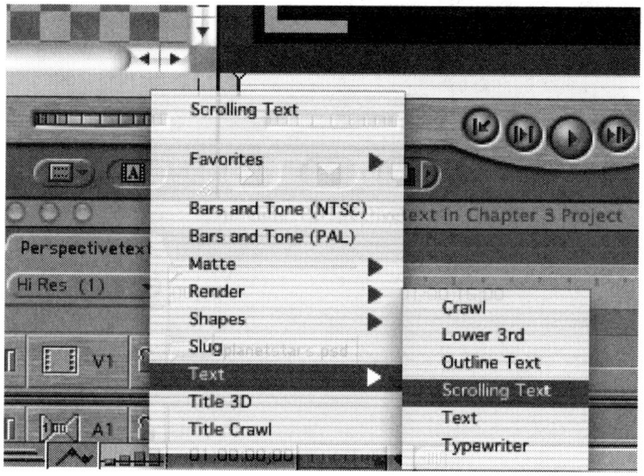

50.1

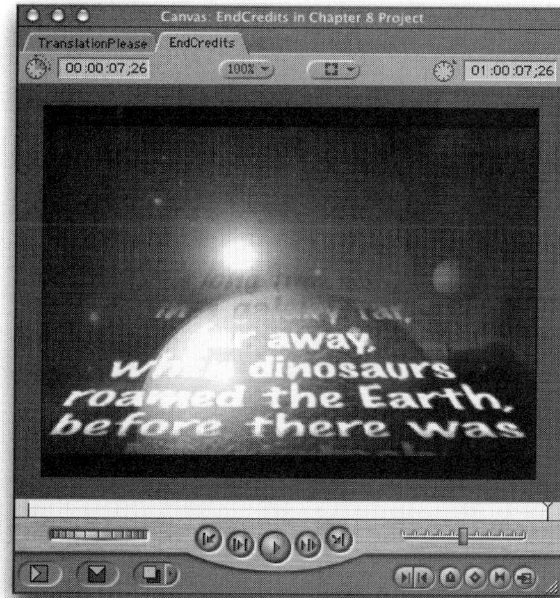

50.2 (CP64)

"A long time ago, in a galaxy far, far away . . ." These words and their unique presentation in the movie *Star Wars* are a part of worldwide culture now. Who will forget this memorable introduction where lines of three-dimensional text scrolled over the movie screen starting from a wide perspective at the bottom and gradually getting smaller, ending at the top of the screen in a series of lines of dashes? This technique is one example of "text in perspective."

Final Cut Pro affords you an easy way to simulate this effect in your own video presentations, which helps you create your own version of text in perspective. After you get accustomed to this technique, you will find there are literally thousands of ways to display text in perspective that adds many interesting options to your video presentation.

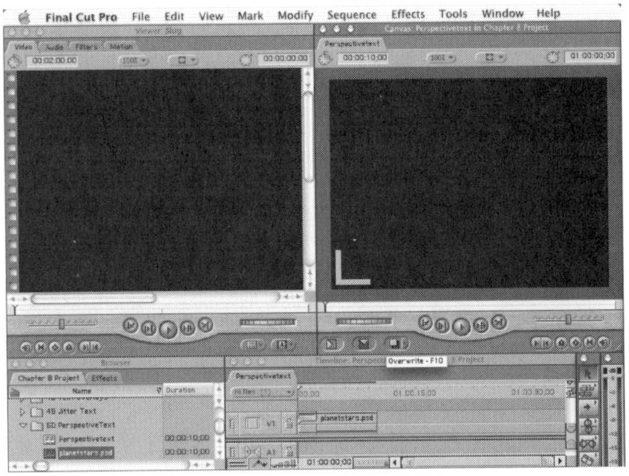

50.3

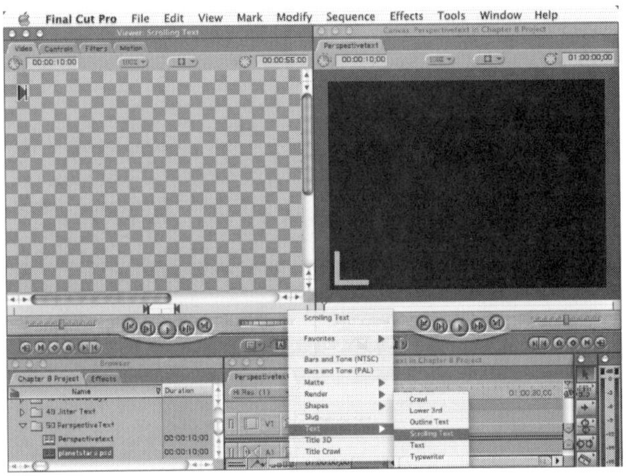

50.4

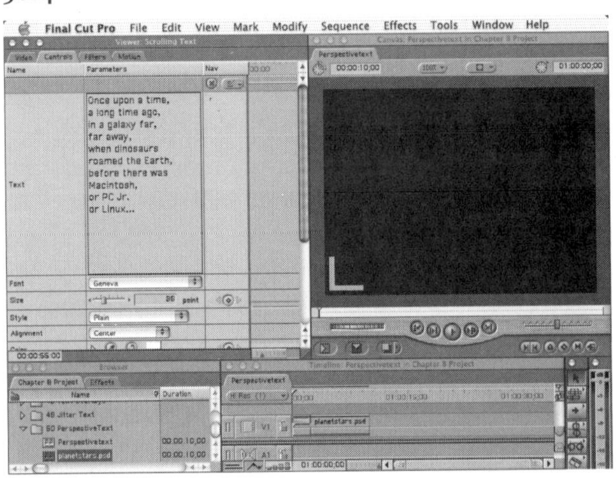

50.5

STEP 1: OPEN THE PERSPECTIVE TEXT SEQUENCE

- Make sure you close any previously opened project tabs.
- In your Chapter 8 Projects folder, open the bin titled **50 Perspective** text.
- In **Figure 50.3** you see a sequence already in place containing a video clip backdrop, which your perspective title scroll effect appears against.

STEP 2: CREATE THE SCROLL

- Before adding your dramatic perspective title to the sequence, you have to create it and define all the attributes.
- Choose the pop-up generator menu icon in the **viewer** window and then choose **Text ➢ Scrolling Text** as you see in **Figure 50.4**.

STEP 3: ADD YOUR TEXT

- Click the **Controls** tab and type in some preliminary text, such as **A long time ago, in a galaxy far, far away. . . .** **Figure 50.5** shows the Controls tab settings and a little extra text.

STEP 4: ASSIGN SOME ATTRIBUTES

- Set the Size of the type sample to **72** points.
- Make sure the Alignment is set to **Center**.
- Choose a bright color that stands out against the background, yet won't contrast so much that it gets lost against the background colors in your video clip.
- Set the Fade size to **33%**.
- Set the Direction to up, which makes the text scroll from bottom to top. All of these settings are shown in **Figure 50.6**.

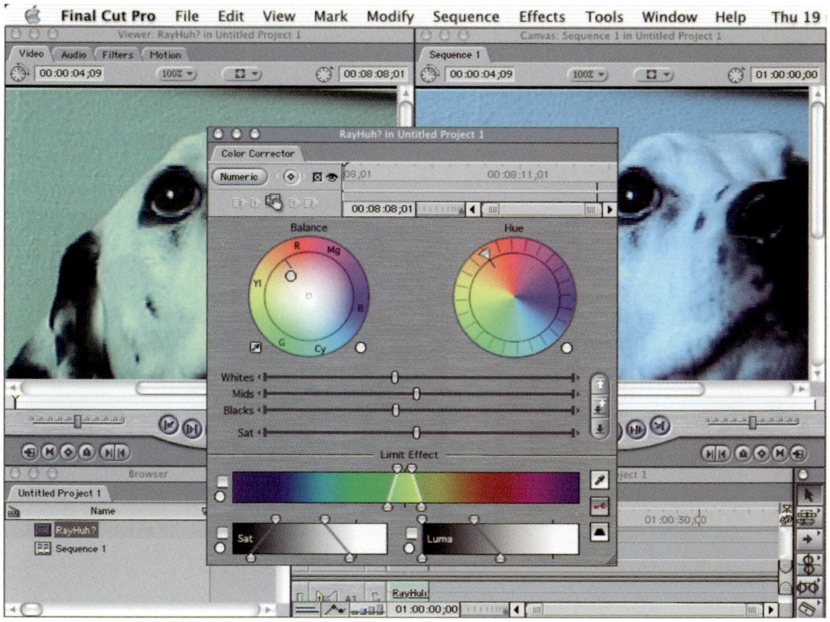

Technique 6: Simple Contrast Correction

Final Cut Pro 3 adds powerful image enhancement utilities like color correction to improve your video output.

CP1

CP2

Technique 10: Sepia Tone and Aged Film

Enhancing a video sequence to make its appearance that of a very old film clip is as simple as applying a few image adjustment filters.

CP3

CP4

CP5

CP6

Technique 15: Adding An Inset Window with Video

Placing a floating video window above your background video is easy and can be easily enhanced with ornaments such as drop shadows and image effects.

Technique 16: Moving Inset Window

An extension of the floating video window, this one moves across the video frame over time.

CP7

CP8

CP9

CP10

Technique 17: The Overlaid Inset Window

Another technique for creating an inset video window; this one by defining a different composite mode. You can change the composite mode of video tracks across layers just as you would using an image editing program such as Photoshop.

Technique 18: Text Overlays

Just like a floating inset window, you can also create layers of text that overlay on top of your video tracks. Final Cut Pro has powerful text editing tools producing nearly limitless text effects.

CP11

CP12

Technique 19: Art Overlays (Logos)

Again, as with floating video windows, you can add your own artwork and apply it on top of your video track as a layer, changing the composite mode and adding filter effects.

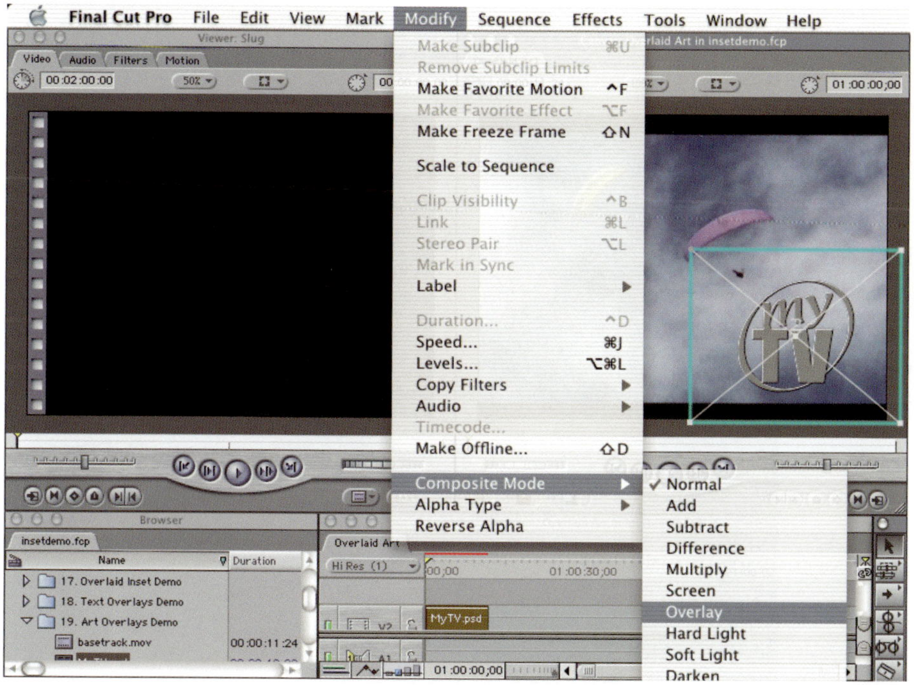

CP13

CP14

Technique 20: Cartoon Balloons

A practical application of the concept of applying a layer of artwork on top of your video track. In this instance, the artwork layer's composite mode is "normal" and the opacity is 100%. Powerful text controls allow you to place any message you want in the cartoon balloon.

CP15

CP16

Technique 21: Imagination Balloons

Another interesting use of the layer concept. This example uses the artwork layer as a "window" through which another video image is visible. The technique is called a "travel matte" and is used in Hollywood all the time.

CP17

CP18

Technique 22: Planets and Moons

A simple application of the layering concept, with a change in the composite mode to simulate the appearance of planets hanging in the night sky. You can easily add your own photographic or video elements into any scene to place anything you want into the sky.

CP19

CP20

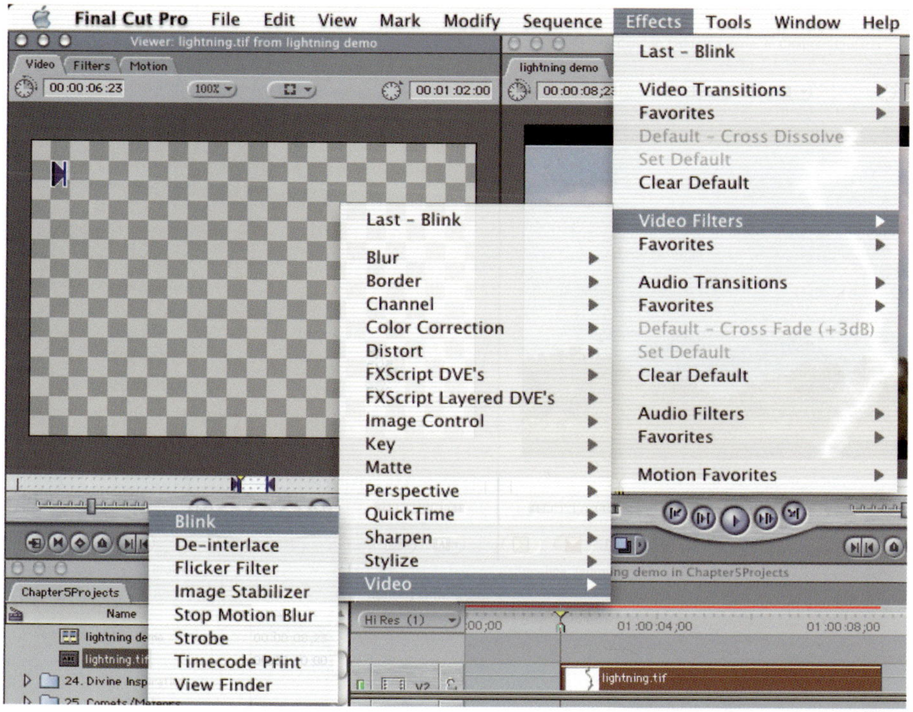

CP21

Technique 23: Lightning Bolts

The artwork here is easily created in a paint or photo editing program, then added as an overlaid video track. The secret to this effect is in the strobe filter effect to make the lightning flash. See the sample video result for the final look of the piece.

CP22

Technique 24: Divine Inspiration

Another simple application of an artwork layer on top of the video track to simulate heavenly rays of light. As a separate layer, you can aim and position the inspiration on any subject.

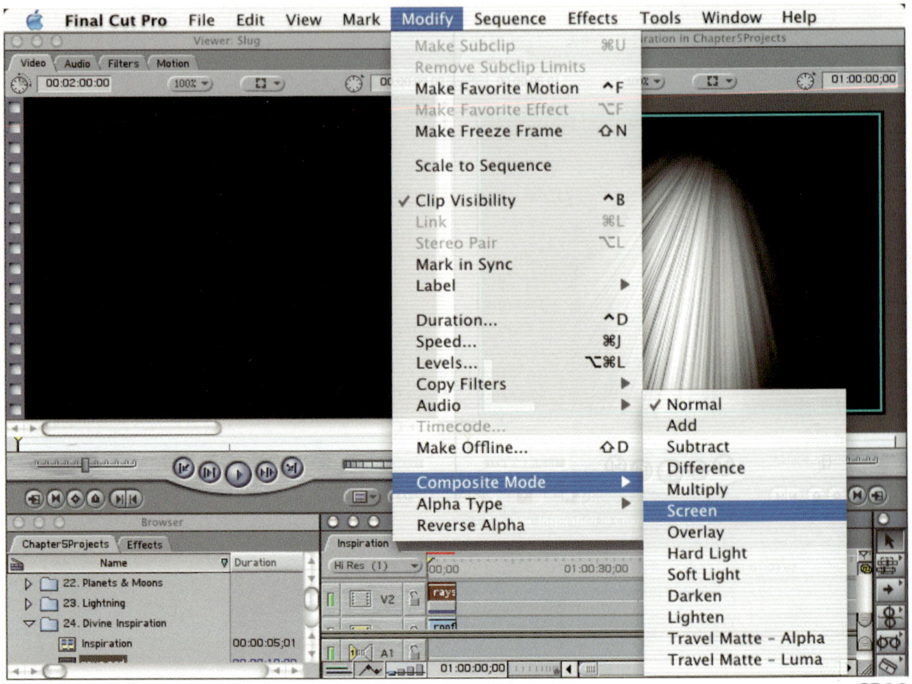

CP23

CP24

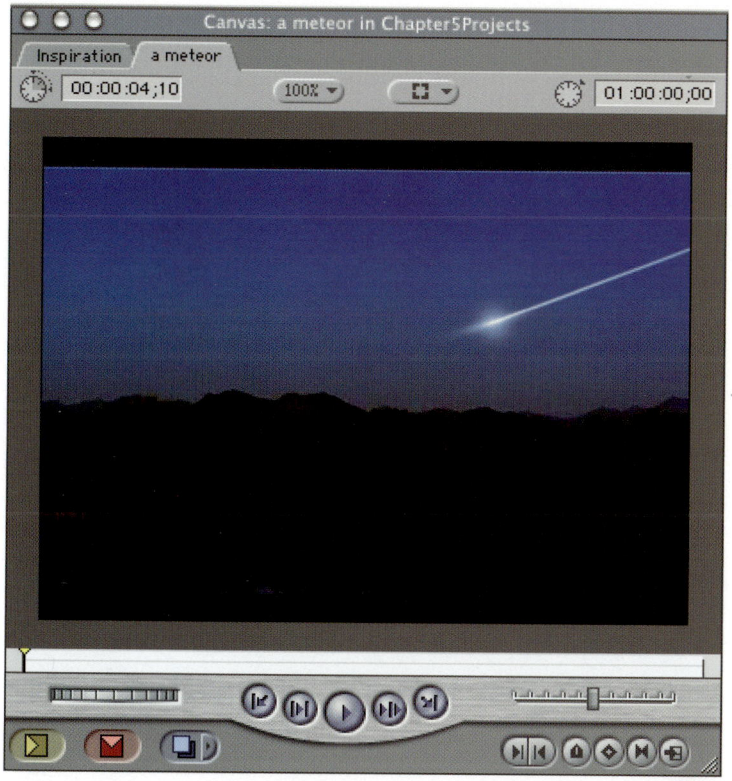

CP25

CP26

Technique 25: Comets and Meteors

Using a simple overlaid image, you can create the illusion of a comet or meteor streaking across the night sky. A comet will appear to float still in the sky, while a meteor streaks across the heavens at thousands of miles per hour.

Technique 26: Overcast Clouds

In this example, an ominous layer of gray clouds has been added to the sky using a simple application of the powerful color key filter in Final Cut Pro. The clouds can be created in a few easy steps in any paint or photo editing product, then imported as artwork to Final Cut Pro.

CP27

CP28

CP29

Technique 27: Monster Eyes

A fantastically striking effect achieved using only the filters and effects found within Final Cut Pro. No outside art to create, no layers or media to import.

CP30

Technique 28: Green Faces

Another easily applied effect using only the tools found in Final Cut Pro. A simple generated mask effect with a color enhancement is all it takes to turn anyone green (or blue, pink, purple, or yellow).

CP31

CP32

Technique 29: Laser Beams

Add your own laser beams to any video sequence. In this example, some artwork was imported, then colorized in a separate video track.

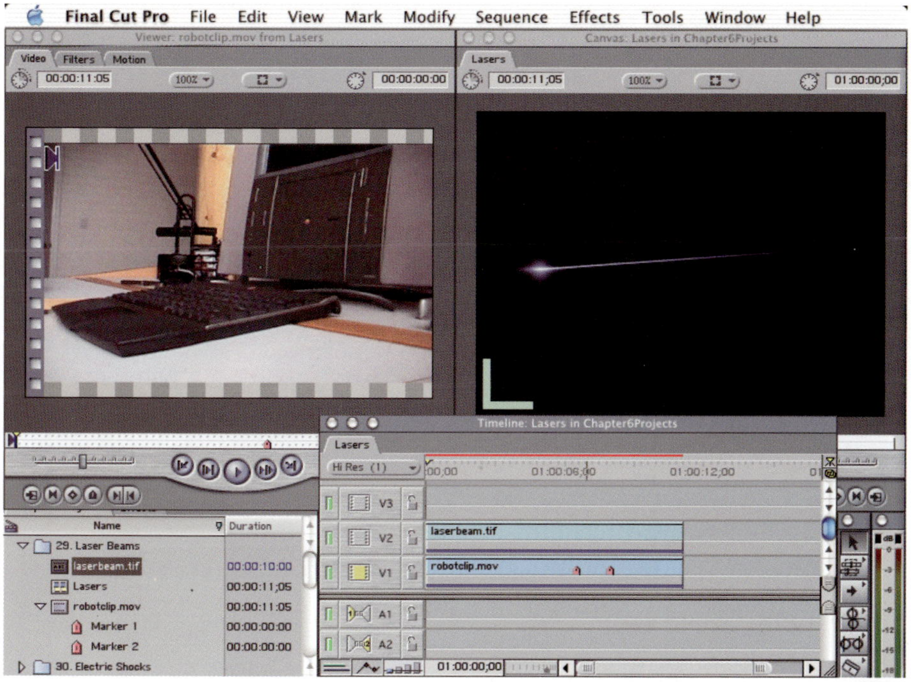

CP33

CP34

Technique 30: Electric Shocks

Shocking developments are easy to add if you know the secrets. Similar to the lightning effect, this technique makes use of imported artwork with a simple composite mode enhancement.

CP35

CP36

Technique 31: Background Flames

You can add fire and flames to almost any image. The secret in this example is the way the background colors are easily selectable using the color key effect.

CP37

CP38

Technique 32: Foreground Flames

Foreground flames can be easily placed in almost any image. The sample seen here employs a commercially available sample clip from Artbeats. The secret to this effect is creating a travelling matte that allows the flames to show through a matte window realistically against your background.

CP39

CP40

CP41

CP42

Technique 33: Fire Breath

This is a great example of applied video mischief. This technique relies on sharp control of short clips and accurate placement of the flame layer.

Technique 34: Indoor Explosions

Indoor Explosions are easy to simulate when you have a product like ArtBeats' explosion clips to add to any video sequence. The secret here is to include an endframe mask using a still image to fool the viewer into thinking the subject has really been destroyed in a fiery blast.

CP43

CP44

CP45

CP46

Technique 35: Miniature People and Things

Using a simple matte window, generated within Final Cut Pro, you can add the appearance of almost any miniature subjects to your video sequences. In this example, a symmetrical oval mask was added, then blurred and used as a window through which some video footage of ducks is visible.

Technique 36: Gigantic House Pets

Another simple effect that takes advantage of Final Cut Pro's powerful mask and matte features. The secret to this technique is in matching as closely as possible the camera angle between your foreground and background elements.

CP47

CP48

CP49

CP50

Technique 37: Matte Windows in Objects

Placing a matte window into any flat surface is an easy task with Final Cut Pro. Starting with a simple inset video layer, you can distort the shape of the video track with a simple tool to match the shape and proportions of the object where the inset appears.

Technique 38: Doorway into the Unknown

In this example, the doorway into the unknown is in a simple square hatch of a personal computer. It's as easily created in any rectangular shape (like any closet door in your house) using an inset video window and a simple wipe transition.

CP51

CP52

CP53

CP54

Technique 41: Looking into the Crystal Ball

Using a simple matte window and distortion filter, you can make just about anything you want appear within the spherical globe of a crystal ball. All of these effects are built into Final Cut Pro, requiring no external effects or tools.

Technique 42: Glowing Orbs

Another example of the power and simplicity of Final Cut Pro's suite of filter and effects generators. This effect was performed without any imported artwork or external tools. Simple matte effects and image control filters are all that were required for this powerful technique.

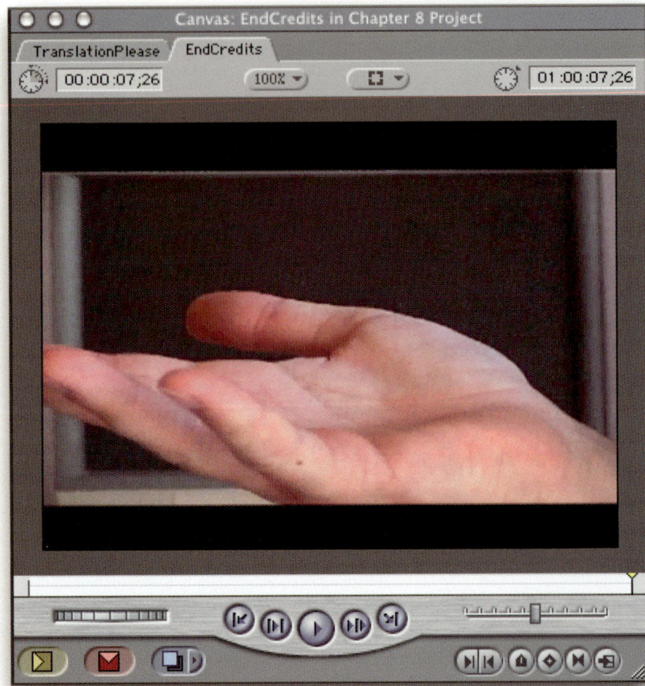

CP55

CP56

CP57

CP58

Technique 47: Text with Drop Shadows

Adding a drop shadow to any imported object is a simple task with the built-in capability in the motion tab of the viewer window. The magic in this technique happens due to the ability to change the effect over time using keyframes.

Technique 48: Text Overlays

Text overlays are an easy technique to accomplish using the built-in effect generators in Final Cut Pro. Several different variations are available within the program.

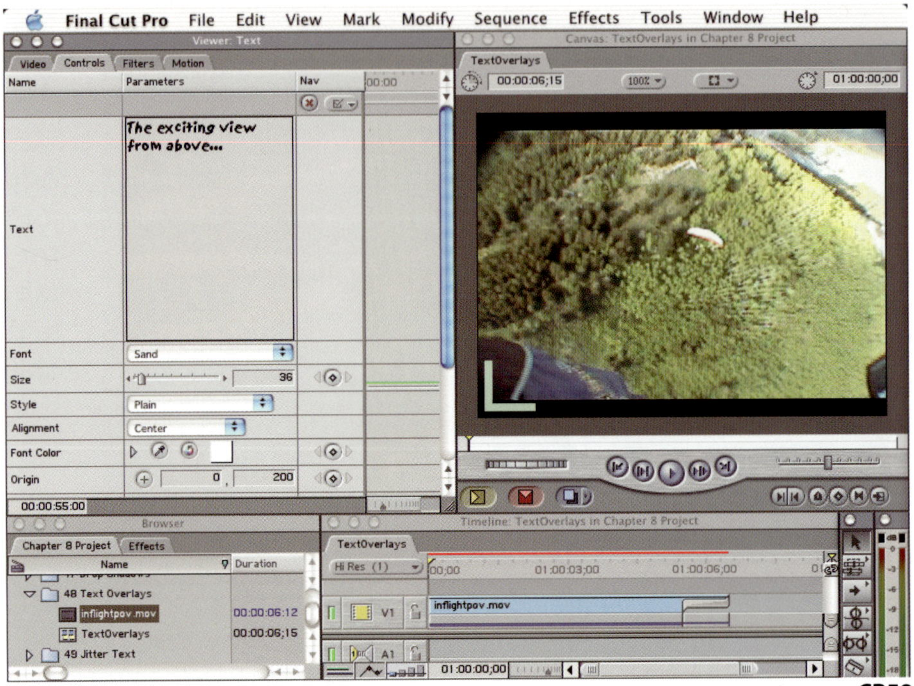

CP59

CP60

CP61

Technique 49: Jitter Text

Simple and powerful, this technique works by adding filter effects to generated effects (such as text) within Final Cut Pro.

CP62

Technique 50: Text in Perspective

Creating "Star Wars" type scrolling perspective text is now an easy process in Final Cut Pro. The scrolling text is a generated effect with a simple manual distortion applied to it.

CP63

CP64

STEP 5: ADD THE TEXT TO YOUR TIMELINE

- Click the Video tab to see a preview of the text attributes.
- You won't see anything there except an empty frame because the text scroll hasn't started yet and begins outside the screen boundaries.
- Click and drag the clip from the viewer window onto the canvas window and choose the Superimpose overlay. The results should appear similar to **Figure 50.7**.
- Drag the play head in the viewer window back and forth to preview the scroll.

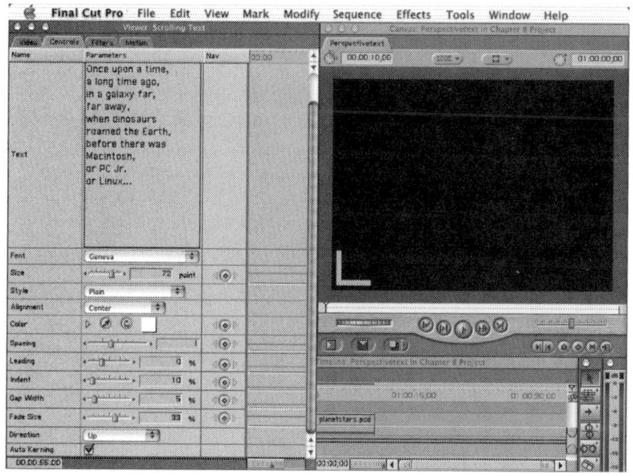

50.6

STEP 6: ADJUST THE DIMENSIONS

- Click to select the text track in the timeline window.
- Enable the Image + Wireframe view under the View menu (or toggle with the "w" keyboard shortcut).
- Preview the scrolling text by Option-dragging the play head back and forth to see the rough preview of the text scroll.
- Activate the arrow tool (keyboard shortcut "a")
- Hold down the Shift key and Click and drag the upper-left wire frame control handle vertically towards the center of the frame, which shortens the height of the text scroll as shown in **Figure 50.8**.

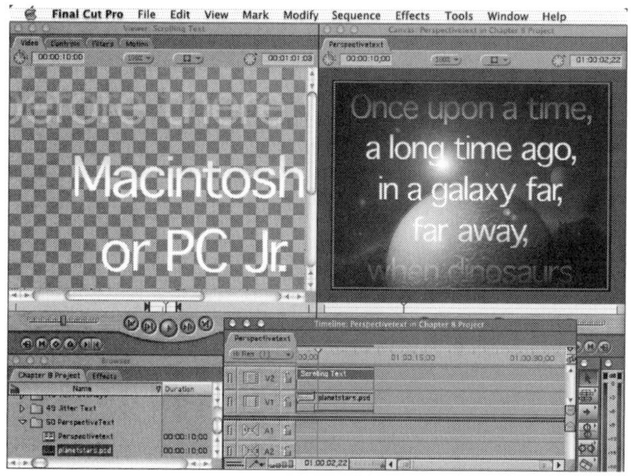

50.7

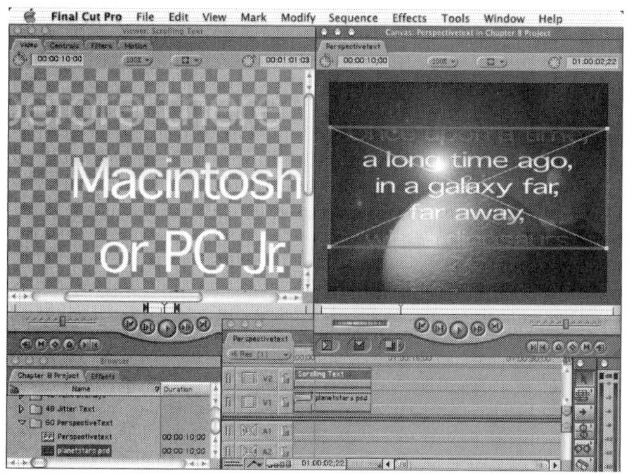

50.8

> **NOTE**
>
> ***Fade size*** **is the space between the top and bottom margins of the frame and the type mask, which allows for a smooth blend and helps simulate the illusion of distance as the text fades into the distance while it scrolls by.**

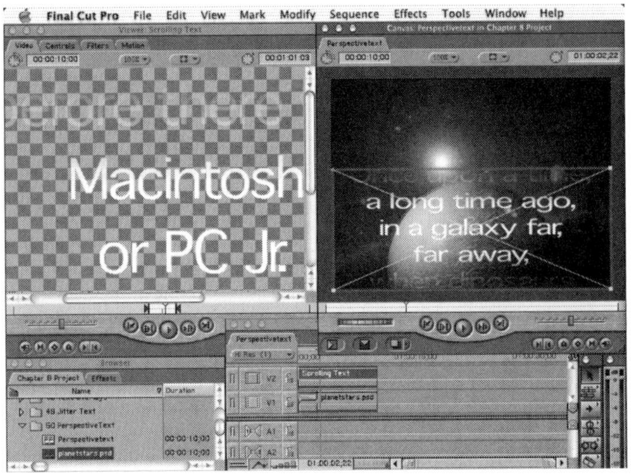

50.9

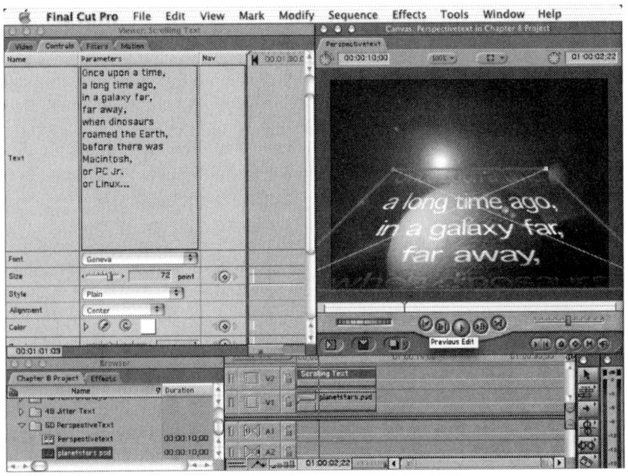

50.10

WARNING

It's sometimes easy to mis-click and accidentally begin dragging the corner handle vertically instead of horizontally. If this happens, undo the action and try again.

STEP 7: CHANGE THE LOCATION OF THE TEXT SCROLL

- Click and drag the center of the text object towards the bottom of the frame so that the bottom edge of the wire frame matches the bottom edge of the video frame as you see in **Figure 50.9**.

STEP 8: ADD THE PERSPECTIVE

- Change tools by selecting the Distort tool (keyboard shortcut "d").
- Hold down the Shift key and Click and drag the upper-left corner of the wire frame indicator towards the center of the frame.
- Notice that as you drag the upper-corner of the wire frame, the lower-corners of the wire frame spread out equally and opposite the amount moved in the upper wire frame corners as shown in **Figure 50.10**.
- Experiment with the look of the perspective. You notice that the distortion is not a true 3D effect and stretches the next line unnaturally as it moves into the distance.

TIP

One magic feature of this technique is that the text you applied in the V2 video track remains "live" after you apply the effect. This means that after you apply the technique, you can go back, change the text, correct spelling, add supplemental text effects, or whatever changes you can imagine. The changes are instantly applied to the effect in V2. All you have to do then is re-render the sequence to see the changes in your final video.

STEP 9: RENDER THE CLIP

■ Choose **Sequence ➢ Render All** as shown in **Figure 50.11** to see how your text travels into the distance in perspective (just like in that famous movie . . .).

With this technique, you can add your own bit of unique American culture to your video presentation. The technique is simple to create, easy to apply, and fun to present.

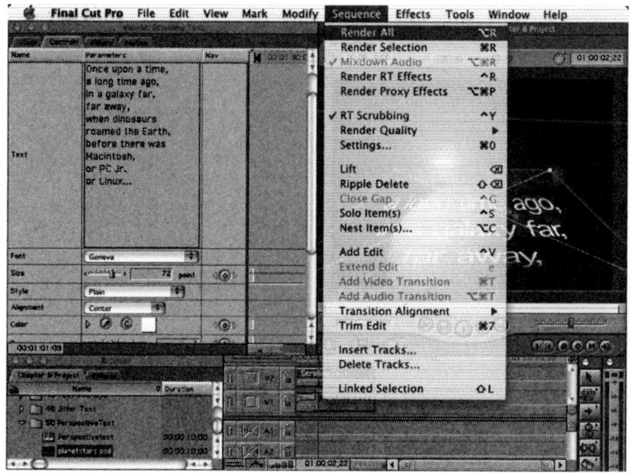

50.11

APPENDIX

WHAT'S ON THE CD-ROM

This appendix provides you with information on the contents of the CD that accompanies this book. Here is what you will find:

- System Requirements
- CD-ROM Installation Instructions
- What's on the CD
- Troubleshooting

SYSTEM REQUIREMENTS

Make sure that your computer meets the minimum system requirements listed in this section. If your computer doesn't match up to these requirements, you may have a problem using the contents of the CD.

- Mac OS computer with a G3 or G4 processor running MacOS 9.2 or later
- At least 256MB of total RAM installed on your computer; for best performance, I recommend at least 512MB

QUICKTIME VERSION 5 PRO OR LATER

If you already installed and are successfully using Final Cut Pro 3, then it is likely you already have the system and software required to view and work with the QuickTime video content on this disc. Most of the files supplied are examples for the Final Cut Pro sample projects demonstrated in this book:

Consult your user documentation that came with your computer and with Final Cut Pro 3 for installation instructions and system requirements. For the latest information on Final Cut Pro, QuickTime and any MacOS-based computer, visit `www.apple.com` on the World Wide Web.

Paramount to any advanced software installation is checking for the most recent updates before you endeavor to begin any critical project. In some cases, the consequences of having the latest OS without the latest application software can be severe; loss of data and potential corruption of your project files can result.

CD-ROM INSTALLATION INSTRUCTIONS

To install a particular piece of software, open its folder and double-click on the Installer file.

1. For the best performance, you may want to copy the files on this CD onto your internal hard disk. Make sure that your hard disk has enough space to accommodate all the files you want to install.
2. Look for a `ReadMe.txt` file or a `.doc` or `.htm` document in the folder with any installable demonstration software. If this document is present, it should contain installation instructions if any are necessary and other useful information.

WHAT'S ON THE CD

The following sections provide a summary of the software and other materials you find on the CD.

50 TECHNIQUES

All the techniques from the book, including samples, are on the CD in individual chapter folders.

PROJECT FILES

- Each technique in the book has an accompanying project file to assist you in following along with the tutorials. In addition, you find QuickTime media imports that go along with the demonstrations. These are found in folders listed by chapter.

- To help you visualize the results of each example, each chapter's folder includes a corresponding results file saved in low-resolution QuickTime format.

SAMPLE MEDIA FILES

- ArtBeats has provided high resolution digital video media samples to promote its library of digital media solutions. The ArtBeats samples are found in the ArtBeats folder in the CD's main directory.

APPLICATIONS

The following applications are on the CD:

Adobe Acrobat Reader, a free portable document format viewing utility, also available via free download from `www.adobe.com`.

Shareware programs are fully functional, trial versions of copyrighted programs. If you like particular programs, register with their authors for a nominal fee and receive licenses, enhanced versions, and technical support. *Freeware programs* are copyrighted games, applications, and utilities that are free for personal use. Unlike shareware, these programs do not require a fee or provide technical support.

Trial, demo, or *evaluation versions* are usually limited either by time or functionality (such as being unable to save projects). Some trial versions are very sensitive to system date changes. If you alter your computer's date, the programs will "time out" and may no longer be functional.

EBOOK VERSION OF 50 FAST FINAL CUT PRO 3 TECHNIQUES

The complete text of this book is on the CD in the Adobe Portable Document Format (PDF). You can read and search through the file with the Adobe Acrobat Reader (also included on the CD, and available as a free download from `www.adobe.com`).

The PDF file also contains all the illustrations, diagrams, and complete text of all the techniques shown in the book. The file is provided for you here as a convenient searchable reference tool.

TROUBLESHOOTING

If you have difficulty installing or using any of the materials on the companion CD, try the following solutions:

- **You have all the software installed.** The standard MacOSX install that came with your Macintosh included Adobe Acrobat Reader. Make sure that it is not already on your hard drive before installing the version on this CD-ROM.
- **Final Cut Pro 3 includes QuickTime Pro.** Your Final Cut Pro 3 install disks include the QuickTime Pro Player edition of QuickTime. Read your final Cut Pro and QuickTime Pro installation instructions to make sure that both are properly installed.
- **Turn off any antivirus software that you may have running.** Installers sometimes mimic virus activity and can make your computer incorrectly believe that a virus is infecting it. (Be sure to turn the antivirus software back on later.)
- **Close all running programs.** The more programs you're running, the less memory is available to other programs. Installers also typically update files and programs; if you keep other programs running, installation may not work properly.
- **Reference the ReadMe.** Please refer to the ReadMe file located at the root of the CD-ROM for the latest product information at the time of publication.

If you still have trouble with the CD, please call the Customer Care phone number: (800) 762-2974. Outside the United States, call 1 (317) 572-3994. You can also contact Wiley Customer Care by e-mail at `techsupdum@wiley.com`. Wiley provides technical support only for installation and other general quality control items; for technical support on the applications themselves, consult the program's vendor or author.

INDEX

G

H

I

J

K

L

M

Q

R

S

T

U

V

Continued

W

Z

ABOUT THE AUTHOR

An Apple Consultant Network member, with 25 years' experience in the design and publishing field, **Tim Meehan** has been at the forefront of both the Desktop Publishing and Desktop Digital Video revolutions. In addition to being the author of several best-selling books on Desktop Publishing, he continues to share his knowledge and experience integrating these two exciting new technologies for his clients worldwide and as an instructor at the University of Colorado in Boulder.

COLOPHON

This book was produced electronically in Indianapolis, Indiana. Microsoft Word 97 was used for word processing; design and layout were produced using Quark Express 4.11, Adobe Illustrator 8.0.1, and Adobe Photoshop 7.0 on Power Macintosh computers. The typeface families used are: Chicago Laser, Minion, Myriad, Myriad Multiple Master, Prestige Elite, Symbol, Trajan, and Zapf Dingbats.

Acquisitions Editor: Mike Roney
Project Editor: Amanda Peterson
Technical Editor: John Matson
Copy Editor: Jerelind Charles
Permissions Editor: Carmen Krikorian
Production Coordinator: Nancee Reeves
Cover Art: Anthony Bunyan
Production: Sean Decker, Joyce Haughey, Kristin McMullan, Shelley Norris, Erin Zeltner
Proofreading: Sossity R. Smith
Quality Control: Laura Albert, Andy Hollandbeck, Susan Moritz
Indexing: Richard T. Evans

WILEY PUBLISHING, INC.
END-USER LICENSE AGREEMENT

READ THIS. You should carefully read these terms and conditions before opening the software packet(s) included with this book "Book". This is a license agreement "Agreement" between you and Wiley Publishing, Inc. "WPI". By opening the accompanying software packet(s), you acknowledge that you have read and accept the following terms and conditions. If you do not agree and do not want to be bound by such terms and conditions, promptly return the Book and the unopened software packet(s) to the place you obtained them for a full refund.

1. **License Grant.** WPI grants to you (either an individual or entity) a nonexclusive license to use one copy of the enclosed software program(s) (collectively, the "Software", solely for your own personal or business purposes on a single computer (whether a standard computer or a workstation component of a multi-user network). The Software is in use on a computer when it is loaded into temporary memory (RAM) or installed into permanent memory (hard disk, CD-ROM, or other storage device). WPI reserves all rights not expressly granted herein.
2. **Ownership.** WPI is the owner of all right, title, and interest, including copyright, in and to the compilation of the Software recorded on the disk(s) or CD-ROM "Software Media". Copyright to the individual programs recorded on the Software Media is owned by the author or other authorized copyright owner of each program. Ownership of the Software and all proprietary rights relating thereto remain with WPI and its licensers.
3. **Restrictions On Use and Transfer.**
   (a) You may only (i) make one copy of the Software for backup or archival purposes, or (ii) transfer the Software to a single hard disk, provided that you keep the original for backup or archival purposes. You may not (i) rent or lease the Software, (ii) copy or reproduce the Software through a LAN or other network system or through any computer subscriber system or bulletin-board system, or (iii) modify, adapt, or create derivative works based on the Software.
   (b) You may not reverse engineer, decompile, or disassemble the Software. You may transfer the Software and user documentation on a permanent basis, provided that the transferee agrees to accept the terms and conditions of this Agreement and you retain no copies. If the Software is an update or has been updated, any transfer must include the most recent update and all prior versions.
4. **Restrictions on Use of Individual Programs.** You must follow the individual requirements and restrictions detailed for each individual program in the What's on the CD-ROM appendix of this Book. These limitations are also contained in the individual license agreements recorded on the Software Media. These limitations may include a requirement that after using the program for a specified period of time, the user must pay a registration fee or discontinue use. By opening the Software packet(s), you will be agreeing to abide by the licenses and restrictions for these individual programs that are detailed in the About the CD-ROM appendix and on the Software Media. None of the material on this Software Media or listed in this Book may ever be redistributed, in original or modified form, for commercial purposes.

5. **Limited Warranty.**

   (a) WPI warrants that the Software and Software Media are free from defects in materials and workmanship under normal use for a period of sixty (60) days from the date of purchase of this Book. If WPI receives notification within the warranty period of defects in materials or workmanship, WPI will replace the defective Software Media.

   (b) **WPI AND THE AUTHOR OF THE BOOK DISCLAIM ALL OTHER WARRANTIES, EXPRESS OR IMPLIED, INCLUDING WITHOUT LIMITATION IMPLIED WARRANTIES OF MERCHANTABILITY AND FITNESS FOR A PARTICULAR PURPOSE, WITH RESPECT TO THE SOFTWARE, THE PROGRAMS, THE SOURCE CODE CONTAINED THEREIN, AND/OR THE TECHNIQUES DESCRIBED IN THIS BOOK. WPI DOES NOT WARRANT THAT THE FUNCTIONS CONTAINED IN THE SOFTWARE WILL MEET YOUR REQUIREMENTS OR THAT THE OPERATION OF THE SOFTWARE WILL BE ERROR-FREE.**

   (c) This limited warranty gives you specific legal rights, and you may have other rights that vary from jurisdiction to jurisdiction.

6. **Remedies.**

   (a) WPI's entire liability and your exclusive remedy for defects in materials and workmanship shall be limited to replacement of the Software Media, which may be returned to WPI with a copy of your receipt at the following address: Software Media Fulfillment Department, Attn.: *50 Fast Final Cut Pro 3 Techniques*, Wiley Publishing, Inc., 10475 Crosspoint Blvd., Indianapolis, IN 46256, or call 1-800-762-2974. Please allow four to six weeks for delivery. This Limited Warranty is void if failure of the Software Media has resulted from accident, abuse, or misapplication. Any replacement Software Media will be warranted for the remainder of the original warranty period or thirty (30) days, whichever is longer.

   (b) In no event shall WPI or the author be liable for any damages whatsoever (including without limitation damages for loss of business profits, business interruption, loss of business information, or any other pecuniary loss) arising from the use of or inability to use the Book or the Software, even if WPI has been advised of the possibility of such damages.

   (c) Because some jurisdictions do not allow the exclusion or limitation of liability for consequential or incidental damages, the above limitation or exclusion may not apply to you.

7. **U.S. Government Restricted Rights.** Use, duplication, or disclosure of the Software for or on behalf of the United States of America, its agencies and/or instrumentalities "U.S. Government" is subject to restrictions as stated in paragraph (c)(1)(ii) of the Rights in Technical Data and Computer Software clause of DFARS 252.227-7013, or subparagraphs (c) (1) and (2) of the Commercial Computer Software - Restricted Rights clause at FAR 52.227-19, and in similar clauses in the NASA FAR supplement, as applicable.

8. **General.** This Agreement constitutes the entire understanding of the parties and revokes and supersedes all prior agreements, oral or written, between them and may not be modified or amended except in a writing signed by both parties hereto that specifically refers to this Agreement. This Agreement shall take precedence over any other documents that may be in conflict herewith. If any one or more provisions contained in this Agreement are held by any court or tribunal to be invalid, illegal, or otherwise unenforceable, each and every other provision shall remain in full force and effect.